EXCHANGE RATE REGIMES AND POLICY INTERDEPENDENCE

Edited by A. W. Hooke

The proceedings of the National Bureau of Economic Research/International Monetary Fund conference reproduced from Volume 30, No. 1, the March 1983 issue of *Staff Papers*

INTERNATIONAL MONETARY FUND
Washington, D.C. 1983

International Standard Book Number:
ISBN 0-939934-21-3

Prefatory Note

The National Bureau of Economic Research and the International Monetary Fund jointly sponsored the conference on Exchange Rate Regimes and Policy Interdependence at the International Monetary Fund on August 31, 1982. The conference was conceived and organized by John F. O. Bilson of the University of Chicago and the National Bureau of Economic Research and Azizali Mohammed, Director of the Fund's External Relations Department.

The conference was hosted by J. de Larosière, Managing Director of the Fund. The sessions were chaired by Jagdish Bhagwati, Professor of Economics at Columbia University, and by William B. Dale, Deputy Managing Director of the Fund. In addition to 4 authors of papers and 8 discussants, the sessions were attended by more than 40 active participants drawn from a variety of international, national, and research organizations, and by about 50 observers from universities, banks, and the Fund. These proceedings were edited for publication by A. W. Hooke, with the assistance of O. Mary Price and Paul Gleason.

The role played by exchange rates and the policies that governments can and should adopt to influence them have been subjects of critical concern, especially since the advent of generalized floating among the currencies of the major industrial countries. In view of this concern, it was decided to publish the proceedings of the conference. It is hoped that this will help to sustain the lively and very useful discussions that took place at the conference.

NORMAN K. HUMPHREYS
Chief Editor

CONTENTS

List of Active Participants

Jacques de Larosière, Managing Director
International Monetary Fund

Chairmen

Jagdish Bhagwati
Columbia University, *New York*
William B. Dale, Deputy Managing Director
International Monetary Fund

Authors

Rudiger Dornbusch
Massachusetts Institute of Technology and National Bureau of Economic Research
William H. Branson
Princeton and National Bureau of Economic Research
Alexander K. Swoboda
Graduate Institute of International Studies, *Geneva*
Ricardo H. Arriazu
Banco Comercial del Norte, *Argentina*

Discussants

Ernesto Hernández-Catá
International Monetary Fund
Willem H. Buiter
London School of Economics and National Bureau of Economic Research
Bijan B. Aghevli
International Monetary Fund
Ryutaro Komiya
Tokyo University
Jacques R. Artus
International Monetary Fund
Jacob A. Frenkel
University of Chicago and National Bureau of Economic Research

Discussants (concluded)

Mohsin S. Khan
International Monetary Fund
Michel Aglietta
Centre d'études prospectives et d'informations internationales, *Paris*

Other Participants

Miguel Beleza
Banco de Portugal
Fred Bergsten
Institute for International Economics, *Washington, D.C.*
John F.O. Bilson
University of Chicago and National Bureau of Economic Research
Ralph Bryant
The Brookings Institution, *Washington, D.C.*
Michael Casey
Alternate Executive Director, International Monetary Fund
John Crow
Bank of Canada
Charles H. Dallara
Alternate Executive Director, International Monetary Fund
Bruno de Maulde
Executive Director, International Monetary Fund
Tom de Vries
Alternate Executive Director, International Monetary Fund
Jacob Dreyer
U.S. Treasury
Richard D. Erb
Executive Director, International Monetary Fund
José R. Gabriel-Peña
Alternate Executive Director, International Monetary Fund
T. Gyohten
Ministry of Finance, *Japan*
Walter O. Habermeier
International Monetary Fund
Dale Henderson
Federal Reserve Board, *Washington, D.C.*
Teruo Hirao
Executive Director, International Monetary Fund

Other Participants (continued)

John A. Holsen
World Bank, *Washington, D.C.*
William C. Hood
International Monetary Fund
Juan Carlos Iarezza
Executive Director, International Monetary Fund
Ulf Jakobsson
Ministry of Economic Affairs, *Sweden*
P.N. Kaul
International Monetary Fund
Anne Krueger
World Bank and National Bureau of Economic Research
Gerhard Laske
Executive Director, International Monetary Fund
Anne Le Lorier
Alternate Executive Director, International Monetary Fund
A.F. Mohammed
International Monetary Fund
Kari Nars
Bank of Finland
J.J. Polak
Executive Director, International Monetary Fund
Lionel Price
Bank of England
Wolfgang Rieke
Deutsche Bundesbank, *Federal Republic of Germany*
Heinrich G. Schneider
Alternate Executive Director, International Monetary Fund
Anna Schwartz
National Bureau of Economic Research
Peter Sedgwick
U.K. Treasury
Hans Seidel
Ministry of Finance, *Austria*
A.S. Shaalan
International Monetary Fund
Jón Sigurdsson
Executive Director, International Monetary Fund
Robert Solomon
The Brookings Institution, *Washington, D.C.*

Other Participants (concluded)

Vijit Supinit
Alternate Executive Director, International Monetary Fund
Christopher T. Taylor
Alternate Executive Director, International Monetary Fund
Tun Thin
International Monetary Fund
Leiv Vidvei
Alternate Executive Director, International Monetary Fund
Tadaie Yamashita
Alternate Executive Director, International Monetary Fund
J.B. Zulu
International Monetary Fund

Opening Statement

J. DE LAROSIÈRE
Managing Director, International Monetary Fund

I AM very happy to greet you here this morning. I also wish to thank those who have participated in the organization of this conference, especially the National Bureau of Economic Research, and all of you who have been kind enough to attend it.

I have prepared some notes on such topics as the timeliness of the conference, the importance of greater stability in the exchange rate system, the need for increased convergence of economic policies to foster this greater stability, and the difficulties stemming from large fluctuations in exchange rates. I have decided, however, that as you know exactly what I would say on these subjects, I will draw on my experience in the Fund over the last four years to make some rather different observations.

First, there is an important need for more research to be done on exchange rate matters. A conference such as the present one affords a valuable opportunity for renewing our thinking on the subject.

Second, the Fund appears to have clearer ideas on what an equilibrium exchange rate is for the currency of a small country than of a large country. Why is it so difficult for the Fund to make pronouncements on the exchange rates of major currencies? I think there are two possible reasons: one, that there is a more explicit frame of reference for the currency of a small country and, two, that the fluidity of capital movements makes it easier for a large country with access to capital markets to maintain a "wrong" or "out-of-line" exchange rate. The Fund is concerned, among other things, to improve the allocation of resources when prescribing a correction of the exchange rate. Should this concern not be greater for large countries? If these countries maintain exchange relationships that distort the allocation of resources, the international repercussions are more far-reaching. There is little published work available that can help us formulate a grid of parities that can be regarded as optimal from the viewpoint of the efficiency of resource allocation, the equilibrium of the balance of payments, and the configurations of international trade. I recognize the difficulties in the way of constructing a formal grid of exchange rates. However, I do feel that it may be possible to construct an informal frame of reference that could prove useful at different stages of the business cycle.

Third, the cost of exchange rate variability in recent years has been quite high. Variability engenders uncertainties for investors, traders, and, indeed, the exchange rate system itself. Little research has been done, however, that would permit us to estimate with some precision just how large these costs are. Before the breakdown of the Bretton Woods system, there was clearly less variability of exchange rates. I am uncertain of the reasons for this, but I believe that greater convergence of economic policies among the principal countries played an important part. What has caused this convergence to break down? Have external shocks been more disturbing than those experienced earlier? Has the cutting of the theoretical link of the U.S. dollar to gold caused an important stabilizer to fall away? I hope that today's conference will facilitate our search to find answers to questions such as these.

Flexible Exchange Rates and Interdependence

RUDIGER DORNBUSCH*

> The fundamental argument for flexible exchange rates is that they would allow countries autonomy with respect to their use of monetary, fiscal and other policy instruments. . . . The argument for flexible exchange rates can be put more strongly still: flexible exchange rates are essential to the preservation of national autonomy and independence consistent with efficient organization and development of the world economy.
>
> Harry G. Johnson (written in late 1960s)[1]

IN MOVING FROM the exchange control and trade discrimination of the 1950s to the open economic system of the 1960s, the world economy briefly returned to the liberal order that has been credited with fostering economic progress during the 40 years before World War I. There can be little doubt that the 1960s were the best decade the world economy has experienced in this century. But the very source of the success—active management of the macroeconomy that included designing the monetary and fiscal mix to achieve satisfactory, sustained growth—eventually created economic problems that fostered disintegration in the world economy. Differences in inflation preferences between the United States and Europe were irreconcilable, and productivity growth differentials were too large to accommodate a world economy using fixed exchange rates.

Harry Johnson's perceptive assessment, quoted above, was widely shared during the late 1960s. Flexible exchange rates were

*Rudiger Dornbusch is Professor of Economics at the Massachusetts Institute of Technology.

Financial support for this study was provided by a grant from the National Science Foundation. The author wishes to acknowledge helpful comments made by Franco Modigliani and John Williamson and efficient research assistance done by Alberto Giovaninni and Larry Schembri.

[1]See Johnson (1973), p. 199.

then seen as an essential further step toward a liberal world system that would allow countries to enjoy the advantages of free markets in goods and assets and yet enjoy domestic macroeconomic independence. Now, after ten years of experience with flexible exchange rates, there is much less confidence that flexible rates and domestic policy autonomy are reconcilable. On the contrary, the exercise of policy autonomy becomes nearly impossible under flexible rates, because many economies are too small and open to accept the exchange rate variations induced by policy. Alternatively, the effects of policies of countries with large economies are exported and interfere with foreign internal stability. What flexible exchange rates are still credited with is an ability to isolate a country from the world inflation *trend,* while it is recognized that they cannot isolate a country from either the effects of policies that initiate a *change in trend* or from any other disturbances. The traditional argument against flexible exchange rates, derived from the experience of the interwar period, is that flexible rates are unstable, move about erratically, and often aggravate the macroeconomic stability problem. The experience of the last ten years would certainly lead an observer to endorse that view. Anytime there is monetary and fiscal dislocation in a major country, as there was in the United States in the 1970s, flexible rates perform poorly, because they lead to excessive real exchange rate changes and to the export of inflation or deflation. Flexible rates leave us with as much interdependence, or even more, as there is under a fixed rate regime. This paper reviews the channels of interdependence and asks in what directions one should look for a system that maintains an open world economy but more effectively comes to terms with the high priority given to national policy autonomy.

There are, broadly speaking, three avenues: (1) making exchange rates more fixed, (2) making them less flexible, or (3) as suggested by Modigliani and Tobin, limiting the incentives for short-run capital mobility, either permanently or on an ad hoc basis. It seems certain that free market economics bar consideration of a capital account tax, which might be seen as embodying a wicked infringement on individual freedom. It is also likely that U.S. macroeconomic policies and policies abroad remain unpredictable and uncoordinated to an extent sufficient to preclude establishment of an exchange rate band or even fixed rates. What is left, then, is the spirit of Versailles—that is to say, the recognition that there may be circumstances where it is not impossible that there might be intervention, which could turn out not to be small. Consequently, a strong case can be made for a different domestic policy mix to go with flexible rates.

I. Channels of Interdependence

This section sketches a model of interdependence on the aggregate demand and supply sides. The purpose of the model is to draw attention to distinct channels and to identify the relevant parameters in assessing the importance of these sources of interdependence. The section begins by considering a standard macroeconomic model, focusing on prices, aggregate demand, perfect asset substitutability, and rational expectations. Extensions follow in subsequent sections.

EXCHANGE RATES, EMPLOYMENT, AND WAGES[2]

To study cyclical interdependence, this paper considers a country that faces a given world interest rate, given import prices, and a given world demand (except for real exchange rate effects) for its exports. The log-linear model is presented in equations (1) and (6):

$$y = a\theta - br + f; \ \theta \equiv e + p^* - w \tag{1}$$

$$m - q = hy - ci \tag{2}$$

$$q \equiv \beta w + (1-\beta)(e + p^*) \tag{3}$$

$$r \equiv i - \dot{q} \tag{4}$$

$$i = i^* + \dot{e} \tag{5}$$

$$\dot{w} = \gamma y + \alpha(q - w) \tag{6}$$

Equation (1) represents the IS (investment-savings) schedule with θ denoting the real exchange rate, and f denotes a domestic or foreign shift variable. The real interest rate is denoted by r. The LM (demand for money = supply of money) schedule is represented by equation (2), where the price level is denoted by q. The price level is a weighted average of domestic prices, which are set

[2]This section combines sticky price, rational expectations models of exchange rate dynamics and the sticky real wage literature. See Sachs (1979), Branson and Rotemberg (1980), Dornbusch (1980), Argy and Salop (1979), Buiter and Miller (1981, 1982), Marston (1982), Modigliani and Padoa Schioppa (1978), and Obstfeld (1982).

equal to wages, and of import prices. Equation (4) defines the domestic real interest rate, and equation (5) expresses the assumption of perfect asset substitutability, with an adjustment made for anticipated depreciation. Wage dynamics are specified in equation (6) and are linked to the gross national product (GNP) gap, y, and to the real wage level. The term $q - w$ represents a rigid real wage effect.[3]

This model is appropriate to short-run cyclical issues. It neglects trend inflation, foreign inflation, productivity growth, and the impact of capital formation. It concentrates on aggregate demand and the cyclical interaction between wages, interest rates, and exchange rates. At any point in time—given home wages, money, and fiscal policy—an exchange rate and a depreciation rate can be found that satisfy the international interest rate relation. The wage level and the exchange rate determine external competitiveness and, hence, aggregate demand and employment. The system can be simplified by noting the relation between home and foreign interest rates:

$$r \equiv r^* + \beta\dot{\theta};\ i = r^* + \dot{\theta} + \dot{w} \tag{7}$$

The model is slightly more complex than the extended Mundell-Fleming model because of two modifications. On the one hand, care is taken to allow for an impact of import prices on the price level used to deflate real balances and real wages and to define the real interest rate. On the other hand, the domestic producer price index (which, here, is the wage) responds not only cyclically but also to the real wage level.

The role of wage behavior can be appreciated by looking at the long-run behavior of the system as shown in Figure 1. For a given world interest rate, the IS schedule shows equilibrium in the domestic goods market. A real depreciation creates excess demand, which is met by an increase in output. Along $\dot{w} = 0$, money wages are constant. A real depreciation, because it reduces real wages, leads to wage increases. To keep wages constant, the reduction in the standard of living owing to depreciation must be offset by unemployment that dampens wage demands. Hence, $\dot{w} = 0$ is downward sloping. The slope of the constant wage schedule is determined by the relative response of wages to the cyclical position and to the standard of living via the real exchange rate

[3]The foreign price level and the full employment level output are chosen to be equal to one, and thus their logs are zero.

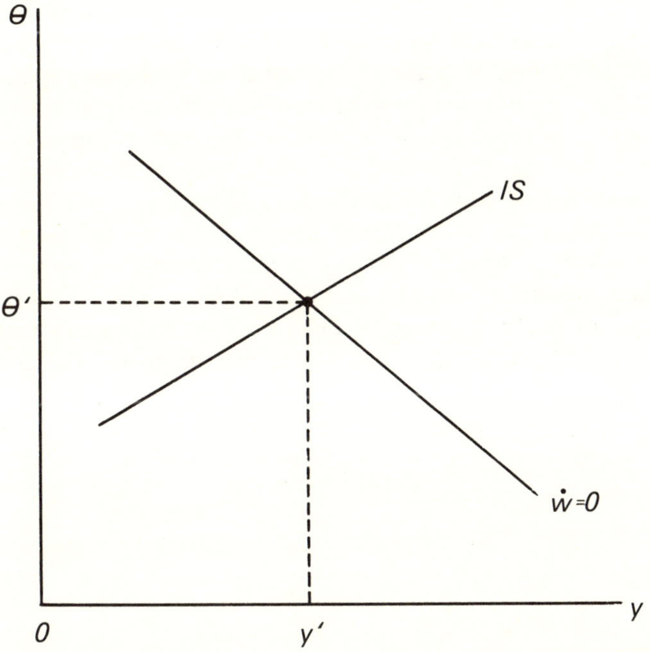

FIGURE 1

$$\left.\frac{d\theta}{dy}\right|_{\dot{w}=0} = \frac{\gamma}{\alpha(1-\beta)} \equiv \lambda \tag{8}$$

The pattern of wage response will determine the long-run effects of disturbances on output and the real exchange rate. A reduction in foreign demand or a rise in world interest rates, for example, will shift the IS schedule upward and to the left. The decline in employment is larger, the flatter the $\dot{w} = 0$ schedule or the lesser the cyclical responsiveness of wages relative to the real wage stickiness as measured by the parameter λ. If the wage is highly responsive cyclically and real wage rigidity is nearly absent, λ tends toward infinity and the economy behaves as if it had full wage and price flexibility, which ensures rapid adjustment to full employment. Conversely, when cyclical flexibility is limited and real wage resistance is strong, λ tends toward zero. Adverse disturbances then can lead to a large impact on the price level combined with unemployment.[4]

The model described in equations (1) to (6) can be reduced to the behavior over time of money wages and the real exchange rate (see Appendix). Figure 2 shows the dynamics by reference to the loci along which wages and the real exchange rate, respectively, are constant. Moving up along the $\dot{w} = 0$ schedule, an increase in the wage raises the price level and thus reduces real balances and exerts deflationary pressure, which causes wages to fall unless a cut in the real wage owing to real depreciation exerts an offsetting impact. The schedule *FF* shown in Figure 2 represents the stable trajectory under perfect foresight. Given any initial money wage, the corresponding point on *FF* shows the equilibrium level of the

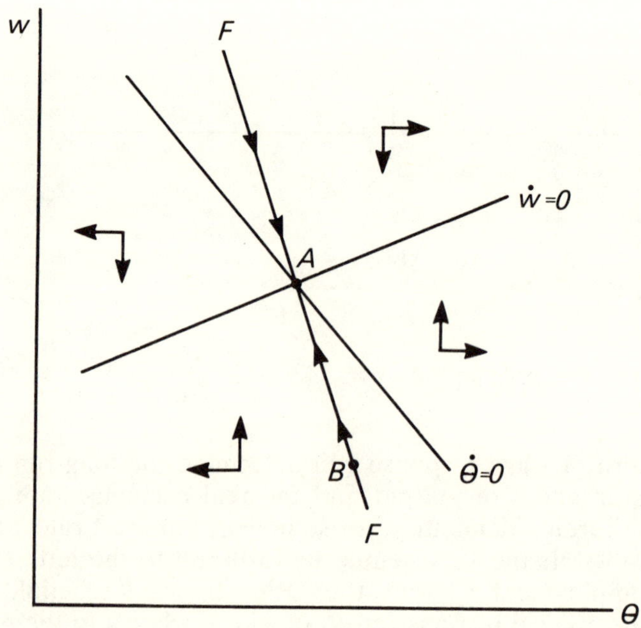

FIGURE 2

[4]From equations (1) and (6), setting $\dot{w} = \dot{\theta} = 0$, we obtain $y = (f - br)/(1 + a\lambda)$.

nominal and real exchange rates such that the economy converges to long-run equilibrium at point *A*.

At point *B*, for example, the wage is low, and thus the price level tends to be low, which makes for high real balances and low nominal interest rates. To maintain international interest parity, the exchange rate must appreciate, which means that the real exchange rate must be above the steady-state level. At point *B*, as one can verify by looking at Figure 2, the real exchange rate favors the home country; and because of real appreciation, by equation (7), the real interest rate is below the world level. Thus, aggregate demand and employment are high. High employment and the high real exchange rate or the low real wage exert upward pressure on the wage, which pushes the economy toward point *A*.

The framework can now be used to investigate the impact of foreign disturbances on home wages and employment. Using Figure 3, the effect of an increase in foreign interest rates can be

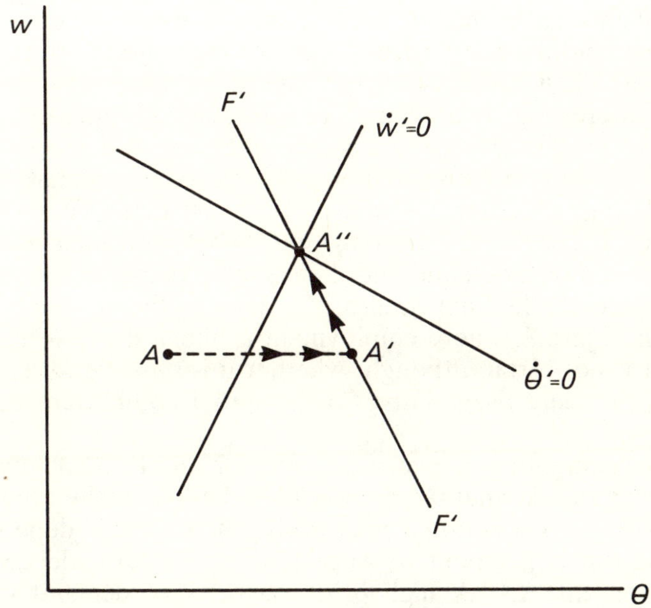

FIGURE 3

studied. Assume that wages increase in the long run and that the exchange rate depreciates. As Figure 3 shows, the exchange rate will overshoot, moving immediately from the initial equilibrium at point A to a short-run equilibrium at A'. The rise in foreign interest rates creates an incipient capital outflow, which leads to exchange depreciation. When point A' is reached, home interest rates have risen somewhat, and there is now expected appreciation, which assures a sufficient return on domestic securities. Changes in employment and in the standard of living combine to generate wage pressure that moves the economy over time to A''. In the long run, of course, there will be some unemployment.

The adjustment pattern is shaped by all the parameters, including particularly the dynamics of wages, income and interest responses of money demand, and the price elasticity of demand for goods. What is crucial to the initial behavior of the exchange rate is the long-run adjustment of money wages. If wages increase in the long run, then the exchange rate must overshoot in the short run, as is shown in Figure 3. In contrast, if wages decrease in the long run, then there will be an immediate depreciation of the nominal and real exchange rate, but a more moderate one. In the subsequent adjustment process, the exchange rate will continue to depreciate. This case is shown in Figure 4.

It is interesting to note that either exchange rates or unemployment *must* overshoot. As shown in Figure 4, unemployment must overshoot, because at point A' the real exchange rate is depreciating, which means that real interest rates are above the world level, and the real exchange rate is below its long-run level. For both reasons, demand and, hence, employment at A' will be less than at A'', the final equilibrium. Exactly the opposite occurs at A' in Figure 3, where employment is above the new long-run level. It is not certain, though, whether it is possible for employment to actually rise relative to the initial equilibrium at A in Figure 4.

The overshooting of exchange rates or employment makes it interesting to ask what factors would make one or the other case more likely. As was noted previously, the outcome depends on the long-run adjustment of wages, which, in turn, depends on several parameters. A high price elasticity of demand implies small changes in equilibrium real exchange rates and, therefore, relatively little pressure on wages and output. A high price elasticity thus implies a long-run increase in wages to accommodate the reduced demand for real balances and the consequent ex-

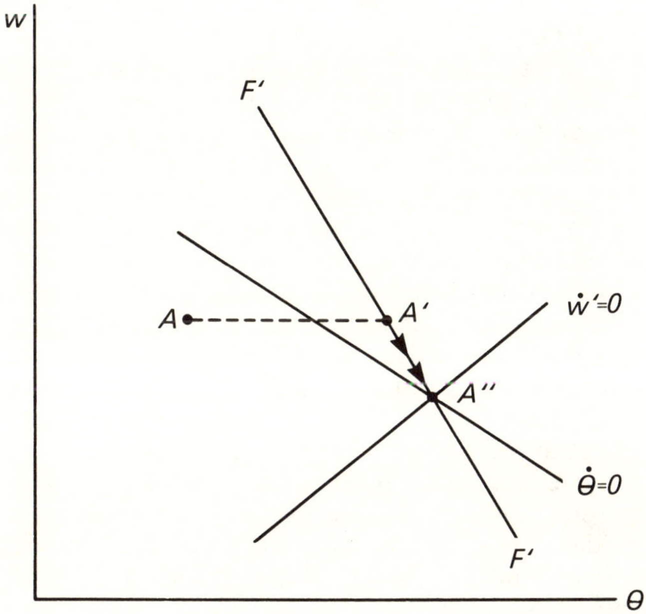

FIGURE 4

change rate overshooting shown in Figure 3. A high interest rate elasticity or income elasticity of money demand works in the same direction. In contrast, a high cyclical response of wages implies that wages could fall in the long run.[5] In the same way, one can analyze the impact of foreign demand disturbances or changes in domestic fiscal policy. Again, one finds that employment or exchange rate overshooting is possible, depending on the pattern of wage flexibility relative to the parameters of aggregate demand.

The effects of disturbances on domestic employment and on wages will presumably differ, depending on the direction of change. One would expect an asymmetry in the real wage resistance, in that workers accept gains in real wages but resist cuts. This extends also to the cyclical behavior of wages; wages rise more rapidly in a boom than they fall in a recession. In terms of

[5]See the Appendix for the long-run solutions to w and θ.

the model, this amounts to saying that the coefficient of wage flexibility, λ, depends on the cyclical and real wage positions. Specifically, starting from full employment, a decrease in foreign demand or an increase in world interest rates will lead to unemployment and to a decline in real income. But an increase in foreign demand or a decrease in world interest rates brings about a real appreciation at full employment rather than a lasting real expansion beyond capacity.

The asymmetry issue is relevant once one considers transitory disturbances. Suppose, for example, that a transitory increase in world demand, caused by a boom abroad, leads to a real appreciation at full employment. Once the boom abroad subsides, the issue arises whether workers are willing to accommodate themselves to a cut in real income brought about by the ensuing real depreciation. There is no reason to dismiss the possibility of a ratchet effect in the operation of real wage resistance.

But if ratchet effects are present, the cyclical variability of real exchange rates, under a flexible exchange rate regime, necessitates consideration of an incomes policy that accommodates the changes in the standard of living associated with real exchange rate movements. Alternatively, active fiscal policy needs to be used to stabilize real exchange rates over the cycle to avoid the real appreciation that cannot, afterward, be undone without adverse effects on employment. But that, of course, raises the question whether there is more fiscal resistance than real wage resistance. In any event, it is clear that transitory disturbances abound; that transitory real appreciation owing to strong demand raises the standard of living cyclically; and that instruments are necessary to dampen or to accommodate the subsequent decline.

So far, this paper has dealt with the case of a country that takes world demand and interest rates as exogenous. It is worthwhile to comment briefly on the changes brought about by repercussion effects. Without going into details, this study recalls the Mundell-Fleming results specifying that with prices given, a monetary expansion in one country has adverse employment effects abroad. Conversely, a fiscal expansion has favorable employment effects abroad. These results depend critically on the behavior of the real money stock in each country. They may cease to hold the moment import prices enter the real balance deflator. Specifically, as a fiscal expansion spreads abroad through real appreciation, it reinforces the expansion in the initiating country, but it reduces real balances abroad, thus tending to confine the expansion. If real wage resistance is an issue, this adverse effect of depreciation is strongly reinforced. In contrast, a monetary expansion may, in such circumstances, raise income abroad.

INTEREST RATES AND RISK PREMIA

The discussion in the previous section was based on the assumption that securities are perfect substitutes once anticipated exchange depreciation is taken into account. Under that assumption, real interest rates are equalized in long-run equilibrium and in the short run can only differ by an amount equal to the rate of change of the real exchange rate. But the assumption of perfect asset substitution is not warranted once real exchange rates fluctuate.

Movements in real exchange rates introduce negative correlation in the real returns on domestic and foreign securities and thus create an incentive for portfolio diversification. Only in a very special case, when relative asset supplies match the minimum variance portfolio shares *and* when there are identical consumption baskets across countries, will there be no risk premium. In general, there is a risk premium that is related to relative asset supplies and to the distribution of world wealth.

In the presence of a risk premium, the interest rate relationship becomes

$$i = i^* + \dot{e} + \rho(V/E\widetilde{W},\ W/E\widetilde{W});\ \rho_1 > 0\ \rho_2 > 0 \qquad (9)$$

where V and W denote, respectively, domestic outside debt and domestic wealth, each measured in home currency, and $\widetilde{W}$ denotes world wealth measured in foreign currency. Equation (9) thus introduces a relationship between interest rates, expected depreciation, the nominal exchange rate level, nominal wealth, and asset supplies. Where in the earlier model nominal money was the only asset to play a role, now the supply of domestic outside nominal assets also appears.[6] An increase in the relative supply of domestic assets, $V/\widetilde{W}E$, must be accommodated by either a more rapid rate of appreciation or a higher nominal interest rate differential or else must be offset by depreciation of the exchange rate *level.*

The link between exchange rates and portfolio balance can be inferred from equation (9), taking the case of a small country, so

[6] For references to the extensive risk premium literature, see the review in Dornbusch (1983) and Krugman (1981).

that world wealth $\widetilde{W}$ is taken as given. Furthermore, assuming given interest rates and a given rate of depreciation, $i - i^* - \dot{e}$, one can find the relation between changes in domestic currency asset supplies, changes in wealth, and the corresponding changes in equilibrium exchange rates, which can be expressed by

$$\hat{E} = \hat{V} + \frac{\rho_2}{\rho_1 + \rho_2}(\hat{W} - \hat{V}) \tag{10}$$

Equation (10) shows that for a given depreciation-adjusted interest differential, an increase in domestic currency assets and wealth, in the same proportion, leads to equiproportionate depreciation. An increase in wealth, given asset supplies, leads, in contrast, to appreciation. On the one hand, an increase in wealth reduces, via domestic habitat effects, the risk premium and thus brings about appreciation; an increase in domestic currency asset supply, on the other hand, leads to a higher risk premium and, thus, to depreciation.

The risk premium introduces two important considerations. The first is that the composition of domestic assets, between money and debt (money being the medium of exchange for which there is a specific demand), is of importance and that open market operations therefore exert an effect on exchange rates that is independent of the effect of the change in money. This point can be illustrated in the following manner: The macro model sketched out previously determines interest rates as functions of the real money stock and real income. The model is closed by finding an exchange rate that satisfies both the macro model and the risk premium equation. An increase in debt or in home relative wealth then must affect both interest rates and exchange rates.

The second consideration introduced by the risk premium is that it constitutes a link between wealth distribution in the world, interest rates, and the exchange rate. A rise in domestic wealth leads to changes in both interest rates and exchange rates. Interest rates at home decline and/or the exchange rate appreciates. This effect is added to the macro model and provides a channel through which dynamic effects associated with the current account and the budget have implications for the exchange rate.

Intervention policy must be considered in relation to the risk premium. Intervention, viewed from that perspective, takes one of two forms. If purchases of foreign exchange are allowed to change the domestic money stock, intervention will be effective. But if there is sterilization, this has implications for the relative supply of domestic debt and, thus, for the risk premium. Sterilized intervention, it has been argued, is simply a reshuffling of the composition of domestic government liabilities. It has an effect on exchange rates only through the impact on the risk premium. Thus, it can work only when a risk premium exists. Moreover the effectiveness—the bang per buck—depends on risk aversion being high and the variability of real interest differentials being large. Thus, intervention policy works well when uncertainty is large and risk aversion is pervasive.

The risk premium has been singled out as an important channel through which the current account affects the exchange rate. While the current account qualifies in principle as a determinant of exchange rates, it stands to reason that changes in wealth that are not included in the current account should really move to the center of attention. In particular, capital gains resulting from stock market movements certainly have a far larger impact on relative wealth than the current account does. In addition to the stock market, total domestic saving is a source of changes in relative wealth. Again, the current account's share of saving is typically, though not necessarily, small. Except in special cases, the role of the current account in affecting exchange rate movements, via the risk premium, is not a large one.

THIRD COUNTRY EFFECTS

The perspective that this paper has adopted so far has been that of a country faced with external shocks. The paper now shifts to the perspective of the system to examine the important cyclical interdependence that arises from the behavior of materials prices and import demands of peripheral countries. These countries are predominant exporters of materials and importers of manufactures. They are also debtors.

Table 1 reports regressions of various measures of the *real* prices received by developing countries affected by the world business cycle, the real price of oil, and the real U.S. dollar exchange rate. The cyclical variable is the Organization for Economic Cooperation and Development (OECD) unemployment rate, which is taken from the OECD's *Economic Outlook*, and the real exchange rate is measured by the relative wholesale prices of manufactures of the United States (relative to trading partners), which are taken from the Fund's *International Financial Statistics*. Equation (1) in Table 1 shows export prices relative to import prices of non-oil developing countries. The real oil price and the

TABLE 1. DETERMINANTS OF THE TERMS OF TRADE AND REAL COMMODITY PRICES, 1964–81[1]

Equation	Dependent Variable	Constant	OECD Unemployment	Real Oil Price	Real Dollar Exchange Rate	R^2	D-W	*Rho*[1]	*Rho*[2]
(1)	Terms of trade	1.64 (0.70)	−0.01 (0.02)	−0.001 (0.0004)	−0.31 (0.14)	0.76	1.79		
(2a)	Real materials prices (Fund)	9.04 (1.58)	−0.06 (0.028)	—	−0.88 (0.32)	0.39	1.94	0.07	
(2b)	Real materials prices (Fund)	2.96 (1.31)	−0.15 (0.03)	0.16 (0.05)	−0.78 (0.26)	0.68	2.17	0.28	−0.73
(3a)	Real materials prices (World Bank)	2.22 (1.63)	−0.05 (0.023)	—	−0.64 (0.34)	0.25	1.81		
(3b)	Real materials prices (World Bank)	−1.18 (1.36)	−0.16 (0.03)	0.19 (0.05)	−0.49 (0.27)	0.66	2.02	0.29	−0.59
(4)	Real minerals and metals prices	−4.53 (1.30)	−0.20 (0.027)	0.22 (0.05)	0.78 (0.26)	0.89	1.97		
(5)	Real agricultural prices	3.71 (2.0)	−0.04 (0.03)	—	−0.98 (0.41)	0.28	1.85	0.15	

[1]Standard errors are in parentheses. The left-hand-side variable and the real dollar exchange rate are expressed in logs, as is the real oil price, except in equation (1). D-W denotes the Durbin-Watson statistic. *Rho*[1] and *Rho*[2] denote the coefficients for correction of first-order and second-order serial correlation.

real dollar exchange rate are significant explanatory variables; a dollar appreciation or an increase in real oil prices leads to deterioration of developing countries' terms of trade. So does a rise in OECD unemployment, although here the coefficient is not precisely estimated. Equation (1) shows that a 1 percent real dollar appreciation would lead to a deterioration of developing country terms of trade by ⅓ of 1 percent. This is, of course, a very sizable effect.

In equation (2a), the dependent variable is the Fund's index of the prices of all commodities (reported in *International Financial Statistics*) deflated by the dollar price of manufacturers' exports from developed countries (reported in the United Nations' *Monthly Bulletin of Statistics*). Again, real dollar appreciation has a significant adverse impact on the real prices of materials. For this measure of real prices, a 1 percent real dollar appreciation leads to a nearly proportional deterioration in real commodity prices. In equations (3a), (3b), (4), and (5), it is shown that the results are not consistent, differing significantly between commodities. Equation (3a) reports the results for the World Bank's index of 33 commodities (see Grilli (1982)) deflated by the dollar prices of manufactures as was done for equations (2a) and (2b). The results are substantially the same as those for equations (2a) and (2b). The index is made up of agricultural commodities (70.6 percent), metals and minerals (24.3 percent) and timber (5.1 percent). Equations (4) and (5) show that real dollar appreciation leads to an *increase* in the real price of minerals and metals, but to a *decrease* in the real price of agricultural commodities. The latter, presumably because of their predominant weight in the index, carry the results in the regressions for the total commodity group. The difference in the more disaggregated results suggests that the whole question, including the important issue of using alternative cyclical variables,[7] should be studied further.

Consider now how these third country effects operate when, say, the United States tightens its monetary policy. This would lead to increased nominal and real interest rates and to a slowdown in demand in the United States. The dollar would appreciate in nominal and real terms. This paper has already discussed the direct effects on industrial countries of higher interest rates

[7]Regressions using residuals from a regression of the OECD industrial production index on two time trends (as the cyclical variable) performed more poorly in establishing significant determinants of the left-hand variable than the regressions whose results are shown in Table 1.

and reduced exports; they unambiguously translate into unemployment unless there is no real wage rigidity. But now there are additional effects caused by the impact of events in the United States on the material producing debtor countries. Higher real interest rates worsen those countries' current accounts. This is reinforced by the decline in demand by industrial countries for both manufactures and materials and, finally, by the effect of dollar appreciation on the real prices of materials. This combination is quite devastating for material exporting debtor countries. Typically, they will be forced to limit their own growth because of balance of payments constraints.

As seen from the perspective of industrial countries, the adjustments in material exporting debtor countries have two sides. Industrial countries as a group achieve a direct terms of trade improvement relative to material exporters, both for cyclical reasons and because of dollar appreciation. This gain may, however, be dampened, perhaps substantially, by the decline in developing countries' imports of manufactures.

Changes in the real prices of commodities during the cycle or as a by-product of changes in key exchange rates play an important role in relation to real wage rigidity. The deterioration in developing countries' terms of trade may well offset some of the real income loss an individual industrial country experiences as a result of, say, higher U.S. interest rates.

BUBBLES, PESOS, AND RUNS

The preceding sections have focused on *actual* changes in exchange rate fundamentals, cyclical or permanent, that affect goods or asset markets and then affect the rest of the world through asset demands, demands for goods, exchange rate movements, and prices. However, many of the disturbances in the world economy are not the result of actual changes in fundamentals but rather of changes in expectations about the future course of these fundamentals. These revisions in expectations exert effects on interdependence that are as powerful as those exerted by actual changes in fundamentals.

When asset markets are dominated by expectations about the future course of fundamentals, exchange rates may move in ways that do not promote macroeconomic stability. Three ways in which this situation may come about deserve special attention. The first is familiar from recent literature on financial markets and concerns the possibility that exchange rates, in part, are determined by irrelevant information. Market participants may have the wrong model of fundamentals, and their expectations, based on the wrong model, will affect the actual exchange rate. If there is sufficiently high serial correlation in the irrelevant variables, it may be impossible to discern the systematic forecast errors using conventional efficiency tests. But the exchange rate will be significantly more volatile than is warranted by the true model.

This point is important because market participants may be impressed by a plausible fundamentals variable, attribute explanatory power to it, and, consequently, make their expectations actually come true. Then, when some other variable moves, attention may shift to a different "main factor," which, in turn, comes to dominate the exchange rate for a while. Exchange rates carried by irrelevant beliefs are troublesome, not only because of the excess variance but also because shifting from one irrelevant factor to another will precipitate major exchange rate collapses. The possibility that exchange rates are sometimes far out of line with the fundamentals cannot be discounted. It is important to recognize this, because in the past economists may have given excessive weight to the notion that the market knows "the model" and, at the same time, is rational. It is quite conceivable that a number of fashionable factors, such as fiscal discipline, basic monetary control, long-run strength in manufacturing, and *Angebotsfreundliche Gesellschaftspolitik* (supply side policy) play a role, one at a time.

The second source of disequilibrium exchange rates is expectations about the possibility of regime changes and has been called the "peso problem." In this perspective, exchange rates are influenced not only by current fundamentals but also by agents' expectations that there are given probabilities that these fundamentals may change in specific directions. If market participants have sufficiently strong beliefs that a given course of policy will not be followed, they may, in fact, make it impossible for the authorities to follow that course. Under flexible exchange rates, this problem may become acute because the exchange rate is so flexible a price and so much governed by expectations. It may well be argued, as was done in the discussion of the French stabilization experience under Raymond Poincaré, that speculators are the true judges of fundamentals and that a collapse of the exchange rate brought about by adverse capital flows is irrevocable evidence of a program of stabilization that was out of touch with fundamentals. But such an argument must be viewed as simplistic by anyone who recognizes that stabilization policy has a wide range of indeterminacy.[8]

The third source of disequilibrium exchange rates can be explained using the analogy of bubbles. A bubble exists when holders of an asset realize that the asset is overpriced but are nevertheless willing to hold it, since they believe there is only a limited risk of a price collapse during a given holding period; therefore, asset holders expect to be able to sell eventually at a price that will provide them with sufficient capital gains to compensate them for running the risk of a collapse.[9] An analogous situation occurs when a currency has appreciated more than can be considered justified by fundamentals and overvaluation is widely thought to prevail, but appreciation is expected to continue until some disturbance causes the crash. There are no models of such a crash as yet, but it should be clear that an essential ingredient is the arrival of new information that diverts a sufficient number of speculators from keeping the bubble growing.

Bubbles, peso problems, and irrelevant information all move the exchange rate away from the particular equilibrium implied by current fundamentals. In each of these cases, there is a re-evaluation of beliefs. When this occurs, exchange rates change markedly, which, in turn, may force an accommodating change in policies. Unless policies are very exogenous, instability of policies may be provoked by instability of expectations. That means flexible exchange rates may require, as an institutional setting, that policies be more exogenous than, in fact, they are today. Without such an anchor, flexibility of exchange rates may aggravate macroeconomic instability.

II. Coping With Interdependence

In the late 1960s, discussion of international monetary arrangements centered on the idea of "flexing" the system. Exchange rates were too inflexible to be compatible with an overvalued dollar and the one-way street that overvaluation created for internationally mobile, speculative capital. Today much of the ex-

[8]See Flood and Garber (1982 a, 1982 b), Salant and Henderson (1978), Lizondo (1980), and Blanchard (1982) for discussions of regime changes.

[9]See Tirole (1982) and Blanchard (1979).

change rate debate starts from the recognition that it is desirable to reduce excessive fluctuations that exert undesirable interdependence effects. The quest then is for "flixed" exchange rates: the optimal exchange rate regime would prevent *persistent* overvaluation or undervaluation of a currency that would ultimately lead to protection or an undesirable monetary-fiscal policy mix. The rate system would also have to be flexible enough to yield *long-run* inflation autonomy. But, at the same time, short-run real exchange rate variability should be reduced and the export of inflation through appreciation limited. There is little question that a flexible exchange rate system has desirable long-run features and that these should not be readily sacrificed. But, at the same time, the short-run implications of unsynchronized policy actions are sufficiently severe to raise the question whether exchange rates are too flexible at present. That question, of course, can be answered by comparing arrangements with a set of alternative arrangements.

Three alternative methods of reforming the present system are (1) returning to fixed or quasi-fixed rates, (2) limiting the incentives to move capital, and (3) permitting limited exchange rate flexibility. Brief comments will be made on aspects of each of these.

A return to outright fixed exchange rates appears adventurous. Such a move would be difficult because of large discrepancies in inflation rates among key industrial countries. The willingness of major industrial countries to impose trade restrictions seems striking confirmation that these countries are not disposed to abide by rules. An outright commitment to peg would yield, at best, a variety of the European Monetary System. The difficulties posed by a fixed rate system are aggravated by the economic instability in at least two key industrial countries—the United States and the United Kingdom.

An alternative to fixed rates has been proposed by McKinnon (1982). He argues that exchange rate instability and the instability of world inflation are outgrowths of misconceived monetarism. The right kind of monetarism would look at the world quantity of money. Specifically, he argues (p. 331) that

> . . . the solution to international currency instability is straightforward: the Federal Reserve System should discontinue its policy of passively sterilizing the domestic monetary impact of foreign official interventions. Instead, a symmetrical nonsterilization rule would ensure that each country's money supply mutually adjusts to international currency substitution in the short

run, without having official exchange interventions destabilize the world's money supply.

The basic premise of this prescription, and its flaw, is that it assumes that exchange rate instability is induced by shifts in the currency denomination of the public's money holdings—that is, by currency substitution. But surely international currency speculation is not carried out by shifts between different countries' M_1s (currency plus demand deposits) but by shifts between interest-bearing assets. The proposal also encounters the not negligible issue of the transition to low inflation in the United States. It certainly does not help to overlook the fact that inflation is significantly higher today in the United States than it is in Japan and the Federal Republic of Germany. As noted previously, however, monetary policy seeks to achieve a transition to low inflation, and it is the by-product of that transition that causes the real exchange rate havoc.

Proposals for more limited exchange rate flexibility take the form of intervention rules. They may either involve an exchange rate band (fixed or moving) with full intervention at the margin and none in between or an intervention rule that seeks to dampen exchange rate movements relative to some notion of a fundamentals rate.

Proponents of band proposals are reluctant to specify how the band would actually be set. They emphasize, as does Bergsten (1982, p. 11), that

> there is no suggestion here of a return to fixed exchange rates, nor even to seeking "correct rates" within narrow margins. It should be possible, however, to reach international agreement on the existence of "wrong rates"—as was indeed done in November 1978, and seems largely possible today. Rates could then be pushed back toward appropriate zones through direct intervention, alterations in domestic policies and public pronouncements.

One objection to an exchange rate band is that such an arrangement actually promotes exchange rate instability within the band. The presence of a band reduces risk to portfolio holders and, therefore, increases portfolio shifts in response to perceived changes in mean returns. Thus, given random movements in mean return expectations, there will be more exchange rate variability within the band than there would be without such limits and the greater risk of speculation. Moreover, it is not clear why a rate should be allowed to change dramatically, only to be pushed back afterward. If there can be agreement on what constitutes an excessive exchange rate change, then there can be agreement on a limiting point. But, of course, this question is one on which national interests may differ, as was seen so clearly in the debate over the valuation of the U.S. dollar throughout the 1960s. It also stands to reason that authorities who take a view on what an excessive exchange rate change is will also take a view on what is too rapid a correction. Thus, intervention might dampen the correction of exchange rates and, in this way, reduce the risk of speculation, thus enhancing actual capital flows.

The basic objection to a band proposal is that it makes no sense to set limits for exchange rates but not for other key macroeconomic variables. Exchange rate targets without an accompanying, well-understood macroeconomic support program can hardly be expected to be effective. Macroeconomic policies geared exclusively to exchange rate targets rather than a broader range of targets—including real interest rates, the real value of corporate stock, inflation, and unemployment—may well lead to a deterioration of macroeconomic performance. In the absence of such a broader range of targets, one can only expect poor results from intervention policy, such as the results observed during the 1979 Carter period of overexpansion.

An alternative approach to limited exchange rate variability is based on the idea that it is possible to extract, at least approximately, from market data the sources of exchange rate disturbances. To the extent that these disturbances are portfolio shifts between currency denominations, they should be accommodated by intervention. This is the standard argument used in the literature about interest rate versus money stock targets. In that context, the rule is to peg interest rates, allowing money to vary if disturbances are primarily financial. In the present context, the rule is to stabilize exchange rates if disturbances are primarily portfolio shifts rather than events that require changes in the equilibrium real exchange rate. Specifically, if disturbances can unambiguously be identified as shifts between domestic and foreign currency debt, the appropriate policy is *sterilized* intervention that keeps the exchange rate as well as interest rates fixed. The same is true for portfolio shifts between home money and home securities, although in this case the maintenance of fixed exchange rates and interest rates would not require intervention.

When disturbances are both real and financial and identification becomes ambiguous, the case for rigid intervention disappears. Formal models, in these mixed cases, suggest that managed floating becomes the optimal exchange rate regime.[10] The extent to which the exchange rate would be more nearly fixed depends on the relative variability of real and financial shocks, the authorities' concern with the composition of aggregate demand as well as the level of activity, the perceived durability of shocks, and the structure of the economy. The strong case that can be made for sterilized intervention when all disturbances are pure portfolio shifts is no longer valid, and few sturdy rules are available to guide policymakers.

Intervention policy cannot cope with the main source of exchange rate movements—namely, *divergent national monetary policies*. When money is tightened in one country to reduce inflation, the financial disturbance is, in fact, deliberately produced by the government in the hope of reducing inflation. Moreover, the initial real appreciation, because it reduces inflation, is a welcome part of the disinflation process. Intervention would mean forcing the monetary contraction on the rest of the world, even though cyclical conditions abroad might not call for tight money. Of course, the rest of the world might pursue tight money to stabilize the exchange rate but, at the same time, implement a fiscal expansion to maintain aggregate demand in the face of higher interest rates and lower net exports. This policy is open to the objections that fiscal policy is overused and that cyclical expansions can rarely be undone.

III. Concluding Remarks

The preceding discussion argues that active policy measures, as much as the business cycle itself, cannot fail to spill from one country into another, whatever the exchange rate regime. What the exchange rate regime does determine is the particular shape of the spillover—namely, whether it takes the form of a decline in employment with relatively unchanged competitiveness and inflation, or whether there are large changes in inflation and real exchange rates (and, therefore, in real income) but relatively smaller changes in employment. The effects of fixed and flexible rates differ markedly and are influenced by the domestic economic structure. Real wage rigidity has a particularly strong influ-

[10] See Henderson (1982) and Frenkel (1976).

ence on exchange rate effects. It is here that one has to recognize Robert Mundell's point that the case for flexible exchange rates rests fundamentally on money illusion, in the sense that real wage rigidity must be absent.

Flexible exchange rates can work well when financial disturbances are indentifiable and can be accommodated by the appropriate sterilized intervention and when, in addition, real disturbances can be accommodated by changes in real exchange rates that do not conflict with full employment. Even if neither of these two requirements is met, there are long-run benefits in using a flexible rate system. But there are also short-run costs, which may be quite high, that are brought about by the very fact that the exchange rate is too flexible. These short-run costs, in turn, are higher, the more fervently policymakers (mistakenly) believe that the use of flexible rates is tantamount to the achievement of macroeconomic independence. If many policymakers hold this erroneous view, the use of flexible rates may well have a destabilizing effect on the world economy. This was already recognized in the 1960s, as evidenced by the following statement made by the Government of the Federal Republic of Germany in 1964:

> Fixed exchange rates are an indispensable element in a world committed to integration; with a system of flexible rates the existing readiness to cooperate and integrate might be destroyed at the first appearance of serious difficulties since flexible rates would offer such an easy opportunity for isolated action.[11]

If flexible exchange rates, in the course of stabilization policy, lead to excessive real exchange rate changes, and if the latter are the source of adverse spillover effects, a reduction in incentives for international capital movements may be a remedy. The case for restrictions on international capital flows of one kind or another is old. Specifically, Modigliani argued

> . . . there may arise a need, at least in the short run, for holding private capital movements in line with the achievable transfer of real capital. To achieve this goal, without outright limitations on the freedom of capital movements, countries could rely on general fiscal policy as one of the possible devices for influencing incentive to capital movements. But they should also be allowed to opt, just as freely, for the alternative approach relying on specific tax and related incentives, which, we have argued, is likely to be superior under most circumstances.[12]

[11]Quoted in Cooper (1968), p. 233.
[12]Modigliani (1973), p. 252.

The same view has been articulated by Tobin (1978) and Liviathan (1979).

The argument for specific taxes, often referred to as interest equalization taxes, to reduce the incentives for international capital flows, has been objected to on three grounds. The first, and most serious, is that such flows limit exchange rate movements and therefore imply a transmission of macroeconomic disturbances through the current account. A tight money policy in a large country would lead to a decline in real income worldwide, as would a regime of fixed exchange rates, thus avoiding the effects of exchange rate movements on real wages and on the price level. The second objection is that taxes on capital flows cannot work because they lead rapidly to all kinds of evasions, including the use of offshore markets. There is no doubt some truth to this argument, although its force is limited for transitory taxes, which would be appropriate during a period of divergent policy in a particular country.

The last objection to interest equalization taxes is that they interfere with the efficient operation of the world capital market. This argument is, in the opinion of the author, actually wrong. It mistakes the short-term money market rate for the social productivity of capital. Suppose a country reduces money growth and this leads (as it will) to an increase in the interest rate on financial assets. Incipient capital flows will lead to currency appreciation and a current account deterioration financed by borrowing abroad.[13] It is hard to argue that the current account deficit is a reflection of enhanced investment opportunities or increased time preference that, in an efficient and integrated capital market, would call for redirection of lending toward the home country. On the contrary, the decline in demand would reduce the profitability of domestic real capital. It therefore would not be optimal for capital to flow toward the country with a tightened monetary policy. Policy intervention, in these circumstances, could well enhance the efficiency of capital allocation in the world. Needless to say, not much research has been done on this topic.

Even if restrictions were imposed on capital flows, so that less adjustment took place through relative prices and adverse spillover effects on inflation, disturbances would still be transmitted through the current account. The simple fact is that whatever the exchange rate regime, real disturbances will be transmitted in

[13]See Dornbusch (1980) or Buiter and Miller (1981, 1982).

some form. This suggests that what should be sought is a policy mix that makes disinflation less of a real disturbance. The mix that is most frequently suggested consists of incomes policy and a monetary rule. Experience with incomes policy is not encouraging by any means. Nevertheless, it is widely held that a flexible exchange rate system without a firm anchor consisting of both monetary rules and effective supply side policies severely disrupts the established liberal world order based on economic growth and openness in trade and capital markets.

APPENDIX

Macro Model and Data Sources

Macro model

Combining equations (1) and (2) and using equations (3)–(5) and (7) leads to the following system of equations:

$$m - w - (1-\beta)\theta = h(f + a\theta - br^* - b\beta\dot{\theta}) - c(r^* + \dot{\theta} + \dot{w}) \qquad (11)$$

$$\dot{w} = \gamma(f - br^* - b\beta\dot{\theta} + a\theta) + \alpha(1-\beta)\theta \qquad (12)$$

which defines the rates of change of wages (in equation (13)) and of the real exchange rate (in equation (15))

$$\dot{w} = \{[(1-\beta)(b\beta(\gamma - \alpha h) - \alpha c) - a\gamma c]\theta - \gamma cf - \gamma b\beta(m - w) + \gamma cb(1-\beta)r^*\}/\Delta \qquad (13)$$

By assumption,

$$\Delta \equiv b\beta(c\gamma - h) - c < 0 \qquad (14)$$

and

$$\dot{\theta} = [(m - w) + (a(c\gamma - h) + (c\alpha - 1)\,(1-\beta))\theta + (c(1 - b\gamma) + hb)r^* + (c\gamma - h)f]/\Delta \qquad (15)$$

The slopes of the schedules in Figure 1 are given by the following two equations:

$$\left.\frac{dw}{d\theta}\right|_{\dot{w}=0} = \frac{(1-\beta)\,(b\beta(\gamma - \alpha h) - \alpha c) - a\gamma c}{\gamma b\beta} \qquad (16)$$

and

$$\left.\frac{dw}{d\theta}\right|_{\dot{\theta}=0} = a(\gamma c - h) + (c\alpha - 1)\,(1-\beta) \qquad (17)$$

The long-run solutions for wages and the real exchange rate are as follows:

$$\theta = (b\lambda r^* - \lambda f)/(1 + \alpha\lambda) \tag{18}$$

and

$$w = m + (c + b(h - \gamma/\alpha)\Big/(1 + a\lambda))r^* - ((h - \gamma/\alpha)\Big/(1 + a\lambda))f \tag{19}$$

and are obtained by setting $\dot{w} = \dot{\theta} = 0$ in equations (11) and (12).

Data sources

In Table 1, the cyclical variable is the OECD unemployment rate, which is available only as far back as 1964. The real oil price is measured as the dollar price of oil deflated by the U.S. GNP deflator. The terms of trade of the non-oil developing countries are measured by the ratio of export to import prices reported in the Fund's monthly publication, *International Financial Statistics* (see World Tables, "Export Unit Values," line 74d/country code 201 and "Import Unit Values," line 75d/country code 201). The real exchange rate for the dollar is reported in the same source (see World Tables, "Cost and Price Comparisons for Manufacturing," the relevant subsection of which is entitled "Relative Wholesale Prices").

The real materials price in equation (2) is the index of the prices of all commodities found on line 76ax of the "Commodity Prices" section of the World Tables in *International Financial Statistics,* deflated by the dollar export price of manufactures of industrial countries reported in the United Nations' *Monthly Bulletin of Statistics.* In equation (3), an index of 33 commodity prices is used. The index is prepared by the Commodities and Export Projections Division of the World Bank's Economic Analysis and Projections Department, and the most recent data are contained in Table 13 on page 31 of Grilli (1982). The indices for agricultural prices and the prices of the metals and minerals group are drawn from the same source.

BIBLIOGRAPHY

Argy, Victor, and Joanne Salop, "Price and Output Effects of Monetary and Fiscal Policy Under Flexible Exchange Rates," *Staff Papers,* Vol. 26 (June 1979), pp. 224–56.

Artus, Jacques R., "Monetary Stabilization With and Without Government Credibility," *Staff Papers,* Vol. 28 (September 1981), pp. 495–533.

Basevi, Giorgio, and Paul de Grauwe, "Vicious and Virtuous Circles," *European Economic Review,* Vol. 10 (1977), pp. 277–301.

Bergsten, C. Fred, *The International Implications of Reaganomics,* Kieler Vorträge, No. 96 (Tübingen, 1982).

Blanchard, Olivier J., "Speculative Bubbles, Crashes and Rational Expectations," *Economics Letters,* Vol. 3 (1979), pp. 387–89.

———, "Credibility, Disinflation and Gradualism" (unpublished, Harvard University, April 1982).

Branson, William H., and Julio J. Rotemberg, "International Adjustment with Wage Rigidity," *European Economic Review,* Vol. 13 (May 1980), pp. 309–32.

Buiter, W., and M. Miller, "Monetary Policy and International Competitiveness: The Problems of Adjustment," *Oxford Economic Papers,* New Series, Vol. 33, Supplement (July 1981), pp. 143–75.

———, "Real Exchange Rate Overshooting and the Output Cost of Bringing Down Inflation," *European Economic Review,* Vol. 15 (1982), pp. 83–123.

Caves, Richard E., "Flexible Exchange Rates," *American Economic Review: Papers and Proceedings of the Seventy-Fifth Annual Meeting of the American Economic Association,* Vol. 53 (May 1963), pp. 120–29.

Cooper, Richard E., *The Economics of Interdependence: Economic Policy in the Atlantic Community* (New York, 1968).

Dornbusch, Rudiger, *Open Economy Macroeconomics* (New York, 1980).

———, "Equilibrium and Disequilibrium Exchange Rates," *Zeitschrift für Wirtschafts und Sozialwissenschaften,* Vol. 6 (1982), pp. 573–99.

———, "Exchange Risk and the Macroeconomics of Exchange Rate Determination," in *The Internationalisation of Financial Markets and National Policy,* ed. by R. Hawkins, R. Levich, and C. Wihlborg (1983).

Drèze, Jacques H., and Franco Modigliani, "The Trade-Off Between Wages and Employment in an Open Economy," *European Economic Review,* Vol. 15 (January 1981), pp. 1–40.

Flood, Robert P., and Peter M. Garber (1982 a), "A Model of Stochastic Process Switching," International Finance Discussion Papers, No. 201 (Board of Governors of the Federal Reserve System, January 1982).

——— (1982 b), "Collapsing Exchange Rate Regimes: Some Linear Examples" (unpublished, Board of Governors of the Federal Reserve System, 1982).

Frenkel, Jacob A., "The Optimal Dirty Float" (unpublished, University of Chicago, 1976).

———, "Flexible Exchange Rates, Prices, and the Role of 'News': Lessons from the 1970s," *Journal of Political Economy,* Vol. 89 (August 1981), pp. 665–705.

———, and Michael L. Mussa, "The Efficiency of the Foreign Exchange Market and Measures of Turbulence," *American Economic Review: Papers and Proceedings of the Ninety-Second Annual Meeting of the American Economic Association,* Vol. 70 (May 1980), pp. 374–81.

Genberg, Hans, "Effects of Central Bank Intervention in the Foreign Exchange Market," *Staff Papers,* Vol. 28 (September 1981), pp. 451–76.

Grilli, Enzo R., ed., *The Outlook for Primary Commodities,* World Bank Staff Working Paper No. 9 (Washington, July 1982).

Henderson, Dale W., "The Role of Intervention Policy in Open Economy Financial Policy: A Macroeconomic Perspective," International Finance Discussion Papers, No. 202 (Board of Governors of the Federal Reserve System, February 1982).

International Monetary Fund, *World Economic Outlook: A Survey by the Staff of the International Monetary Fund* (Washington, 1982).

Johnson, Harry G., "The Case for Flexible Exchange Rates, 1969," in his book, *Further Essays in Monetary Economics* (Harvard University Press, 1973), pp. 198–222.

Krugman, Paul, "Consumption Preferences, Asset Demands, and Distribution Effects in International Financial Markets," National Bureau of Economic Research, Working Papers Series, No. 651 (March 1981).

Liviathan, N., "Neutral Monetary Policy and the Capital Import Tax" (unpublished, Hebrew University of Jerusalem, 1979).

Lizondo, J. Saúl, "Foreign Exchange Futures Prices Under Fixed Exchange Rates" (unpublished, ITAM, Mexico, 1980).

McKinnon, Ronald I., "Currency Substitution and Instability in the World Dollar Standard," *American Economic Review,* Vol. 72 (June 1982), pp. 320–33.

Marston, Richard C., "Wages, Relative Prices and the Choice Between Fixed and Flexible Exchange Rates," *Canadian Journal of Economics,* Vol. 15 (February 1982), pp. 87–103.

Modigliani, Franco, "International Capital Movements, Fixed Parities, and Monetary and Fiscal Policies," in *Development and Planning: Essays in Honour of Paul Rosenstein Rodan,* ed. by Jagdish Bhagwati and Richard S. Eckaus (MIT Press, 1973), pp. 239–53.

———, and Tommaso Padoa Schioppa, *The Management of an Open Economy with "100% Plus" Wage Indexation,* Essays in International Finance, No. 130, International Finance Section, Department of Economics, Princeton University (1978).

Mussa, Michael L., *The Role of Official Intervention,* Group of Thirty, Occasional Papers, No. 6 (New York, 1981).

Obstfeld, Maurice, "Relative Prices, Employment, and the Exchange Rate in an Economy with Foresight," *Econometrica,* Vol. 50 (September 1982), pp. 1219–42.

Sachs, Jeffrey D., "Wages, Profits and Macroeconomics Adjustment: A Comparative Study," *Brookings Papers on Economic Activity: 2* (1979), pp. 269–319.

———, "Wage Indexation, Flexible Exchange Rates and Macroeconomic Policy," *Quarterly Journal of Economics,* Vol. 64 (June 1980), pp. 731–47.

Salant, Stephen W., and Dale W. Henderson, "Market Anticipations of Government Policies and the Price of Gold," *Journal of Political Economy,* Vol. 86 (August 1978), pp. 27–48.

Tirole, Jean, "On the Possibility of Speculation Under Rational Expectations," *Econometrica,* Vol. 50 (September 1982), pp. 1163–81.

Tobin, James, "A Proposal for International Monetary Reform," Cowles Foundation for Research in Economics, Yale University, Discussion Paper No. 506 (October 20, 1978).

Williamson, John, *The Open Economy and the World Economy* (forthcoming in 1983).

Comments

Ernesto Hernández-Catá

This commentary covers three topics briefly. The first relates to the model presented in the first section of Mr. Dornbusch's paper and some of its implications for the appropriate conduct of monetary and fiscal policies against the background of a tightening of monetary conditions in the United States. The second topic relates to the problem of modeling expectations in the context of uncertainty regarding the future of policies. The final topic relates to the external implications of monetary restraint in the United States.

The Dornbusch model suggests that a small, open economy with flexible exchange rates would experience a long-run decline in output and a long-run real depreciation of its currency as a result of a tightening of monetary policy in the rest of the world (referred to, for simplicity, as "the United States"). In addition, there would be an increase in consumer prices, partly because of the real depreciation of the domestic currency but also because the decline in the demand for money stemming from lower output and higher interest rates must be offset, in long-run equilibrium, by a decline in the real money supply.

The question one may ask is how, on the basis of the model, the small, open economy should adjust its macroeconomic policies in response to a tightening of monetary conditions in the United States. First, it can be noted that in long-run equilibrium, monetary policy in the small economy has no effect on domestic interest rates (which are determined by world interest rates) or on domestic output (which is fully determined in the goods and labor markets, as shown in Figure 3).[1] Domestic monetary policy does, however, influence the long-run behavior of domestic consumer prices through the money demand function. Thus, it might be argued that monetary policy in the small, open economy should be tightened in response to a rise in real interest rates abroad. Such tightening would prevent a permanent increase in consumer prices and would probably moderate any overshooting of the real exchange rate.

[1]By contrast, the assumption that a tightening of monetary conditions in the United States would result in a permanent increase in world interest rates implies that U.S. monetary policy *does* have long-run effects.

It can also be noted that an expansionary fiscal policy in the small country would stimulate domestic output and lead to a real appreciation of the domestic currency (in the language of Figure 3, a fiscal expansion at home shifts the IS schedule to the right). Thus, in terms of the model, fiscal expansion at home would appear to provide an offset to the effects of monetary restriction abroad. There are, of course, well-known practical problems with this prescription. Today, budget deficits are generally perceived to be excessive; a fiscal expansion would strain further the financial position of the government and might give rise to expectations of future monetization of the deficit.

Questions can also be asked about what would be the appropriate fiscal policy in the United States from the standpoint of its partners. In the Dornbusch model, fiscal policy abroad affects the small, open economy in two ways: (1) by changing world interest rates and (2) by changing external demand, thereby influencing the current account balance of the small country.

It is difficult to ascertain the net effect of these changes, because the structure of the U.S. economy is not specified in the Dornbusch model. Presumably, a tightening of fiscal policy in the United States would lower U.S. interest rates and lead to a worldwide reduction in crowding out. However, the net effect of U.S. fiscal policy on other countries would depend to a large extent on whether aggregate demand in the United States would ultimately rise or fall as a result of fiscal restraint. If aggregate demand were to decline in the United States (as it would if the effects of fiscal policy in that country were similar to those described in the context of the small economy model), there would be an adverse effect on the current account of the small country. The fall in external demand and the decline in world interest rates would affect output in the small country in opposite directions; therefore, the final outcome would depend upon the parameters of the model and could not be determined a priori. However, there is at least the possibility that the effect of lower demand in the United States could outweigh the effect of the decline in interest rates. Under this scenario, a fiscal contraction in the United States would aggravate the recessionary impact of U.S. monetary policy on the small country and would also result in a further real depreciation of the small country's currency.

Of course, it may be more realistic to assume that (beyond the short run) fiscal restraint in the United States would stimulate domestic output by improving expectations concerning the outlook for monetary control and inflation. In this case, a tightening of fiscal policy in the United States would stimulate output and employment in the small, open economy. This result would be consistent with the widespread belief that action to cut the U.S. budget deficit would alleviate the adverse external effects of tight monetary policy in the United States.

Mr. Dornbusch remarks that "many of the disturbances in the world economy are not the result of actual changes in fundamentals," such as macroeconomic policies, "but rather of changes in expectations about the future course of these fundamentals."[2] He adds that when expectations are formed in certain ways, movements in exchange rates and other variables will not necessarily promote macroeconomic stability. For example, market participants may have the wrong model of fundamentals in mind. Expectations based on this erroneous model will affect the exchange rate and, as a result, the "exchange rate will be significantly more volatile than is warranted by the true model."[3]

An equally serious problem for both the model builder and the policymaker is that, under certain circumstances, it may be impossible for market participants to know what the "true model" is. Suppose that market participants are well informed and have adequate knowledge of the various structural relationships that govern the behavior of the private sector. Suppose further that the monetary authorities have announced their intention of bringing down the growth rate of the monetary aggregates with the aim of reducing inflation. Even if market participants are convinced that the authorities are willing (and technically able) to pursue the policy that has been announced, they might be uncertain as to how long the government will continue to support the policies of the central bank in a context of rising unemployment. Specifically, market participants might reasonably assume that there is a "politically unbearable rate of unemployment" at which the government will stop supporting monetary restraint and will exert pressure on the central bank to relax monetary policy.

For the model builder, the problem is that the "politically unbearable" unemployment rate, a key parameter of the model, is unknown and cannot be estimated on the basis of historical information. At best, individuals can form judgments as to what kinds of political pressures are likely to arise and as to how the govern-

[2]See p. 18.
[3]See p. 19.

ment will react to such pressures; but it is clear that judgments of this kind will be very difficult to make.

Under such circumstances, market participants are likely to assess monetary policy by focusing on deviations of monetary growth from the announced target. As unemployment rises, any initial estimate of the "politically unbearable" unemployment rate will be revised upward if, and only if, monetary expansion remains at or below the target rate for a significant period. According to this scenario, expectations about underlying inflation will adjust only slowly—as doubts concerning the persistence of monetary restraint are dispelled by actual performance—and monetary policy will have adverse effects on output and employment. This expectational mechanism resembles the backward-looking adaptive expectations scheme used in many econometric models. This is the case not because individuals believe that the future is necessarily the mirror image of the past, but because they do not know whether or when the authorities will cave in under pressure.

Ultimately, if monetary restraint persists, those who have based their behavior on the assumption that inflation will continue will suffer, not necessarily because they were "fooled" or because they did not use existing information in an efficient way, but because the parameters of the decision-making process could not be known in advance. Conversely, failure to persevere in the effort to reduce monetary growth would seriously undermine any future stabilization attempts, as it would convince market participants that there is a critical unemployment rate above which the government will stop supporting monetary restraint and will call for a relaxation of policy.

In Mr. Dornbusch's paper, a long list of ills is attributed to monetary tightness in the United States during the past several years. Monetary restraint in the United States causes high nominal and real interest rates and increases unemployment abroad, even in long-run equilibrium; it leads to exchange rate overshooting and causes the currencies of U.S. trading partners to depreciate in real terms, thus raising consumer prices abroad. Furthermore, a tightening of monetary conditions in the United States worsens the current account balances of developing countries by raising the interest payments on their external debt; it also hurts developing countries by depressing the prices of commodities relative to manufactured goods prices through a reduction in demand in industrial countries and an appreciation of the U.S. dollar.

There is no doubt that the policies aimed at reducing inflation in the United States have had effects on other countries. However, the effects have not been unequivocally damaging. For example, the real appreciation of the dollar has reduced the competitiveness of U.S. exports, thereby contributing to an improved current account performance by other countries (particularly those that export largely manufactured goods). Moreover, while it is true that monetary restraint in the United States has contributed to a decline in the real prices of commodities, it would appear that in some cases (petroleum, for example) the decline has been greeted with relief in many countries, developing as well as industrial.

More fundamentally, it should be noted that without a lasting reduction in inflation, there is little hope for significant improvements in the long-term growth of productivity and output in the United States—improvements that are clearly important to the rest of the world. Mr. Dornbusch is correct in stating that a move toward fixed exchange rates would be complicated by policy instability in major countries, and it should also be recognized that such instability is impairing the functioning of a flexible exchange rate system. It is precisely for this reason that the restoration of price stability in the United States would be a major contribution to the stability of the world economy.

Willem H. Buiter

As regards the traditional debate on the relative merits of floating versus fixed exchange rates, Dornbusch argues quite clearly and convincingly that floating exchange rates are desirable and useful for accommodating and permitting differences in trend inflation rates and differences in trend rates of productivity growth between countries, but that they are not a means of insulating a country against external shocks, let alone a means of avoiding external spillovers from domestic policy changes. So, from the point of view of a single country operating in a given world system, the question of fixing versus floating reduces to a variant of the price versus quantity argument, and some form of managed float will obviously be optimal, with precise specification of the rule depending on 750 different parameters. Again, no clear-cut evidence for or against the current regime emerges.

Both fixed rate and floating rate regimes require rules of the game with respect to domestic monetary and budgetary policies in order to operate well. The merit of a floating rate regime is that when the rules of the game are not followed, fixed rate regimes break down while floating rate regimes simply perform poorly but continue to operate. Consequently, industrial countries will be stuck with some measure of exchange rate flexibility for the foreseeable future, given the lack of policy convergence.

When the Dornbusch paper talks about interdependence, it refers to national economies as "coupled," interacting systems. This is structural or model interdependence. An equally important form of interdependence is, of course, strategic interdependence. Dornbusch is most explicit about this. His statement that national policy autonomy must be accepted as a fact amounts to saying that noncooperative or, at best, only partly cooperative behavior by the players in the international arena must be taken as given. Dornbusch goes on to analyze various domestic policy responses to exogenous foreign policy shocks, as well as domestic policy design with foreign policy design and foreign policy rules taken as given.

There are positive and normative assumptions implied by describing policymaking in the international economic system as a noncooperative, non-zero-sum Nash game in which countries take the rest of the world's actions as given. While this description may be accurate for a number of small and medium-sized countries, it is clearly not accurate for the United States, which is more of a Stackelberg leader in the international arena. Therefore, a positive theory of strategic interdependence has to be developed in addition to the theory of model interdependence simply to make sense of the data and to interpret the time-series records presented in the Swoboda paper. This positive theory is needed to enhance analysts' understanding of how countries respond to each other's policy actions and of what games are really being played. Of course, at the normative level, a theory of strategic interdependence is needed to facilitate the design of feasible cooperative schemes and rules of the game that may enhance the performance of the system as a whole. International organizations like the Fund aim to do just that, in order to enable the international economy to achieve some of the potential gains that cooperation promises. Presumably, international economic interaction is not a zero-sum game, even though it is frequently played as if it were.

Some brief comments on the formal model presented in the

Dornbusch paper are in order. The main difference between the analysis contained therein and the familiar Dornbusch analysis is that the former adds real wage rigidity to the latter's nominal wage rigidity. One implication—an important one—is that real shocks, such as changes in world trade, in world interest rates, and in domestic fiscal stances will now have long-run effects on real output and employment. This change in the model is an important one, because it really alters the apparent attractiveness of the real interest equalization tax, which is mentioned in the Dornbusch paper as one means of trying to prevent undesirable real exchange rate overshooting in the international economy. Clearly, if there are only nominal shocks and nominal rigidity in the economy, then a real exchange rate equalization tax that prevents unnecessary change in the real exchange rate will be a sensible second-best policy, provided it can be implemented. However, real shocks in the international economy that require changes in the equilibrium real exchange rate and real wages if full employment is to be maintained should not be countered with a real interest rate equalization tax. The discussion in the Dornbusch paper, especially that concerned with Figure 2, is illuminating in this regard. After there is an increase in world interest rates, there is either an overshooting of the real exchange rate or of unemployment. In a way, the real exchange rate absorbs part of the shock that might otherwise fall on unemployment. Introduction of a real interest rate equalization tax, which in the model is also a real exchange rate stabilization tax, might well lead to higher unemployment.

Another important distinction is very similar to one drawn in the labor market literature between the real product wage relevant to employers and the real consumption wage viewed by workers. When the Dornbusch model talks about real interest rates, it is apparently referring to real intereat rates as viewed by consumers. During the adjustment process, as has been witnessed recently in the United Kingdom, the real interest rate as viewed by consumers—by lenders, in other words—is very different from the real interest rate as viewed by producers, especially by producers in the internationally exposed sector of the economy. These producers, after all, will have to repay their borrowing out of the proceeds from sales of goods that do not follow the same trend as the general inflation rate but instead follow the trend of the inflation rate of internationally traded goods prices. Thus, a huge wedge can open up between consumers' and producers' real interest rates.

The points Dornbusch makes about the volatility of foreign exchange markets and about bubbles, pesos, and runs are very well taken. It gives one very little comfort to know that asset market prices fully reflect all available information, if part of that information is of the sunspot, Henry Kaufman, or other nonfundamental variety. More widespread use of capital controls may, indeed, be the only feasible way of preventing these kinds of disequilibrium changes in the real exchange rate from disrupting the international economy. There is a tendency to confuse the notion of informational efficiency of markets, in the narrow technical sense, and the notion of economic, or allocative, efficiency. Information efficiency simply means that nobody can systematically make a risk-adjusted profit that is above normal. Allocative efficiency relates to the way in which markets expand the consumption possibilities set and determine the economy's position in it. Dornbusch rightly focuses on the allocative efficiency of markets.

An examination of the European response to high U.S. interest rates may serve to illustrate some of Dornbusch's observations on this subject. If there is something in the Mundell view that expansionary monetary policy in a floating-exchange-rate world with capital mobility is a beggar-my-neighbor policy, then appreciation of the U.S. dollar, which corresponds to depreciation of European effective exchange rates, should be welcomed by Europeans as an offset to the contractionary influence of U.S. tight money on European effective demand. The last thing, therefore, one should do in Europe is try to stabilize the exchange rate by raising interest rates and tightening money as the United States is doing. If a depreciating exchange rate, however, has no expansionary effect on European production—say, because there is absolute real wage resistance—then there will be only the inflationary consequences, and European countries might as well allow their interest rates to follow U.S. interest rates upward.

Economic Structure and Policy for External Balance

WILLIAM H. BRANSON*

I. Introduction and Summary

THE TRADITIONAL MACROECONOMICS of the period since World War II, as well as the more recent rational expectations and neo-Keynesian approaches, analyze one-commodity economies. Output, or real gross national product (GNP), is like the *schmoo*[1] that lived in Dogpatch. It is a single good that can be consumed, invested, or exported, and it is produced by a homogeneous labor force and capital stock. The emphasis in these macroeconomic models has typically been on the interaction between the real and financial sectors and on the role of aggregate demand policy. The international version of this model, in its simplified extreme, is the monetary model of the balance of payments or, more recently, of the exchange rate.

During the 1970s emphasis shifted to the role of structure and the supply side. Most of the shocks to the industrial economies came from relative price changes, which cannot be analyzed clearly in a model with one commodity. The oil and raw materials price increases, exchange rate changes, and growth of manufacturing output in developing countries all appear as changes in relative prices in the economies of countries of the Organization for Economic Cooperation and Development (OECD). To analyze these events, structure must be specified.

Research in open economy macroeconomics has responded to

*William H. Branson is Professor of Economics and International Affairs at Princeton University and Director of the Research Program in International Studies at the National Bureau of Economic Research (NBER). He is the author of *Macroeconomic Theory and Policy* and has served as a consultant at the World Bank. He is currently on leave as Visiting Professor at the Athens School of Economics and Business Sciences and concurrently at the Johns Hopkins University Bologna Center.

[1]Character in U.S. cartoon by Al Capp.

the facts. Emphasis has shifted to the supply side and the role of structure in transmitting economic disturbances and effects of policy. Most recently the literature has begun to focus on questions of optimal structure. Examples are Flood and Marion (1982) and Marston (1982), who study optimal wage indexation and choice of exchange rate regimes.

This paper discusses some of the more significant results of the role of economic structure in determining how disturbances are transmitted. In general, the focus is on the exchange rate as an instrument for adjustment to external balance. Section II begins with an exposition of the monetary model of the balance of payments, which assumes virtually no structure. This provides a framework for the sections that follow and that introduce structural differences into the model, one at a time. In Section III the effects of trade structure on the results of changes in exchange rates are studied. The role of supply elasticities is emphasized. In Section IV the effects of wage rigidities and indexation are discussed. In Section V the effects of financial market structure on adjustment and the choice of exchange rate regime are studied.

The basic results can be summarized briefly. First, the effects of changes in exchange rates may be asymmetric between Europe and the United States. Movements in the exchange rate have their main effect on trade in the United States, by changing relative prices, which thus makes the exchange rate an efficient instrument for external adjustment in the United States. But in Europe changes in the exchange rate may have their main effect on domestic prices, making the exchange rate a poor instrument for external balance.

Second, demand policy in countries with real wage stickiness moves the price level in those countries, but influences output only in countries with nominal wage stickiness. Again, there may be a difference between Europe, with sticky real wages, and the United States with sticky nominal wages. Third, only countries with developed and open financial markets can expect a floating exchange rate to be stable. This may be the reason why the industrial countries tend to float, while the developing countries tend to peg their exchange rates.

II. The Monetary Model

In order to set the framework for discussion of the importance of various aspects of economic structure for international adjustment and interdependence, we begin with a simple version of the monetary model of the balance of payments that was a popular tool of analysis in the 1960s and early 1970s. The monetary model assigned virtually no role to economic structure. Much of the research since the early 1970s showing the role of structural aspects can be interpreted as modifying, or making more "realistic," the assumptions of the monetary model. It thus provides a useful organizing concept and benchmark from which to begin the analysis.

The three aspects of economic structure that will be emphasized in the following sections of the paper are (a) structure of trade, (b) wage and price determination, and (c) structure of financial markets. So in setting out the monetary model, we will emphasize the assumptions made on each of these three points. We focus on the fixed exchange rate version of the model for a single country. The exposition here follows Johnson (1972). More sophisticated and complex versions can be found in International Monetary Fund (1977). Khan and Knight (1981) provide an estimated version with more detail in specification and empirical lags, estimated on pooled time-series, cross-section data for a number of developing countries.

The first strong assumption is (a) that goods are perfect substitutes. This means there is essentially one composite commodity produced by all countries in question. If the "law of one price" holds, the domestic currency price of the good P, and the foreign currency price P^* are related by

$$P = eP^* \tag{1}$$

where e is the exchange rate in units of domestic currency. In a multicountry context, e would be an effective nominal exchange rate.

If the country being discussed is a small country, in the sense that it has no influence on world prices, P^* is exogenous and independent of e in equation (1). A modification of the strong one-good assumption is to assume that each country is specialized in producing one (composite) commodity. Then equation (1) could be interpreted as translating the domestic currency price of the domestically produced export good into foreign exchange, and vice versa for imported goods. If the small-country assumption is maintained, so that many other countries are producing the same good as the home country, then all foreign exchange prices P^* are exogenous. This specialization assumption provides the starting point of the analysis of the role of structure in goods markets in Section III below. As long as the small-country assumption is maintained, the basic results of the monetary model obtain under either the one-commodity or the specialization assumption.

The second important assumption of the monetary model is (b) flexible wages and prices. Flexible real wages are not sufficient; the system must be free of all nominal price rigidity or stickiness. In general, all relative prices must be free to move to clear the relevant markets, *and* the nominal price level must be free to adjust real demand to meet full-employment output. The assumption of wage and price flexibility sets domestic output y at its full-employment level $\bar{y}$

$$y = \bar{y} \tag{2}$$

So far we have exogenized P and y by assumptions (a) and (b). It remains to pin down the interest rate by assuming (c) that domestic and foreign interest-earning assets are perfect substitutes. In the fixed rate version of the monetary model this makes the domestic interest r equal to the exogenous world rate r^*

$$r = r^* \tag{3}$$

The law of one price plus the assumption of perfect substitutes establishes the equality; the small-country assumption in asset markets makes r^* exogenous.

Money demand in the monetary model is given by

$$\frac{M^d}{P} = m(r, y), \tag{4}$$

or

$$M^d = P \cdot m(r, y)$$

It can be easily seen that assumptions $(a) - (c)$ have exogenized all the determinants of money demand with fixed exchange rates. Substitution of (1) – (3) into (4) gives us

$$M^{\mathrm{d}} = eP^* \cdot m(r^*, \bar{y}) \tag{5}$$

The demand for money is proportional to the exchange rate, given P^*, r^*, $\bar{y}$. It is useful to note here that wealth is not included as a determinant of money demand in (4). Addition of wealth effects invalidates most of the clear propositions that come from the simple version of the monetary model, as shown, for example, in Branson and Buiter (1982).

The money supply M^s is determined by the central bank's holdings of domestic debt D and foreign exchange reserves R in this simple stylized model

$$M^s = D + R \tag{6}$$

The money multiplier is set equal to unity here; we could multiply $(D + R)$ by a constant multiplier without influencing the results.

Equating money demand and supply gives us money market equlibrium

$$D + R = eP^* \cdot m(r^*, \bar{y}) \tag{7}$$

With the determinants of money demand fixed, the money stock is demand determined. In most applications of the model, movements in D are set by requirements of financing the government budget deficit, $G - T$

$$\dot{D} = \alpha(G - T) \tag{8}$$

where α is the fraction of the deficit that is monetized, and a dot over a variable denotes its time rate of change—for example, $\dot{D} = dD/dt$. With money demand fixed, equation (7) implies

$$\dot{R} = -\dot{D} \tag{9}$$

We can now describe two thought experiments that show how the model works and outline the basic policy package it implies. These are "thought experiments" because they describe the reaction of the model to changes in policy beginning from a full equilibrium position. As the purpose of policy action is generally to eliminate disequilibrium, these experiments do not describe the likely results of actual policy moves. This we will do below. But these experiments do provide a way to describe how the model works. The simulations of Khan and Knight (1981) are exactly such thought experiments.

First, consider the effects of a given expansion of the domestic debt component of the money stock, generated by a temporary government deficit. Initially this increases the money supply by the increment to the domestic debt component ΔD. With the exchange rate fixed, money demand on the right-hand side of equation (7) is unchanged. The expansion of the money supply by ΔD thus creates an excess supply of real balances, which leads to a rise in domestic absorption and a current account deficit. It also puts downward pressure on the domestic interest rate and leads to a capital outflow. Both effects reduce reserves, and the reserve loss continues until $\Delta R = -\Delta D$. This restores real balances to their original value and re-establishes equilibrium. Thus, the increase in the money supply caused by the budget deficit is eliminated by an equal reserve loss.

Second, consider the effects of a devaluation. This is represented by an increase in e given in percentage terms by $\Delta e/e$. Here the difference between the one-commodity and the complete-specialization assumptions plays a role in the analysis. In either case the rise in e reduces real balances M/eP^* by the same proportion. This reduces absorption and puts upward pressure on the interest rate, resulting in a current account surplus and a capital inflow. In addition, in the complete-specialization case there is a reduction in the price of home goods relative to foreign goods, which also stimulates a current account surplus. This is a trade elasticity effect.

The balance of payments surplus adds to reserves, and this increases the money supply until the latter has risen in proportion to the initial change in e—that is, until $\Delta M/M = \Delta e/e$. At this point, the original value of real balances is restored, and the system is back in equilibrium. A devaluation generates a temporary balance of payments surplus. This adds to reserves and increases the money supply until the system is back in equilibrium. Thus, in the monetary model exchange rate policy is really policy to manipulate reserves not the current account balance.

We can now use these properties of the model to describe a policy package for a country in an initial state of disequilibrium. The monetary model, being an equilibrium model, cannot rigorously describe what happens out of equilibrium but it is frequently used to prescribe policy in such cases.

Consider a country with an existing budget deficit, which is being monetized by the central bank, causing the money supply to increase. This generates a rise in domestic spending and inflation. The excess of absorption over domestic output yields a current account deficit, and downward pressure on real interest rates may also produce a capital outflow. Thus, the existing budget deficit generates both inflation and a payments deficit. What is the policy prescription loosely implied by the monetary model?

One draconian possibility would be to unwind the entire process. If we could go back to some initial date when the economy was in equilibrium, this alternative would require reversing to a budget surplus that would diminish the money supply, would reduce prices, and would restore the initial reserve position. This would be a policy of deflation that re-established equilibrium solely through budget and monetary policy, with no change in the exchange rate.

This policy prescription may seem too strong. This is probably because the user of the monetary model to describe long-run equilibrium also has in mind a short-run model with some stickiness in wages and prices and adjustment costs in rearranging production. An actual deflation could mean a protracted spell of unemployment. The economy, or more precisely the existing government, may not reach the long-run equilibrium toward which the policy is aimed.

A less draconian alternative would be to end the budget deficit, halting the growth in the domestic debt component of the money supply, and to devalue in order to "validate" the past increase in M. If we can estimate the parameters of the money demand function m, then for given values of P^*, r^*, and $\bar{y}$ we can estimate the percentage devaluation that would reduce real balances M/eP^* enough to restore equilibrium at the existing level of M. This would end excess absorption and validate the existing M as an equilibrium value.

This is the familiar policy package of balancing the budget to stop money growth and devaluing to end the loss in reserves. It avoids the need for actual deflation by validating the past money growth through devaluation. Preference for this policy over deflation already implies that the policymaker has some structural characteristic of the economy in mind that is not part of the monetary model.

A third alternative would provide a more gradual path to equilibrium. The budget deficit could be reduced to zero gradually. This would be accompanied by a jump devaluation to validate the existing money stock, and then further gradual devaluation at a decreasing rate to keep real balances in equilibrium as the budget deficit was reduced. An announced plan of this sort would be quite similar to the decelerating crawling peg attempts made by the "Southern Cone" countries of South America. These programs have run into a number of problems involving real appreciation of the currency, with devaluation ahead of inflation, as analyzed for example by Calvo (1981), Díaz-Alejandro (1981), Dornbusch (1980), and Krugman (1980). The explanation for the difficulty in all these cases involves specification of structure of the economy beyond the simple monetary model.

Both alternatives to simple monetary contraction imply that at least one of the three simplifying assumptions of the monetary model does not hold, and the alternative assumptions generally require some specification of the structure of the economy. We now turn to questions of the structure of trade.

III. Trade Structure and Devaluation

Under the strong assumption of perfect goods substitution, devaluation influences the current account only through real balance effects on expenditure. To study relative price effects of devaluation, we need to assume at least two separate goods (or commodity bundles), one produced by the home country and the other by the rest of the world aggregate. This adds a channel of effect for exchange rate changes, while preserving the real balance/absorption channel of the monetary model.

In this section we will analyze in a partial equilibrium framework the effect of a devaluation on the trade balance. The framework is the familiar elasticity approach. This can be used to illustrate the impact effect on the trade balance from the change in relative prices caused by the devaluation, which leads to general equilibrium adjustments. The graphs that will be used to illustrate various cases were introduced by Haberler (1949) and were used to analyze the Smithsonian realignments of 1971 by Branson (1972). The formal mathematics are presented in Appendix A of Branson and Katseli (1982).

We will characterize different "types" of trade structure in terms of special values for elasticities of demand or supply for exports, d_x and s_x, respectively, and imports, d_m and s_m. First we will begin with the traditional *small* country case, where d_x and s_m are infinite. The small country cannot influence world prices of its exports or imports. Then we will analyze the case of a *"semismall"* country, where s_m is infinite but d_x is not. The semismall country has "market power" on the export side; it cannot expand sales without reducing price. Most European countries may be in this category. A subcase of the semismall country is the "Keynesian small country," where all supply elasticities are infinite. This is the model of the usual statement of the Marshall-Lerner condition that $|d_x+d_m|>1$ for a "successful" devaluation.

A third example is the *"rigid"* country, where s_x and d_m go to zero. This would be true for a developing country producing a supply inelastic agricultural export, using an intermediate import with fixed coefficients. A fourth case that combines aspects of the semismall and rigid countries would be the *"pure manufacturing"* economy that imports intermediate goods not produced at home and that exports manufactures. Here d_m may approach zero. Japan may be an example of this.

In each case we wish to examine the effect of a devaluation on the trade balance and on the terms of trade. Negative results for either may be a reason for a country to reject devaluation as a way to eliminate a trade deficit, or in general to reject the use of the exchange rate as a tool for stabilizing the current account.

SMALL COUNTRY

We begin with the small country, where devaluation improves the trade balance and leaves the terms of trade unchanged. This case serves to introduce the basic diagrams in Figure 1, Panel A. On the vertical axes are the home currency prices of exports and imports, P_x and P_m, relative to an overall index of domestic opportunity cost. Thus, the changes in exchange rates that are discussed below are changes in real exchange rates, as shown in Branson and Katseli (1982). Quantities are on the horizontal axes. The areas under the supply-demand intersections are the domestic currency values of exports and imports.

In the small country, the infinitely elastic demand curve for exports and supply curve for imports are shifted up by the proportion of the devaluation. This raises both P_x and P_m proportionately, leaving the terms of trade unchanged. This also increases export value but has an ambiguous effect on import value, depending on the elasticity of demand. It should be clear from the diagrams that the limiting case where the increase in import payments equals the increase in export receipts would be where the supply curve for exports and demand curve for imports are both vertical. This is the rigid country case, which we take up below.

In the small country, exchange rate changes stabilize the trade balance with no effect on the terms of trade. This is a clear example of structure that is consistent with the monetary model and with a policy that uses the exchange rate for external stabilization purposes.

SEMISMALL COUNTRY

Next, consider the case of the country that is small on the import side, so that s_m is infinite, but not on the export side. This case is consistent with traditional trade theory, in which each country concentrates on production of goods along its lines of comparative advantage and exports these few goods, but imports the whole range of consumption. Each country might then be "large" in its export markets, but "small" in its import markets. A system of such countries has been called the "world supermarket" by de Melo, Dervis, and Robinson (1977). Each producer is large in selling to the world supermarket, but small when appearing as a consumer. Indices of market power on the export and import sides were computed in Branson and Katseli (1980), and their differences were quite significant. Many medium-sized European countries and developing countries producing agricultural output or minerals and having significant shares of the world markets for these might fit into the semismall country category.

The effects of devaluation on a semismall country are shown in Figure 1, Panel B. The diagrams are the same as in Panel A except for the export demand curve. It is evident that the terms of trade P_x/P_m deteriorate with a devaluation in this case. In general, fluctuations in the exchange rate will generate fluctuations in the terms of trade in the semismall country. The effect of this on real income and welfare was analyzed in Branson and Katseli (1980).

The same ambiguity in the effect of devaluation on import payments appears in Panels A and B, but the gain in export receipts is smaller in Panel B. In the semismall country case the full Marshall-Lerner conditions come into play. Insufficiently elastic demands can result in J-curve effects and lead to dynamic instability in the exchange markets.

A special subcase of the semismall country is the "Keynesian small country," in which the supply elasticity of exports is also infinite. (Jeffrey Frankel reminded me of this terminology when the topic was discussed at the Institut Européen d'Administration des Affaires (INSEAD) in Fontainebleau in July 1982.) The justification for this assumption would be that the export sector of the home country is small relative to the total economy so that resources can be moved into the sector at a constant opportunity cost. In this case the Marshall-Lerner conditions simplify to the traditional $|d_x+d_m|>1$.

In the semismall country, exchange rate fluctuations cause fluctuations in the terms of trade and may cause J-curve effects. The latter can raise problems of dynamic stability in the foreign exchange markets, as discussed in Branson (1977) and Artus (1982). Thus, even with this seemingly minor modification of the structure to conform with the basic ideas from trade theory, the use of exchange rate changes for external stabilization can be open to question.

RIGID COUNTRY

Most analysis using small or semismall country assumptions also implicitly assumes that the traded goods are final goods that substitute in consumption and that they are also substitutes in production for home goods. Consumption substitution yields demand elasticity and production substitution yields supply elasticity. Since the oil price increase in 1973, attention has turned to cases where imports are intermediate goods that may not be produced or consumed at home. The role of intermediate imports is explored extensively in Katseli (1980). In addition, there may be only a small domestic market for some exportables, such as raw materials and minerals, and the elasticity of total supply of some exports may be low.

An illustration (in the extreme) of the difficulties these structures cause might be a (probably developing) country that produces an agriculturally based raw material with an inelastic output supply in the short run. It also uses an imported intermediate input with fixed coefficients in the short run. This makes elasticities of export supply and import demand zero.

Devaluation in the rigid country is shown in Panel C of Figure 1. The terms of trade are not affected since P_x and P_m rise by the same proportion as the devaluation, but for very different reasons than in the small country (compare Panels A and C). Import payments and export receipts both rise by the same proportion. The effect on the balance of trade depends on the initial balance. An initial deficit is magnified by the devaluation, a particularly perverse result. Most devaluations occur in an initial deficit position.

The perverse trade balance results also have macroeconomic implications. Devaluation raises internal prices, reducing real balances and demand for home goods. The increased trade deficit also siphons off income, reducing demand for home goods. This can result in a deflationary devaluation, in which the devaluation itself creates a demand slump and unemployment. This problem was noted by Cooper (1971) and was more recently analyzed by Krugman and Taylor (1978). A similar problem associated with J-curve effects generally was noted by Dornbusch and Krugman (1976).

In the rigid economy, exchange rate fluctuations can magnify

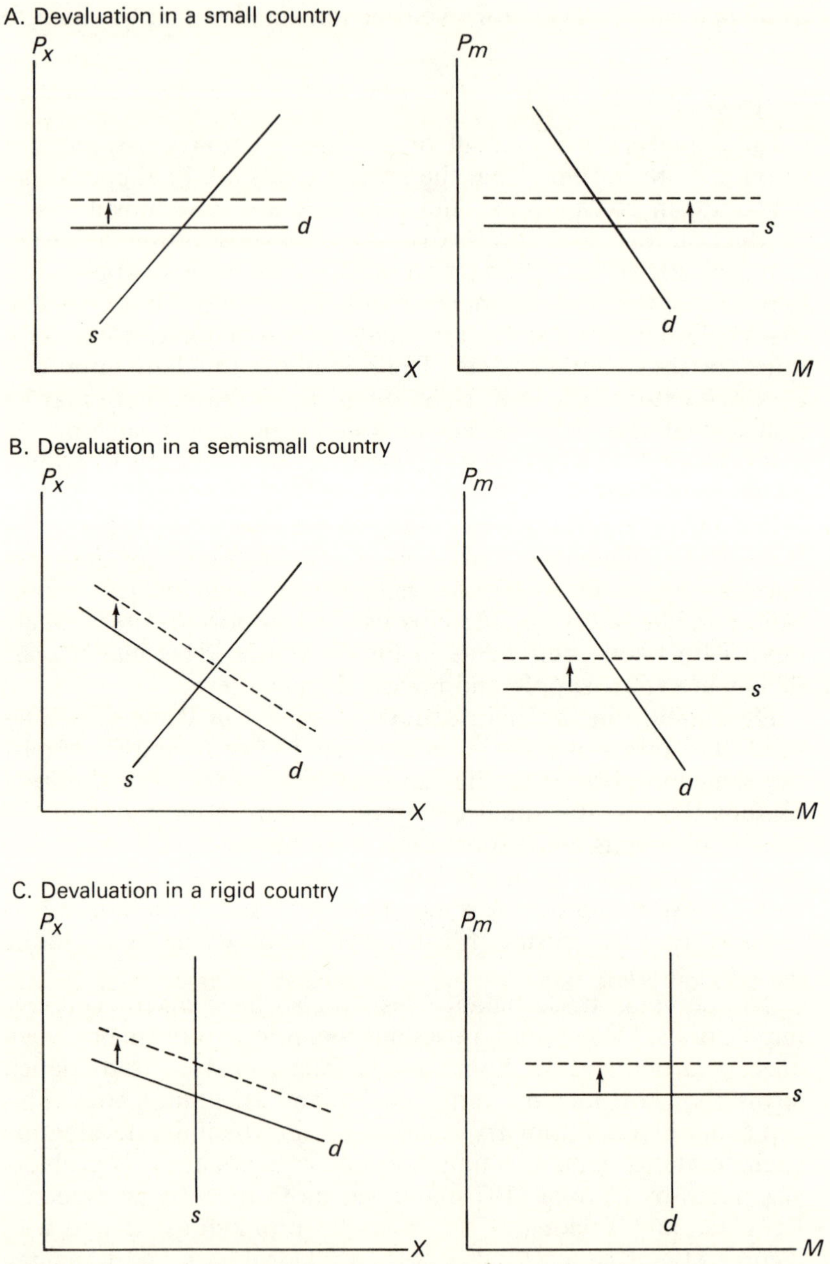

FIGURE 1. EFFECTS OF DEVALUATION

trade imbalances if the usual prescription of devaluation to eliminate a deficit is followed. Exchange rate fluctuations can also generate demand fluctuations in unexpected directions. This is an instance where structure is crucial for the application of external balance policy.

PURE MANUFACTURING COUNTRY

A final example, which is a variant on the rigid economy, is a country with imported intermediate inputs and manufacturing output. In this case export supply will have a positive slope, while import demand will be relatively inelastic. A case in point could be Japan, with 90 percent of its exports manufactured goods and 80 percent of its imports intermediate inputs.

Devaluation in this case can be analyzed with one or two modifications of Panel C in Figure 1. The effect of giving the export supply curve a positive slope is to reduce the increase in P_x; the effect on export earnings depends on the elasticity of demand. If it is inelastic, export earnings fall relative to the rigid economy case, and the effect on the trade balance is even more perverse. Thus, devaluation in this case could worsen the trade balance and cause the terms of trade to deteriorate.

Even more bizarre would be the result if intermediate inputs were tied to final output by fixed coefficients. Then the import demand curve could be positively sloped. As exports rise, intermediate imports rise. This could add to the perversity of the trade balance results while reducing the terms of trade effects.

CONCLUSION ON TRADE STRUCTURE

Traditional elasticity analyses of the effects of exchange rate changes on trade have generally implicitly assumed high supply elasticities and focused on small or semismall country cases, including the Keynesian small country. When I studied effects of the Smithsonian realignments in this framework (Branson, 1972), there was almost no literature on supply elasticities. Since the early 1970s, the problems introduced, especially by imported intermediate goods, have been recognized in the literature, and supply problems have come to the fore.

The literature on the monetary model is generally silent on elasticity conditions, which are usually presented as an alternative to the elasticity approach. The application of these conditions at the policy level, however, frequently assumes implicitly that the structure of trade meets the elasticity requirements. Their extension to the asset market approach to flexible exchange rates makes elasticity conditions important for the dynamic adjustment paths. Thus, empirical questions of trade structure have surfaced as important in the evaluation of exchange rate policy independently of the analytical approach or the degree of flexibility of the exchange rate under analysis.

IV. Wage Rigidity and Policy Interdependence

In this section the effects of sluggish adjustment, or stickiness, of wages and prices on policy interdependence are analyzed. The role of the exchange rate in the transmission of policy effects between countries will be especially focused on.

The monetary model of Section II assumes that flexible wages and prices set output equal to its full employment value. However, the idea that a nominal price or wage might be slow in adjusting to disturbances, policy or otherwise, has long been a part of the literature on output fluctuations. For example, the textbook "Keynesian" model focused on a sticky nominal wage. In the past decade there has been a resurgence of research on nominal wage stickiness as a source of real output fluctuations in the United States. Fischer (1977) and Taylor (1979) present models of multiperiod nominal wage contracts in a framework of rational expectations; the literature is surveyed by Gordon (1981).

In Europe there has been a "neo-Keynesian" development that has studied adjustment of the domestic economy to a temporary equilibrium with rigid wages and prices. While this literature is highly technical, good expositions are provided by Malinvaud (1977) and Muellbauer and Portes (1979). These approaches all share the assumption that *some* nominal price is rigid, and this rigidity results in output fluctuations.

The role of stickiness of nominal or real wages in international adjustment has been studied by Sachs (1980, 1981) and Branson and Rotemberg (1980), among others. They observed that while sticky nominal wages might be an appropriate model for the United States, a more appropriate model for many European countries would be sticky real wages. Japan might be an intermediate case. The nature of the international transmission and adjustment processes then depends crucially on which countries have which rigidities and on where the disturbances originate.

All this is bound to have implications for the use of the exchange rate as an instrument for achieving external balance, depending on the location of rigidities and degrees of indexation. These implications have been worked out in recent papers by Flood and Marion (1982) and Marston (1982). The analysis below will use Marston's graphic framework extensively.

Three aspects of recent research in this area provide excellent examples of the importance of the interaction of wage rigidity and economic structure for policy interdependence. The first is transmission with different kinds of wage rigidities. This can be seen most clearly in a one-commodity model. The second is the role of terms of trade effects in shifting aggregate supply; to study this we need at least two commodities. The third aspect is the pervasive importance of wage indexation, which can be seen by adding a nontraded good to the study. Each of these aspects will be analyzed in turn.

TRANSMISSION WITH WAGE RIGIDITIES

Rather than proceed with an exhaustive taxonomy, let us make the point with a single case. The problem is analyzed in detail in Branson and Rotemberg (1980). Suppose we have two countries, notionally named the United States and Europe. Nominal wages are sticky in the United States and real wages are sticky in Europe, both above their equilibrium levels. In Malinvaud's terms, unemployment in the United States is "Keynesian," and in Europe it is "classical." To make the particular point in the simplest way, let us assume both areas produce and trade the same composite commodity.

In this case, the aggregate supply curve in Europe is vertical at the level of output where the marginal product of labor equals the real wage, but in the United States it has a positive slope. These are shown in Figure 2, where P and y are, respectively, the U.S. gross domestic product (GDP) deflators and real U.S. GDP in dollars, and P^*, y^* are, respectively, the European GDP deflator and real European GDP in European currency units (ECUs). The aggregate demand curves have the usual downward slopes, and for convenience we index the \$/ECU exchange rate at unity so that $P_0 = P_0^*$.

The solid lines in Figure 2 (a) and (b) show an initial equilibrium, where supply equals demand, in both diagrams, so that both current accounts are balanced. The initial price level is given by $P_0 (= P_0^*)$, and outputs are given by y_0, y_0^*.

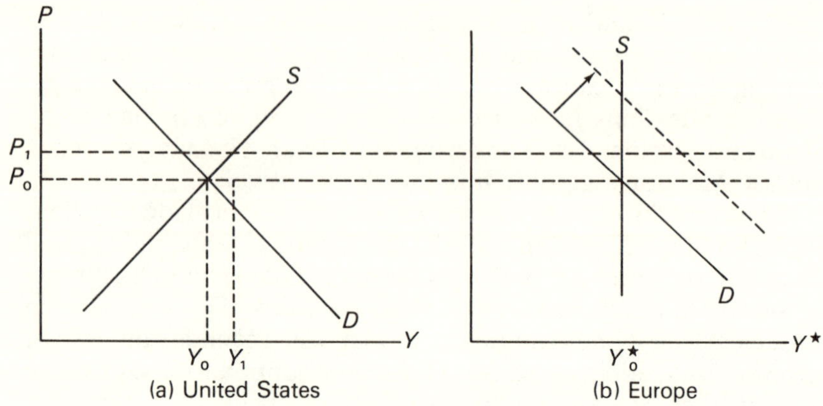

FIGURE 2. DEMAND EXPANSION IN EUROPE

Consider now a policy-induced demand expansion in Europe with the exchange rate held constant. This shifts the European demand curve to the dashed line, and raises world demand. Prices rise to $P_1(=P_1^*)$, where the United States has a current account surplus, given by its excess of supply over demand, equal to Europe's deficit. The outcome of this policy shift is a rise in prices in both areas, an increase in output and reduction in unemployment only in the United States, and a shift in the current account toward surplus in the United States and deficit in Europe.

The gain in output goes to the area with the sticky nominal wage, while the area with the sticky real wage gets inflation and a "deterioration" of the current account. It is, therefore, not surprising that the United States supported the "locomotive" approach in 1977 and Europe rejected it.

As a second policy experiment consider an appreciation of the U.S. dollar relative to the ECU. To keep the example clear we will assume this is achieved by tightening U.S. monetary policy and easing U.S. fiscal policy, which would have a neutral effect on U.S. demand in the absence of appreciation.

The results of appreciation are shown in Figure 3. Demand shifts from the United States to Europe, and prices in Europe rise relative to those in the United States. The final equilibrium shows a deficit in the United States (demand exceeds supply at P_1) equal to the surplus in Europe at P_1^*, where $P_1 = eP_1^*$ at the new exchange rate.

In the one-commodity model, an appreciation of the U.S. dol-

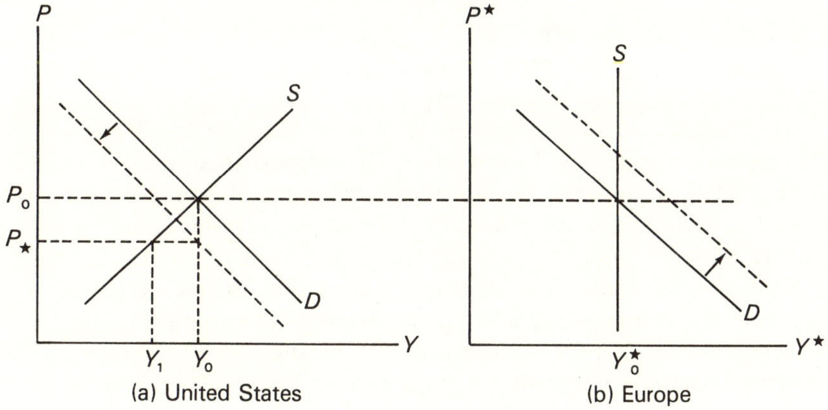

FIGURE 3. APPRECIATION IN UNITED STATES

lar with a demand-neutral tightening of monetary policy raises prices in Europe relative to the United States, reduces output in the United States where the nominal wage is sticky, and shifts the current account toward deficit in the United States and surplus in Europe. Except for the constancy of European output at y_0^*, this is a fairly accurate description of recent economic developments in the two areas. Movement in European output can be explained by going to a two-commodity model with terms of trade effects.

TERMS OF TRADE EFFECTS ON SUPPLY

Consider a more realistic case in which the United States and Europe produce different composite commodities. Then a change in the exchange rate will alter the relative price of the two commodities. Here the difference between the price that is relevant for producer decisions and the price index that defines the real wage becomes important. This point is also discussed at length in Branson and Rotemberg (1980).

In each area the producers equate the marginal product of labor to the product wage W/P^i, where P^i is the price of the output of the area. On the other hand, in our example, workers in Europe are interested in the real wage W/I, where I is a consumer price index (CPI) defined across areas' products

$$I = \alpha P^* + (1-\alpha)\frac{P}{e} \tag{10}$$

Here α is the weight of European goods in the European CPI, and

P/e is the European price of U.S. goods. We now are using P and P^* to denote the domestic currency prices of the U.S. good and the European good, respectively.

An appreciation of the U.S. dollar relative to the ECU, by reducing e, raises the European CPI defined in equation (10). With a sticky real wage W/I, the nominal wage W rises along with I. This raises the product wage W/P^* facing European employers, who react by reducing employment. The result of the dollar appreciation is a reduction in employment and output in Europe because of the terms of trade effect. This effect can be introduced into Figure 2(b), if we reinterpret P^* as the price of European output. The negative terms of trade effect shifts the vertical European supply curve to the left. This reduces European output y^* and further increases the price level P^*. Thus, the result of the U.S. appreciation in this more realistic model is stagflation in Europe—output falls, and unemployment and prices (or the rate of inflation) rise.

A structure with nominal wage stickiness in the United States and real wage stickiness in Europe is consistent both with policy differences in the 1970s and the effects of the shift in the United States toward fiscal ease and monetary tightness in 1981–82. Tentative econometric evidence has been presented by Sachs (1981), Branson and Rotemberg (1980), and Grubb, Jackman, and Layard (1982) that supports this pattern of wage stickiness. On the other hand, the quick adjustment of the real wages in the Federal Republic of Germany to the 1979–80 oil price shock, summarized in my discussion of de Menil and Westphal (Branson, 1982), suggests that real wage resistance may be dissipating in the Federal Republic of Germany. The German model of Artus (1982) assumes nominal rather than real wage stickiness in the German economy.

The basic point that comes out in the examples is that the pattern of structural differences in wage behavior across countries is important for the transmission of policy effects.

WAGE INDEXATION AND NONTRADED GOODS

Wage indexation can provide a channel through which exchange rate changes pass quickly into prices of nontraded goods and thus escalate the entire domestic price level. In this case, changes in nominal exchange rates have no effects on real rates or relative prices, and we are back with the monetary model that relies solely on real balance effects. This is a generally well-known point, so a simple example should suffice to establish it.

Consider a small country that produces and consumes traded and nontraded goods. The nominal wage is indexed to the CPI, and the price of nontraded goods P_N, assuming constant productivity equals the wage rate plus a markup. Then we have the following structure of wage and price movements.

The change in the home currency price of traded goods is the sum of movements in the exchange rate and the world price of traded goods

$$\hat{P}_T = \hat{e} + \hat{P}^* \tag{11}$$

Here $\hat{P}_T$ is the domestic currency price of traded goods, and P^* is the world foreign currency price. A circumflex over a variable denotes percentage rate of change—for example, $\hat{e} \equiv \Delta e/e$.

The price of nontraded goods follows the wage rate

$$\hat{P}_N = \hat{W} \tag{12}$$

The movement in the consumer price index is given by a weighted average of home currency P_T and P_N

$$\hat{I} = \alpha \hat{P}_T + (1 - \alpha)\hat{P}_N \tag{13}$$

and wages are indexed to I

$$\hat{W} = \hat{I} \tag{14}$$

The combination of wage indexation in equation (14) and markup for prices of nontraded goods in equation (12) makes P_N follow the index I

$$\hat{P}_N = \hat{I}$$

If we substitute this into equation (13) for $\hat{P}_N$, and equation (11) into (13) for $\hat{P}_T$, we obtain

$$\hat{I} = \alpha(\hat{e} + \hat{P}^*) + (1 - \alpha)\hat{I}$$

Solving I gives us the basic result

$$\hat{I} = \hat{e} + \hat{P}^*$$

As $\hat{P}_N = \hat{I}$, $\hat{P}_N$ also equals $\hat{e} + \hat{P}^*$

The combination of wage indexation and markup pricing of the nontraded good passes exchange rate changes right through into wages, prices of nontraded goods, and the entire CPI. In this example of a fully indexed economy, exchange rate changes have no effects on relative prices. Thus, any effect on equilibrium output would have to come through real balance effects, which could be achieved direct through monetary policy. In a fully indexed economy, exchange rate fluctuations serve more to destabilize prices than to stabilize the trade balance.

CONCLUSION ON WAGE BEHAVIOR

The structure of labor markets and wage behavior are important in determining the pattern of international transmission of the effects of policy shifts in any one country. In general, countries or areas with relatively sticky nominal wages will experience larger output responses and smaller price responses to demand disturbances than will areas with relatively sticky real wages. Terms of trade effects from an exchange rate change yield output effects even when real wages are sticky by shifting aggregate supply. However, in a fully indexed economy, all prices move with the exchange rate.

These results suggest a pattern of differences in adjustment to exchange rate changes between Europe and the United States. Suppose we think of the latter as having relatively sticky nominal wages and relatively less indexation than Europe. Then an exchange rate change will move relative prices and the balance on current account in the United States, and also influence output, all in the expected "stabilizing" direction. In Europe, however, the movement in the exchange rate will mainly move the overall price level, with minimal effects on the trade balance or output. So the exchange rate is reasonably viewed as an effective instrument for stabilizing the current account in the United States. In Europe, however, exchange rate fluctuations are equally reasonably viewed as essentially destabilizing the price level. The result is policy conflict based on different implicit assumptions about the underlying structure of labor markets and wage behavior.

V. Financial Markets and Exchange Rate Stability

In Section II, we presented the fixed exchange rate version of the monetary model as the initial framework for the analysis of effects of exchange rate changes in Sections III and IV. In this section we turn to the structure of financial markets and the stability of floating exchange rates.

The monetary model can be easily converted into a model of exchange rate determination. Let us retain the strong initial assumptions of the monetary model that (a) goods are perfect substitutes so $P = P^*$, (b) wages and prices are flexible so $y = \bar{y}$, and (c) assets are perfect substitutes so $r = r^*$. The last assumption, combined with floating exchange rates, implies static expectations. The usual statement of perfect asset substitutability with a floating exchange rate is $r = r^* + \tilde{e}$, where $\tilde{e}$ is the expected percentage change in the exchange rate. One robust empirical finding from the 1970s is that spot exchange rates roughly follow random walks. Examples of these results can be found in Branson (1982) or Frenkel (1981). As a result, the best single predictor of the future spot rate is the present spot rate. This is shown, for example, in Bilson (1981). Thus, static expectations are a reasonable rule of thumb and we can retain the simplifying $r = r^*$ assumption.

The monetary model of Section II can be written as

$$M = eP^*m(r^*, \bar{y}) \tag{16}$$

If M is fixed as well as P^*, r^*, and $\bar{y}$, this money market equilibrium condition determines a value for the exchange rate

$$e = M/[P^* \cdot m(r^*, \bar{y})\ ] \tag{17}$$

This is the equilibrium value of the exchange rate that clears the money market. With the assumption that assets are perfect substitutes, equation (17) is a monetary model of exchange rate determination. This serves as a useful starting point for the discussion in this section of the role of financial market structure.

The monetary model provides an interesting way to analyze the monetary policy problems of Section IV. Suppose we interpret the "home" country as Europe, so the asterisk variables are the United States. A tightening of U.S. monetary policy raises r^*. This reduces the demand for real balances in Europe, $m(r^*, \bar{y})$. To keep this excess supply of money from raising e (i.e., depreciating the ECU against the dollar), European M would have to shrink proportionately. Holding the exchange rate constant in the face of tightening monetary policy in the United States would keep the demand curve from shifting upward in Figure 3(b).

The monetary model has strong implications for the relationship between price stability and monetary stability in an open economy. These are shown in the first subsection below. Then we explore the implications of imperfect asset substitutability for monetary and exchange rate policy. Finally, we end with a brief discussion of the effect financial market structure has on the choice between floating and pegging the currency.

MONETARY VERSUS PRICE STABILITY

Consider the problem facing the monetary authority that wishes to stabilize the domestic price level in an open economy described by the monetary model. Since $P = eP^*$, stabilizing P when P^*, the world price level, is fluctuating requires offsetting fluctuations in e. As world prices rise, e must fall, that is, the domestic currency must *appreciate,* to prevent importation of the world inflation. As P^* falls, the currency must depreciate.

How are these movements in the exchange rate to be achieved? From equation (17) we have

$$P = eP^* = M/m(r^*, \bar{y}) \tag{18}$$

Exogenous fluctuations in world interest rates (or full employment output) will move the demand for real balances $m(r^*, \bar{y})$. If fluctuations in the nominal domestic money supply meet these fluctuations in demand, the product $eP^* = P$ will be stabilized. In equation (17), the sole source of fluctuations in the excess demand for money will then be movements in P^*, and these will cause offsetting changes in e, stabilizing P.

An immediate implication of the monetary model with a floating exchange rate is that to maintain domestic price stability the domestic money supply should adjust to meet fluctuations in demand for real balances as world interest rates fluctuate. This would be consistent with a constant money supply, or with a steady growth rate of the money supply equal to $\bar{y}$, only if the international financial environment is stable.

ASSET SUBSTITUTABILITY AND MONETARY POLICY

With $r = r^*$ (and static expectations) changes in the domestic money supply cause the exchange rate to change, as indicated in equation (17), regardless of how these changes are achieved. It makes no difference whether the central bank trades in assets denominated in domestic currency via open market operations, or assets denominated in foreign currency via foreign exchange market intervention; the two are perfect substitutes by assumption. The thing that matters is what happens to the money supply.

However, if home and foreign assets are not perfect substitutes, so that $r \neq r^*$, then it is important whether changes in the money supply are induced by open market operations or by intervention in the foreign exchange markets. Consider a given reduction in the money supply, ΔM. If this is achieved by selling domestic government debt, the interest rate will rise more, and the exchange rate will fall less, than it would if the same ΔM were achieved by selling foreign exchange reserves. This is shown formally in Branson (1977); Henderson (1982) and Obstfeld (1982) provide more up-to-date expositions, complete with rational expectations. The less substitutable the assets the more pronounced these differences will be, as is shown in Katseli and Marion (1982).

These differences could be important if the objective of the monetary restraint is to slow an existing inflation. As we saw in Section III, a reduction in *e* can have a direct influence on domestic prices, even with imperfect goods substitution and nontraded goods. Thus, a monetary tightening that has a maximum effect on the exchange rate will yield a direct effect on domestic prices. This could have an important influence on inflationary expectations.

The extent of imperfect asset substitution and the implied degree of freedom to conduct monetary policy are as yet unclear empirically. One line of research emphasizing calculation of optimal portfolios indicates a wide range of substitutability, and even complementarities. An example is de Macedo (1981). On the other hand, researchers looking for systematic variation of "risk premiums," or interest rate differentials as asset supplies change, lean toward the perfect substitutes result. A good example is Frankel (1982). Thus, no general empirical result on asset substitutability is yet available. Given the rapid change in structure of international financial markets in the last decade, obtaining clear empirical results may remain difficult for some time.

FINANCIAL STABILITY AND CHOICE OF EXCHANGE RATE REGIME

In the short run, the value of a floating exchange rate is determined by equilibrium conditions in asset markets. In the monetary model, only the money market matters; in general, the exchange rate is part of the process of general achieving equilibrium in financial markets. Thus, we should expect a floating exchange rate to exhibit the fluctuations typical of stock prices rather than goods prices, as shown by Frenkel (1981). And the short-run stability of the exchange market depends on overall stability of the financial sector, as shown in Branson (1977). The

Marshall-Lerner condition must be met if there is to be dynamic stability of the feedback process from the exchange rate to the current account, but in the short run it is financial stability that matters.

This implies that free floating is feasible only for countries with financial markets that are thick enough and sufficiently well-integrated into international financial markets to convince monetary authorities that private speculation will generally be stabilizing. The argument is given in detail in Branson and Katseli (1981). In this case a floating rate can be expected to be stable, and it is possible to leave exchange rate determination to the market.

If floating is not feasible, the central bank has to "make" the market in foreign exchange. This means it has to set a price, and the problem of exchange rate policy becomes one of how to determine the equilibrium price and adjustment toward it. One of the interesting developments of the 1970s was the alignment of countries into groups of "feasible floaters" with financial stability—mainly the industrial countries—and "peggers" with exchange rates fixed against one of the major currencies or an average of several of them.

Why might floating not be feasible for any single country? Stable floating requires the existence of a number of agents in the private sector who hold the home currency as part of a portfolio diversified across currencies and who will shift out of the currency when the exchange rate rises above its expected long-run level and into the currency when the exchange rate falls below that level. Agents may hold the currency either for transactions balances or for portfolio diversification. For many countries, the trade denominated in domestic currency is so limited that there is no external transactions demand for that currency. Some small countries, such as Singapore or Switzerland, have created portfolio demand for their currencies by giving them attractive stability or covariance properties. But portfolio diversification into many currencies is minimized, either by political risk that foreign claims on home country institutions denominated in home currency may not be honored, or by capital controls that make up part of a system of financial repression that rules out capital mobility and floating.

Thus, due to underdevelopment of the local financial market structure, floating may not be a feasible option for many central banks. This has led to the advent of more or less floating currencies and blocs such as the European Monetary System, at the center of the international financial system, while countries on the periphery are pegging in many instances.

CONCLUSION ON FINANCIAL STRUCTURE

The assumptions of free capital movement and perfect substitution are perhaps the most powerful and widely used combination in international finance. They permit the analyst to peg domestic interest rates to the world market level and to proceed with an analysis that essentially ignores the structure of financial markets. For some questions, this is the efficient way to proceed. For others—such as the choice of market for monetary policy intervention, or the decision whether to float or peg—consideration of aspects of structure in financial markets is essential. The choices that governments have made in these areas since the early 1970s attest to the governments' views that even financial market structure is important for macroeconomic policy decisions.

The short-run determination of floating exchange rates by financial market equilibrium conditions has put financial structure in the center of analyses of policy interdependence and the choice of exchange rate regimes. Sir Arthur Lewis characterized the results in his Per Jacobssen lecture at the International Monetary Fund in 1977:

> It is now the conventional wisdom that the currencies of the developed countries should float, but the currencies of the less developed countries (LDCs) should not; that is to say that each LDC should choose a more developed country (MDC) as a partner—or the SDR—and tie itself in a fixed relationship.[2]

REFERENCES

Artus, Jacques, "Effects of U.S. Monetary Restraint on the Deutsche-Mark/Dollar Rate and the German Economy," paper presented at the National Bureau of Economic Research Conference on Exchange Rate Theory and Policy (Bellagio, 1982).

Bilson, J., "The 'Speculative Efficiency' Hypothesis," *Journal of Business,* Vol. 54 (July 1981), pp. 435–51.

Branson, William H. "The Trade Effects of the 1971 Currency Realignments," *Brookings Papers on Economic Activity,* No. 1 (1972), pp. 15–69.

[2]"The Less Developed Countries and Stable Exchange Rates," in *The International Monetary System in Operation* (Washington, 1977), p. 33.

———, 1977, "Asset Markets and Relative Prices in Exchange-Rate Determination," *Sozialwissenschaftliche Annalen,* Vol. 1, pp. 69–89. Reprints in International Finance No. 20 (Princeton, June 1980).

———, 1982, "Exchange Rate Policy After a Decade of Floating," paper presented at the National Bureau of Economic Research Conference on Exchange Rate Theory and Policy (Bellagio).

———, and W. H. Buiter, 1982 "Monetary and Fiscal Policy with Flexible Exchange Rates," scheduled to be published in 1982 in J. Bhandari and B. Putnam, eds., *The International Transmission of Economic Disturbances* (Massachusetts).

Branson, William H. and Lauka T. Katseli-Papaefstratiou, 1980, "Income Stability, Terms of Trade, and The Choice of Exchange-Rate Regime," *Journal of Development Economics,* Vol. 7, pp. 49–69.

———, 1981, "Exchange-Rate Policy for Developing Countries," in S. Grassman and E. Lundberg, eds., *The World Economic Order: Past and Prospects* (London), pp. 391–419.

———, 1982, "Currency Baskets and Real Effective Exchange Rates," in Carlos Díaz-Alejandro, Mark Gersovitz, Gustav Ranis, and Mark R. Rosenzweig, eds., *The Theory and Experience of Economic Development, Essays in Honor of Sir W. Arthur Lewis* (London), pp. 194–214.

Branson, William H. and J. J. Rotemberg, 1980, "International Adjustment with Wage Rigidity," *European Economic Review,* Vol. 13, pp. 309–32.

Calvo, G. A., "Trying to Stabilize: Some Theoretical Reflections based on the Case of Argentina" (unpublished manuscript, Columbia University, February 1981).

Cooper, R. N., "Currency Devaluation in Developing Countries," Princeton Essays in International Finance, No. 86 (Princeton, June 1971).

de Macedo, J. B., "Portfolio Diversification Across Currencies," in R. N. Cooper, P. B. Kenen, J. B. de Macedo, J. Van Ypersele, eds., *The International Monetary System Under Flexible Exchange Rates: Global, Regional and National* (Cambridge, 1981), pp. 69–100.

de Melo, Jaime, Kemal Dervis, and Sherman Robinson, "A Global Model of North-South Trade and Growth," Research Program in Development, Discussion Paper No. 73 (Princeton, May 1977).

de Ménil, Georges and Uwe Westphal, 1982, "The Transmission of International Disturbances: A French-German Diometric Analysis, 1972–1982," *European Economic Review,* Vol. 18 (May/June), pp. 41–73.

Díaz-Alejandro, Carlos, "Southern Cone Stabilization Plans," in W. R. K. Cline, S. Weintraub, eds., *Economic Stabilization in Developing Countries,* (Washington, 1981).

Dornbusch, Rudiger, 1980, "Monetary Stabilization, Intervention and Real Appreciation," Ch. 12 in *Open Economy Macroeconomics* (New York), pp. 215–35.

———, and P. Krugman, 1976, "Flexible Exchange Rates in the Short Run," *Brookings Papers on Economic Activity: 3*, pp. 537–75.

Fischer, S., "Long-Term Contracts, Rational Expectations, and the Optimal Money Supply," *Journal of Political Economy,* Vol. 85 (February 1977), pp. 191–205.

Flood, R. P., and N. Marion, 1982, "The Transmission of Disturbances Under Alternative Exchange-Rate Regimes with Optimal Indexing," *Quarterly Journal of Economics,* February, Vol. 96, No. 1, pp. 43–66.

Frankel, Jeffrey, "On the Mark, Pound, Franc, Yen and Canadian Dollar," paper presented at the National Bureau of Economic Research Conference on Exchange Rate Theory and Policy (Bellagio, 1982).

Frenkel, Jacob A., "Flexible Exchange Rates, Prices, and the Role of 'News': Lessons from the 1970s," *Journal of Political Economy,* Vol. 89 (August 1981), pp. 665–705.

Gordon, R. J., "Output Fluctuations and Gradual Price Adjustment," *Journal of Economic Literature,* Vol. 19 (June 1981), pp. 493–530.

Grubb, D., R. Jackman, and R. Layard, "Wage Rigidity and Unemployment in OECD Countries," Centre for Labour Economics, London School of Economics, Discussion Paper No. 135 (July 1982), presented at The International Seminar in Macroeconomics, Mannheim, June 20–22.

Haberler, G., "The Market for Foreign Exchange and the Stability of the Balance of Payments: A Theoretical Analysis," *Kyklos,* Vol. 3 (1949), pp. 193–218. Reprinted in R. N. Cooper, ed., *International Finance* (Middlesex, 1971), pp. 107–34.

Henderson, D., "What Role for Intervention Policy," paper presented at the National Bureau of Economic Research Conference on Exchange Rate Theory and Policy (Bellagio, 1982).

International Monetary Fund, *The Monetary Approach to the Balance of Payments: A Collection of Research Papers by Members of the Staff of the International Monetary Fund* (Washington, 1977).

Johnson, H. G., *Inflation and the Monetarist Controversy,* Ch. 3 (Amsterdam, 1972), pp. 75–108.

Katseli-Papaefstratiou, Louka T., 1980, "Transmission of External Price Disturbances and the Composition of Trade," *Journal of International Economics,* Vol. 10 (August), pp. 357–75.

———, and N. P. Marion, 1982, "Adjustment to Variations in Prices of Imported Inputs: The Role of Economic Structure," *Weltwirtschaftliches Archiv.*

Khan, Mohsin S., and Malcolm D. Knight, "Stabilization Programs in Developing Countries: A Formal Framework," *Staff Papers,* Vol. 28 (March 1981), pp. 1–53.

Krugman, P., 1980, "The Capital Inflows Problem in Less Developed Countries" (unpublished manuscript, Massachusetts Institute of Technology, February).

———, and L. Taylor, 1978, "Contractionary Effects of Devaluation," *Journal of International Economics,* Vol. 8 (August), pp. 445–56.

Lewis, W. A., "The Less Developed Countries and Stable Exchange Rates," in

The International Monetary System in Operation (Washington, 1977).

Malinvaud, E., *The Theory of Unemployment Reconsidered* (London, 1977).

Marston, R. C., "Wages, Relative Prices and the Choice Between Fixed and Flexible Exchange Rates," *Canadian Journal of Economics,* Vol. 15 (February 1982), pp. 87–103.

Muellbauer, J., and R. Portes, "Macroeconomics When Markets Do Not Clear," in W. H. Branson, *Macroeconomic Theory and Policy,* 2nd ed., (New York, 1979).

Obstfeld, M., "Can We Sterilize? Theory and Evidence," National Bureau of Economic Research Working Paper, No. 833 (January 1982).

Sachs, J. D., 1980, "Wages, Flexible Exchange Rates, and Macroeconomic Policy," *Quarterly Journal of Economics,* Vol. 94 (June), pp. 731–47.

———, 1981, "The Current Account and Macroeconomic Adjustment in the 1970s," *Brookings Papers on Economic Activity: 1,* pp. 201–68.

Taylor, J. P., "Staggered Wage Setting in a Macro Model," *American Economic Review,* Vol. 69 (May 1979), pp. 108–18.

Comments

Bijan B. Aghevli

Branson provides us with a general survey of the rapidly growing literature to which he has himself made important contributions. The present paper contains a number of interesting ideas, particularly those relating to the nature of wage rigidities and policy interdependence between the United States and Europe. Following the organization of the paper, I will focus my comments on the structural aspects of the goods market, the labor market, and the financial market.

As pointed out by Branson, simple monetary models of the type described in the first section of his paper are not capable of analyzing the elasticity requirements for successful devaluation. In his section on trade structure, Branson presents a taxonomy of elasticity conditions and analyzes the effect of a devaluation under different circumstances. One certainly would not disagree with the familiar results of this analysis, but it seems to me that the essential policy issue, not discussed in Branson's paper, is an empirical one: what are the numerical values of these elasticities over the relevant time horizon? In their recent survey of the empirical trade literature on this question, Goldstein and Khan[1] find that the estimated magnitudes of price elasticities are such that they would not be a barrier to a successful devaluation over the medium term (two–three years), although in the short run (up to six months) some perverse effects may occur. These results indicate the importance of distinguishing between short- and long-term elasticities. Moreover, the empirical estimates of supply and demand elasticities for exports and imports surveyed by Goldstein and Khan are based on a partial equilibrium specification that does not explicitly take account of the real balance effects of an exchange rate adjustment on absorption and income; it could, therefore, be quite misleading to rely on these results for policy purposes. Recent theoretical and empirical work has extended the simple monetary model to include both traded and nontraded goods, and I do not think it is any longer accurate to argue, as

[1]M. Goldstein and M. Khan, "Income and Price Effects in Foreign Trade," scheduled to be published in 1983 in W. Jones and P. Kenen, eds., *Handbook of International Economics* (Amsterdam).

Branson does, that "the literature on the monetary model is generally silent on elasticity conditions." A main issue in the more recent general equilibrium models is the speed at which output in the traded sector responds to relative price changes. Rigidities in real wages can neutralize the impact of an exchange rate adjustment on relative prices and, thereby, on output. In this context, the trade structure and the rigidities in the labor market are closely related.

This brings me to the second part of Branson's paper, which deals with the implications of the "stylized fact" that in the United States nominal wages tend to be inflexible in the short run, whereas in a number of European countries it is *real* wages that appear to exhibit short-run rigidity. These labor market rigidities will obviously produce different patterns of output, current account, and price responses to exogenous shocks and policy changes in the two regions. In Branson's framework, not only the real wages but also the relative price of traded and nontraded goods are assumed to be fixed in "Europe," and, consequently, there is no room for output adjustment. A relaxation of the particular indexation formula used by Branson—which ties the price of nontraded goods to wages—would allow some real effects through the adjustment of relative prices, even if real wages were kept constant. In addition, a decomposition of traded goods into exports and imports would allow an analysis of the effect of an exchange rate adjustment on the external terms of trade; this phenomenon is particularly important if the country is a price taker in markets for some of its imports. (For instance, to the extent that oil prices are set in U.S. dollars in the short run, an appreciation of the currency in Europe against the dollar would shift the external terms of trade against Europe.)

Notwithstanding the restrictive assumptions made by Branson, however, it is reasonable to deduce, as does Branson, that if real wages are sticky in Europe the impact of a policy change in the United States will be more reflected in inflation in Europe than in the United States. Consequently, European countries would be reluctant to depreciate their currency to correct a current account deficit, as this would increase their domestic inflation. It should be noted, however, that the above argument does not hold in reverse, in the sense that European countries should not be reluctant to accept an appreciation of their currency to correct a current account surplus as this would lead to a reduction in their domestic inflation. I would also note the obvious implication of Branson's analysis that Europe's reluctance to accept a dowr ment of its exchange rate should be based only on the implications for inflation and not on its ineffectiveness to correct an external imbalance. Presumably, the impact of an exchange rate adjustment on the current accounts of Europe and the United States should be of similar magnitude since the bulk of trade of the two is with each other.

I will briefly turn to the relation between financial stability and the choice of the exchange rate regime. The author's proposition that "floating is feasible only for countries with financial markets that are thick enough and sufficiently well-integrated into international markets that the monetary authorities can trust private speculation to be stabilizing" is clearly valid. In practice, however, this seems to be a necessary but not a sufficient condition for stability of a floating rate. By this I mean that for countries that already have reasonably deep financial markets, *more* integration with other financial markets will not necessarily improve exchange rate stability; indeed, it could increase the fluctuations in the exchange rate in response to such factors as monetary shocks or shifts in expectations originating in other countries. This argument provides the basis for the recent upsurge of calls for capital controls to reduce unwarranted exchange rate movements. Whether or not such controls could be effectively implemented, however, is an issue that is open to question.

Recent monetary models have gone a long way in describing the behavior of exchange rates or, more accurately, in explaining why movements in exchange rates cannot be directly related to changes in what Dornbush calls the "fundamentals." This literature is comprehensively analyzed in a recent paper by Frenkel and Mussa.[2] While this literature is technical and does not make easy reading, its implications for policy are quite interesting and intuitively appealing. In Mussa's analysis: "The response of the exchange rate depends not only on the current policy action of the government, but also on the effects of this action on expectations concerning the future behavior of exogenous real and monetary factors. Even a seemingly modest policy change can have a pronounced effect on the exchange rate if this change significantly

[2]J. Frenkel and M. Mussa, "Asset Markets, Exchange Rates and the Balance of Payments: The Reformulation of Doctrine," scheduled to be published in 1983 in W. Jones and P. Kenen, eds., *Handbook of International Economics* (Amsterdam).

alters expectations concerning the future path of government policy." In the presence of wage price rigidities, the immediate response of prices to any policy change is likely to be much greater under a floating rate than under a fixed rate regime. Consequently, if changes in government policy were the major source of instability, a flexible rate system would lead to more instability because the exchange rate would immediately respond to a new information about the course of economic policy and, thus, affect prices. The impact of price fluctuations on output, however, would depend on the nature and extent of wage rigidities; this issue has been dealt with in a number of recent papers, notably those by Mussa[3] and by Argy and Salop,[4] but further theoretical and empirical work is required to incorporate structural factors into the monetary models of the balance of payments.

Ryutaro Komiya

The main message of Mr. Branson's paper, as I understand it, is that in an economy in which various kinds of rigidities exist, such as rigid nominal or even real wages, wage indexation, low price elasticities, or poorly developed financial markets, it is more difficult to achieve full employment and price stability than in an economy in which there are fewer rigidities. I will make four comments of a more or less general nature, drawing upon recent Japanese experience where relevant.

First, I feel that recently governments of various countries have tended to complain too much about what other governments do in the area of macroeconomic policies. Some thirty years ago, Jan Tinbergen said in his *Theory of Economic Policy* that when there are a number of targets for economic policy, there must be at least an equal number of policy instruments in order to reach the given targets simultaneously. About fifteen years ago, Robert Mundell proposed a notion of the assignment problem. Mundell said that it was best to assign to each target a policy variable which exerted

[3]M. Mussa, "The Theory of Exchange Rate Determination," scheduled to be published in *Exchange Rates: Theory and Practice*, eds. John Bilson and Richard Marston (University of Chicago).

[4]V. Argy and J. Salop, "Price and Output Effect of Monetary and Fiscal Expansion in a Two-Country World Under Flexible Exchange Rates," scheduled to be published in 1983 in *Oxford Economic Papers*.

most direct influence on that target. Consider a very simplified model of an international economy, consisting of Europe, the United States, and Japan, and suppose that each of the three has two targets: the inflation rate and the unemployment rate.

Then there are altogether six policy targets, so that in order to *achieve* the six targets simultaneously there must be at least six policy variables. Each country should use its own fiscal, monetary, and/or incomes policies at their disposal to achieve their own policy objectives, and should assign each target a policy instrument that has the most direct influence on it.

Recently, European governments, and also to some extent the Japanese Government, have been complaining about high U.S. interest rates. But from around 1970 to 1973, and also in 1978, Europeans and Japanese complained about the lack of monetary discipline on the part of the United States. Now that the United States has firm discipline on money supply, they complain about high interest rates. I think that the U.S. money supply or the interest rate is not a policy variable that can be reasonably assigned to any target in Europe or Japan.

I am puzzled by Figures 2 and 3 of Branson's paper (pages 54 and 55). If this is the correct picture of the European situation, not much can be done to reduce the unemployment level in Europe anyway. Apparently, the number of policy instruments is insufficient.

It might be said that the complaint is not about the U.S. monetary policy but about the large U.S. budget deficit that brings about high interest rates. The Japanese Government too is now being asked by foreign governments to expand the budget deficit further. But here again, any country's budgetary policy belongs to the domain of its national sovereignty. The U.S. or the Japanese Government cannot be expected to change the size of its budget deficit to accommodate the needs of foreign macroeconomic targets. Unless there are a sufficient number of policy variables, we are bound to have a conflict of interest between countries. As far as Japan is concerned, in my view, there are a sufficient number of policy instruments and enough flexibility so that there is no need to complain about foreign countries' macroeconomic policies.

In this connection I have a question about Branson's statement on page 56. He says that a reduction in real wages due to the worsening of the terms of trade results in a rise in unemployment in Europe. When real wages decline, some workers may cease working because it is not worthwhile to continue to work at lower real wages and because they prefer leisure time or work at home. This is quite understandable: it may well be a rational and economic allocation of time by individuals. Why should one call this an increase in unemployment?

My second comment is on the time dimension of the notion of rigidities. Branson says on page 57 that the real wage resistance in the Federal Republic of Germany may be dissipating. I think that many of the rigidities are not absolute ones but relative to the length of time and that rigid relations can be made more flexible over time by appropriate policies. Even oil consumption, which is inelastic over the short run, is price elastic if one considers the long run. Compared with the level in 1973, Japan's real gross national product (GNP) in 1981 was 40 percent higher, while oil consumption was over 20 percent less. It is encouraging that even in the United States workers in the automobile industry accepted lower wages in the face of major difficulties of the industry. So, various rigidities, such as wage indexation, should not be taken for granted if a country wants to attain high employment.

My third comment is concerned with fluctuations in exchange rates and swings in the balance of payments on the current account. Let me take up the current account balance first. The maximum swing in the current account balance of the United States or Japan has been in the range of 1–2 percent of their respective GNPs, at most. Major European countries have had larger swings, and for smaller countries the swing sometimes goes further, up to 8 and 10 percent. Nowadays, economies of developed countries are closely integrated with each other, by the reduction in tariff and nontariff barriers and in the cost of transportation and communications. In this highly integrated international economy, whatever is the exchange rate regime, the swing in current account balance of the size we have experienced should be taken for granted as a part of the normal macroeconomic adjustment process. Macroeconomic policymakers, and especially U.S. politicians and the general public, should not become excited about the size of Japan's overall current account surplus or the U.S. overall trade deficit experienced from time to time in the past. These surpluses or deficits, which amount to 1 to 2 percent of GNP, cannot be made equal to zero every year, just as it is difficult to stabilize completely the amount of inventory investment or fixed investment in the business sector in any country.

Coming to fluctuations in exchange rates, certainly they have been much larger than most economists thought in years before floating. But if we take the real effective exchange rate, the degree of fluctuations have been generally within the range of 10–15 percent over a quarter, and within, say, 20–30 percent over a year, for most countries. As long as each major country pursues its own independent fiscal and monetary policies, we have to accept this degree of fluctuation in the exchange rate, as there is no better alternative.

Central bank intervention in the exchange market for the purpose of stabilizing exchange rates has not been successful, generally speaking, for two reasons. First, the amount of funds that the central bank can mobilize is too small compared with the private short-term capital flows. Second, nowadays market participants' expectations are not influenced much by central bank intervention.

It seems to me that the mechanism of private speculation and short-term capital flows is not yet well understood. The largest source of speculation, at least in Japan, comes from the forward covering activity of exporters and importers. A predominant part of Japan's exports and imports are denominated in U.S. dollars. Exporters and importers always have a large balance of already made export and import contracts amounting to, say, 4–6 or even 9 months' exports and imports. Nowadays in normal times they cover by forward exchange only a small portion—say, 20 to 40 percent—of already made contracts. When exporters think that the yen has depreciated much from the trend line, they cover a much larger part of the balance by selling forward dollars. When importers think the yen has substantially appreciated, they cover a much larger part by buying forward dollars. Forward covering by exporters and importers initiates the flow of short-term capital through covered interest arbitrage. Exporters and importers can do the forward covering at any time between the time of signing the contract to the final payment, which may sometimes be half a year, nine months or even longer.

At present, the amount of Japan's official reserves is approximately US$26 billion, which is among the largest in the world. Japan's exports plus imports now amount to US$24–25 billion a month. This means that when the central bank intervenes strongly against the expectations of market participants, just one month's leads or lags in forward covering will wipe out the official reserves or double them within a few weeks, depending on whether the intervention is selling or buying. I think that, for the same reason, the target zone approach or the band proposal cannot be workable whenever the exchange rate hits the ceiling or the bottom. Needless to say, there are many other sources of short-term capital flows in addition to the forward covering activity of traders, but even with this source alone, the short-term capital flows could be really large.

Private speculation of this kind does not completely stabilize fluctuations in exchange rates, but it ensures a certain degree of stability, at least in real effective exchange rates.

My final comment is on the feasibility of the floating system. I very much agree with Branson's statement on page 62 that the floating system is feasible only for countries with well-developed financial markets. I still think the floating system is a luxury, in spite of some overshootings or large fluctuations in exchange rates. It enables the country to get rid of import restrictions, the artificial policy of promoting exports, or restrictions on capital flows. Only those countries that have well-developed and liberalized financial markets can have it.

On the other hand, I disagree with Branson on one of the reasons for the feasibility of floating. He says, for a country where the volume of trade denominated in its currency is small, the floating system is not feasible. But, as explained, when the country has liberalized forward covering activity, interest arbitrage, and short-term capital flows, there will be enough speculative activity. Potentially there will be a large amount of short-term capital flows resulting from leads and lags, and therefore even such a small country can have a floating system that will function reasonably well.

Exchange Rate Regimes and European-U.S. Policy Interdependence

ALEXANDER K. SWOBODA*

RECENT EVENTS have cast doubt on simple traditional views as to the relationship between the exchange rate regime and policy interdependence or, more generally, economic interdependence. Fixed exchange rates enforce a great deal of economic and policy interdependence; flexible rates allow a lessening of the transmission of disturbances through markets and for increased policy autonomy. Or so the story went. That story now appears incorrect, or at least incomplete, on both factual and analytical grounds. Theory has suggested new—or rediscovered old—channels of transmission of disturbances under floating exchange rates.[1] National business cycles have been as, or more, closely in phase across major industrial nations under managed floating as in the 1960s.

The aim of this paper is threefold. It broadly discusses the relationship between the exchange rate regime and policy or economic interdependence. This is done in section II, which, after a general discussion of targets and instruments of policy under alternative international monetary regimes, discusses briefly transmission under flexible rates and the notion of a world business cycle.

*Alexander K. Swoboda is Professor of Economics at the Graduate Institute of International Studies and Director of the International Center for Monetary Studies in Geneva, Switzerland. A Yale graduate, Mr. Swoboda has taught at the University of Chicago, Johns Hopkins University Bologna Center, the London School of Economics and Political Science, and Harvard University. His main writings and chief research interests are in international monetary economics, macroeconomics, and international banking and finance.

[1]This paper will touch only briefly on channels of transmission under alternative exchange rate regimes as this is the topic of Dornbusch's paper for this conference.

The section concludes that for many relationships interdependence is likely to be similar under fixed and flexible exchange rates but that the channels of transmission tend to differ. Section III speculates on the implications for the conduct of policy. It begins with a discussion of rules versus discretion, and of consistency versus credibility or commitment. It concludes with a brief discussion of the relevance of the argument to two issues raised by the organizers of this conference—the prospects for a regional arrangement such as the European Monetary System and for the return to fixed rates between Europe and the United States.

Before proceeding to such broad generalities, however, the next section offers some statistical background evidence on the correlation between main macroeconomic variables in six countries: the United States; the Federal Republic of Germany, France, and the United Kingdom; Japan, and Canada. The choice of these countries was dictated by a number of considerations. They are the six major industrial countries, and our analysis is confined to the "Atlantic" world. Data were readily available for most series of interest for these countries. And the division of the sample between the United States, the three European countries, and the two non-European ones should help detect patterns of association specific to these three groups. This should also help to shed some light on the issue of U.S. dominance over the world economy. Further evidence from a few recent studies of the transmission mechanism is cited to round out the section's selective survey of factual evidence.

I. Some Empirical Evidence

Economic interdependence at a macroeconomic level can manifest itself in a variety of ways that range from co-movements (contemporaneously and at various lags) of national target or "endogenous" variables, such as price levels, inflation rates, real output movements, or interest rates, to co-movements (positive or negative) of instrument variables (not necessarily exogenous), such as money stocks or fiscal variables. Such associations across countries are only an indication that some interdependence exists. They reveal little as to the nature and source of the interdependence. In particular, much further analysis would be needed to determine whether causality runs from, say, the United States to the rest of the world; whether, instead, these associations are responses to common outside shocks with differences in national time profiles of response due to differences in national economic structure; whether the similarities in the behavior of output, prices, and interest rates are due to common policy responses rather than to transmission through private markets; or whether there exists a world business cycle, the origins of which may be monetary or real, of which national cycles are a part.[2] Nevertheless, simple measures of association provide a useful start, especially if they help us find similarities and dissimilarities in behavior under fixed and flexible exchange rates.

This section presents, for the six countries mentioned in the introduction, correlations and a principal component analysis of changes in the following variables: the price level (consumer price index—CPI), real output (gross national product—GNP), interest rates (long-term government bond yields), money supplies (M_1), and government spending in real terms. All growth rates are calculated as the percentage change of the value of the variable in the current quarter relative to its value four quarters ago—except for interest rate changes, which are first differences over the previous quarter. The characteristics of the data are shown in Table 1.

All estimates were calculated for three periods: first quarter 1960–first quarter 1981 (or up to second quarter 1982 where available) and two subperiods, first quarter 1960–first quarter 1971 and second quarter 1974–first quarter 1981 (or up to second quarter 1982). The tables only report results for the two subperiods for clarity and to focus on the contrast between the fixed and the flexible exchange rate periods. The flexible rate period starts in the second quarter of 1974, as that observation represents the change of the variable relative to the second quarter of 1973.[3] Quarterly observations of rates of change were calculated relative to the previous year's corresponding quarter in order to smooth the series somewhat and to eliminate part of seasonality.

Table 1 contains few surprises and confirms the well-known broad characteristics of macroeconomic behavior in the 1960s and 1970s. The average rate of inflation almost triples when the flex-

[2]A number of statistical methods that go well beyond the scope of this paper begin to deal with such questions. These include tests of causal ordering, vector autoregression methods, and index models.

[3]Except, of course, for interest rates, where the second quarter of 1974 is the change relative to the first quarter of 1974.

TABLE 1. CHARACTERISTICS OF THE DATA[1]
(*Mean growth rates*)

	United States	United Kingdom	France	Federal Republic of Germany	Canada	Japan	Mean	Standard Deviation
1. Consumer price index (CPI)	2.7/8.9	3.8/14.3	4.0/10.9	2.5/4.7	2.5/9.3	5.4/8.1	3.5/9.4	1.1/3.2
2. Real gross national product	3.8/2.4	2.8/0.09	5.2/1.3	4.6/2.2	5.0/2.6	10.6/3.9	5.3/2.2	2.7/1.1
3. Money (M_1)	3.7/6.2	3.5/12.2	9.2/10.3	7.7/7.5	8.7/5.8	16.3/8.0	8.2/8.3	4.7/2.5
4. Interest rates								
a. Changes	0.04/0.20	0.09/0.05	0.06/0.19	0.03/−0.02	0.03/0.21	. . .	0.05/0.13	0.02/0.11
b. Levels	4.8/9.2	6.9/13.7	5.8/10.6	6.8/8.2	5.9/10.2	. . .	6.0/10.4	0.84/2.06
5. Government expenditure	5.0/3.4	6.3/4.0	4.9/3.8	5.0/4.1	. . .	. . .	5.3/3.8	0.67/0.30

Sources: International Monetary Fund, *International Financial Statistics (IFS)*. Data on the five variables were obtained using the following lines on *IFS* country pages: CPI (line 64); money (line 34); GNP (line 99 ar); interest rates (line 61); government expenditure (line 82); exceptions noted below; Organization for Economic Cooperation and Development (OECD), French industrial production (for GNP); and U.S. Department of Commerce, government expenditure, 1960–67.

[1]The first figure in each cell refers to the 1960, first quarter to 1971, first quarter period. The second figure refers to the period that began in the second quarter of 1974 and ended in the second quarter of 1982 for the CPI, the first quarter of 1981 for GNP, the fourth quarter of 1981 for M_1 and interest rates, the third quarter of 1981 for government expenditure. For interest rate *levels*, the second figure refers to 1973, third quarter to 1981, fourth quarter.

Real government expenditure was obtained by deflating through the CPI. All growth rates, except interest rates, calculated as $\log X_t - \log X_{t-4}$. Interest rate changes are first differences. The series that were not available (indicated by . . .) are either incomplete over the sample period or too unreliable to be included.

ible rate period is compared with the fixed rate period. That flexible rates allow for greater divergence of national inflation rates, as predicted by elementary analysis, is confirmed by the tripling of the standard deviation of mean national inflation rates around the six-country average between the first and second periods. Turning to the growth of output, there is a generalized drop for the second period, as witnessed by a decline in the average growth rate by more than half, from 5.3 percent to 2.2 percent. The decline in output growth is at least as generalized as the preceding high growth performance (compare also the standard deviations). On the surface at least, and contrary to expectations, there does appear to be "real" interdependence under flexible, as well as under fixed, exchange rates.

Averages of first differences in interest rates (row 4a) are not of much interest and are recorded here only for the sake of completeness. As for interest rate level figures (row 4b), they tell a familiar story. There is a significant rise in average interest rates in the second period and the dispersion in interest rate levels across countries rose substantially in the 1970s. As was true of inflation rates, interest rates appear to be more independent across countries during the flexible rate period than the fixed rate period.

As for the remaining two (instrument) variables, no clear pattern emerges at first sight. Nor does theory suggest a priori strong differences in their behavior under alternative exchange rate regimes.[4] Mean money growth rises significantly for the United States and the United Kingdom and falls sharply for Japan. Excluding the latter country, average money growth does rise from 6.6 percent to 8.4 percent for the average of the remaining five countries (while the standard deviation of national money growth rates remains constant). Turning to government expenditure growth in real terms, the sample is limited to four countries only. Mean growth in that variable declines for every country in the sample during the flexible rate period. On average, however, it declines by significantly less than the real growth of output, indicating a rising share of government expenditure in total expenditure and, therefore, some common tendency in fiscal policy.

These broad tendencies are of little help in answering a number of relevant questions, among which five may be listed:

(1) Can one say anything about short- or medium-term inter-

[4]See also the next section.

dependence of inflation rates, output growth rates, etc., across countries?

(2) Can one attribute some of the variation in national series to a common international factor, the remainder to individual country variation?

(3) Are answers to these questions the same for innovations in the series as well as for the series themselves?

(4) Are there systematic differences in the degree of association (interdependence?) across the two subperiods of our sample? Do these hold for all variables?

(5) Can one detect regional groupings in the degree of interdependence? Specifically, do European countries behave differently from, say, the United States?

The correlations and principal component analysis contained in Tables 2 to 5 may help to begin to answer these questions. A word of caution, however: correlations and principal components are essentially descriptive statistics, ways of organizing the data, that cannot in themselves provide any answer to a number of questions that are as interesting as, or more interesting than, those asked above. In particular, they cannot tell us anything about the source of a change in behavior between our two subsample periods, however much we may suspect that the change in the exchange rate regime or raw material shocks may have played a dominant role. Furthermore, they do not allow any inference as to causality or the nature and time profile of the "transmission mechanism."

Tables 2–5 are each divided into two parts. Panel A reports simple correlations of the relevant variable (see Table 1 for definitions). Each cell contains two correlation coefficients, the first referring to the first subsample period, the second to the second subperiod. Panel B contains the results of the analysis of the principal components for both the original series and innovations in the series. Innovations were obtained by regressing, for each sample period separately, the variable on a constant, a time trend, three seasonal dummies, and four lags of the variable. The residuals are the innovations.

Principal component analysis is convenient for searching for a common element (or a number of common elements) that could explain the variance of a number of individual time series.[5] Prin-

[5]For an exposition of principal components analysis, see, for instance, Theil (1971) or Dhrymes (1970). For a relevant application in the present context, see Genberg (1977 a).

cipal components are linear combinations of the original variables that explain increasingly higher proportions of the total variance of the variables. The first principal component is the linear combination that, by itself, explains the greatest portion of the variance (explainable by a single component), and so on for the second and other components. When the number of components is equal to the number of variables, all the variance has been accounted for. Obviously, series whose variance has a strong common element will require few principal components to explain a large fraction of the total variance. Tables 2–5 list the cumulative percentage of variance explained by the first three principal components (line CPVE at the bottom of the tables). Each column (P_1, P_2, P_3) reports the factor loadings of each individual country series on, respectively, the first, second, and third principal component. These loadings are a measure of the association of each country's series with the appropriate principal component.[6] Provided that (as is true here) the original series have been appropriately standardized, the square of the factor loading is a measure of the variance of each country's series explained by the corresponding principal component. Moreover, some inference as to regional groupings can be made by an examination of the pattern of factor loadings. Finally, note that in what follows the analysis is limited to contemporaneous correlations and no formal statistical test is used to support statements as to differences in various coefficients.[7]

Table 2 presents results for CPI inflation rates. The first clear implication is that contemporaneous correlations of quarterly observations of changes in national CPIs are much less strong than those among CPI levels, at least under fixed exchange rates, as is well known.[8] Second, these correlations appear, if anything, stronger under flexible than under fixed exchange rates, contrary

[6]In fact, the factor loading of a variable is the regression coefficient of the variable on the appropriate principal component.

[7]As a check, correlations and principal components were also calculated on *levels* of prices, output, money, and interest rates for the countries in the sample, except Japan. Briefly stated, the results are as follows. Price levels are highly correlated in both subperiods and the CPVE by the first principal component is 0.98 and 0.99, respectively. Similiar results obtain for money levels. For real output levels, correlations are higher in the first subperiod, P_1 accounting for 0.97 of total variance, whereas, in the second subperiod, P_1 accounts for 0.87, and P_1 and P_2 for 0.96, of total variance. For interest rates, correlations are again higher in the first subperiod; the first two principal components account for, respectively, 0.97 and 0.89 of total variance.

[8]See, for instance, Genberg (1977 a).

TABLE 2. INFLATION RATES

A. Correlations

	United States	United Kingdom	France	Federal Republic of Germany	Canada	Japan
United States	1	0.61/0.17	0.54/0.74	0.03/0.54	0.77/0.57	0.12/0.17
United Kingdom		1	0.31/0.20	0.47/0.57	0.27/0.06	0.41/0.49
France			1	0.02/0.83	0.22/0.76	0.42/0.44
Germany, Federal Republic of				1	−0.12/0.69	0.50/0.58
Canada					1	−0.06/0.18
Japan						1

B. Principal Components: Factor Loadings

	Original Series			Innovations		
	P_1	P_2	P_3	P_1	P_2	P_3
United States	0.86/0.74	0.45/0.39	0.08/0.34	0.21/0.73	0.75/0.20	0.10/0.33
United Kingdom	0.80/0.48	−0.22/−0.73	0.32/0.45	0.77/0.76	−0.29/−0.41	−0.17/0.37
France	0.67/0.93	0.05/0.24	−0.69/−0.11	0.62/0.70	0.61/0.47	−0.01/0.06
Germany, Federal Republic of	0.39/0.94	−0.74/−0.15	0.39/0.01	0.22/0.68	−0.40/−0.64	0.88/−0.18
Canada	0.59/0.78	0.66/0.44	0.25/−0.11	−0.55/−0.04	0.71/−0.54	0.30/0.82
Japan	0.54/0.59	−0.64/−0.60	−0.30/−0.46	0.81/0.70	0.20/0.36	0.11/0.21
CPVE[1]	44/58	71/80	86/89	34/42	62/63	77/80

[1]CPVE = cumulative percentage of variance explained.

to what mean rates of inflation over longer time spans indicate. Third, no very clear regional pattern emerges. These findings are confirmed by the results of the principal component analysis of the original series. The first and second principal components account for, respectively, 14 percent and 9 percent more of the cumulative variance under flexible than under fixed exchange rates. Under flexible rates, the factor loadings of the first principal component turn out to be fairly high except for Japan and the

United Kingdom, which also have fairly high negative loadings on the second principal component. This is the only weak regional pattern of note. Somewhat the same story is told by the results for innovations, although both the CPVEs and the edge of flexible over fixed rate explanatory power are substantially reduced. No clear regional pattern emerges. In brief, the main finding is the increased correlation ("commonality") of price level changes during the second subsample period.

Results for the contemporaneous association of real output changes are more clear-cut. They are presented in Table 3. In terms of correlation coefficients, there is a notable increase of their value from fixed to flexible rates. Moreover, under flexible rates, all correlation coefficients are positive. In that second period, the highest coefficient is for France–Federal Republic of Germany, the lowest for Canada–Japan. For the second period, correlation coefficients are usually higher for output than for CPI changes. Turning to principal components, the explanatory power of the first principal component under flexible rates is quite high and equal to 69 percent of the original series. The edge of the CPVE under flexible rates over that under fixed rates is 37 percent and 21 percent, respectively, for the first and second principal components. In terms of factor loadings, consider first fixed exchange rates. The loadings on the first principal component (P_1) are not high, except for Canada and the United States. Loadings on P_2 are negative, except for these two countries. This indicates a regional pattern of variation of real output with one grouping composed of the North American countries, another of the other countries. For the second subsample period, factor loadings on P_1 are higher for all countries except Canada. In terms of the fraction of variance in each country's output changes that is accounted for by the first principal component (the square of factor loadings), the lowest is 51 percent for Japan, the second highest is the United States with 81 percent, and the highest is Germany with 90 percent. The regional pattern is less clear-cut than for the fixed rate period, although the United States and Canada may again constitute one group.

Turning to innovations in the real output series, the pattern resembles that obtained for the original series. A "reasonable" portion of variance is still explained by the first and second factors under floating rates. A United States–Canada versus other country groupings appears again for both the fixed and the flexible rate periods. In the first period, the factor loadings on P_1 are positive

TABLE 3. REAL GNP GROWTH

A. Correlations

	United States	United Kingdom	France	Federal Republic of Germany	Canada	Japan
United States	1	−0.11/0.61	−0.07/0.64	−0.04/0.80	0.83/0.69	0.10/0.73
United Kingdom		1	0.10/0.54	0.20/0.66	−0.09/0.59	0.41/0.50
France			1	0.38/0.89	0.05/0.65	0.26/0.41
Germany, Federal Republic of				1	0.13/0.63	0.22/0.71
Canada					1	0.15/0.24
Japan						1

B. Principal Components: Factor Loadings

	Original Series			Innovations		
	P_1	P_2	P_3	P_1	P_2	P_3
United States	0.82/0.90	0.48/0.13	0.10/0.04	0.56/0.59	0.55/0.65	0.34/0.32
United Kingdom	0.12/0.78	−0.64/−0.06	0.59/0.52	−0.63/0.74	0.37/−0.29	−0.32/−0.46
France	0.28/0.84	−0.58/−0.26	−0.56/−0.41	−0.68/0.77	−0.07/−0.01	0.42/0.46
Germany, Federal Republic of	0.35/0.95	−0.58/0.06	−0.43/0.23	−0.59/0.83	0.29/−0.26	0.56/0.09
Canada	0.89/0.77	0.35 − 0.52	−0.03/0.14	0.29/0.41	0.79/0.74	−0.47/0.01
Japan	0.46/0.72	−0.57/0.68	0.40/0.01	−0.29/0.77	0.60/−0.32	−0.57/−0.11
CPVE[1]	32/69	61/82	78/91	28/49	54/69	71/82

[1]CPVE = cumulative percentage of variance explained.

only for the North American countries and are higher than those of other countries (except Japan) for P_2. For the second period, the loadings for Canada and the United States on P_1 are the lowest and are the only positive ones for P_2. In brief, output changes seem more strongly associated under flexible than under fixed rates, with a strong contemporaneous common element (the first principal component) under flexible rates. Furthermore, a distinction between a European versus North American cycle does seem to make sense under both exchange rate regimes.

The results on money growth rates presented in Table 4 are, in contrast, much less clear. Some correlation coefficients are positive, some are negative; they are, on the whole, fairly low although they may tend to be slightly higher in the second than in the first period. The highest coefficients appear in the second

TABLE 4. MONEY GROWTH RATES

A. Correlations

	United States	United Kingdom	France	Federal Republic of Germany	Canada	Japan
United States	1	0.20/0.16	−0.38/−0.16	−0.05/0.12	0.15/0.22	0.19/−0.23
United Kingdom		1	−0.13/0.39	−0.05/0.66	0.15/0.42	0.19/0.40
France			1	0.21/0.78	−0.04/−0.01	0.26/0.49
Germany, Federal Republic of				1	0.00/0.66	−0.07/0.49
Canada					1	−0.18/0.15
Japan						1

B. Principal Components: Factor Loadings

	Original Series			Innovations		
	P_1	P_2	P_3	P_1	P_2	P_3
United States	0.81/0.09	0.01/0.73	0.20/0.61	0.55/0.61	0.00/0.35	0.55/0.34
United Kingdom	0.31/0.83	0.71/0.07	0.19/0.23	0.79/0.14	−0.25/0.76	−0.15/−0.39
France	−0.64/0.50	−0.09/−0.61	0.43/0.46	−0.12/−0.62	−0.78/0.50	0.35/0.22
Germany, Federal Republic of	−0.02/0.88	−0.42/0.22	0.49/0.23	0.53/0.40	0.25/0.45	−0.58/0.55
Canada	0.60/0.65	0.03/0.52	0.30/−0.34	0.71/0.78	0.21/−0.38	0.36/0.10
Japan	−0.51/0.68	0.61/−0.51	0.23/0.08	0.23/0.47	−0.77/0.21	−0.39/−0.68
CPVE[1]	30/43	47/68	58/82	30/29	53/52	70/70

[1]CPVE = cumulative percentage of variance explained.

period and are those that relate German money growth to that of France, the United Kingdom, and Canada. Some confirmation of these tendencies appears in the figures of Panel B of Table 4. CPVEs for the original series are higher in the second period than in the first period. Under flexible rates, all factor loadings on P_1 are positive but the factor loading for the United States is very small, the one for Germany highest. This is in contrast to the fixed rate period where the factor loading on P_1 is highest for the United States and lowest for the Federal Republic of Germany (in addition to a varied sign pattern for P_1).

These patterns are not confirmed by the principal components analysis of innovations in money growth. This is the only time in all tables when the cumulative percentage of variance explained under flexible rates is not higher than under fixed rates. Moreover, the CPVEs are rather low. Also, the factor loadings on P_1 for Canada and the United States are similar for the two periods and are high relative to the others, although fairly low in absolute value. In fact, there is reduced association for the Federal Republic of Germany in the second period. To summarize, no strong pattern of association among money growth appears across countries, nor are regional groupings suggested except in tenuous fashion. It remains true that the association appears somewhat higher under flexible than under fixed rates for the original series.

Finally,[9] consider interest rate changes as in Table 5. Here correlation coefficients are all positive. Most (8 out of 10) are larger in the second than in the first period. The Canadian–U.S. interest rate correlation is highest for both periods. The cumulative percentage of variance explained by the first two principal components is quite high for the second period. Again, more association appears for the second period than for the first, both for the original series and for innovations. A regional grouping of North America versus Europe also finds some support in both periods. The factor loadings on P_1 are highest for the United States and Canada and negative factor loadings on P_2 appear for two of the other three countries in both periods. Furthermore, note that the results for innovations are quite similar to those for the original series. This is not surprising to the extent that interest

[9]We do not consider government expenditure in the text, as there are only four series. Suffice it to say here that principal components show the association to be substantially higher under flexible rates for the original series but not for innovations.

TABLE 5. INTEREST RATE CHANGES

A. Correlations

	United States	United Kingdom	France	Federal Republic of Germany	Canada
United States	1	0.29/0.23	0.35/0.47	0.36/0.50	0.76/0.82
United Kingdom		1	0.35/0.15	0.21/0.34	0.06/0.21
France			1	0.07/0.55	0.18/0.52
Germany, Federal Republic of				1	0.30/0.48
Canada					1

B. Principal Components: Factor Loadings

	Original Series			Innovations		
	P_1	P_2	P_3	P_1	P_2	P_3
United States	0.90/0.86	0.19/0.20	0.18/0.37	0.85/0.88	0.33/0.05	0.18/0.36
United Kingdom	0.49/0.42	−0.68/−0.88	−0.31/0.16	0.48/0.63	−0.66/0.61	0.01/−0.28
France	0.53/0.75	−0.60/0.16	0.36/−0.51	0.52/0.55	−0.56/−0.74	0.41/−0.22
Germany, Federal Republic of	0.55/0.77	0.21/−0.18	−0.73/−0.38	0.60/0.70	−0.15/0.01	−0.75/−0.57
Canada	0.78/0.86	0.47/0.25	0.26/0.33	0.73/0.85	0.57/−0.02	0.12/0.45
CPVE[1]	45/56	67/75	85/88	42/54	66/72	82/88

[1]CPVE = cumulative percentage of variance explained.

rates follow a stochastic process that is close to a random walk. The major portion of changes in interest rates will then actually be innovations.[10] Thus, factor loadings are very similar for the original series and for innovations. The latter have the highest CPVEs of the innovation series in the tables; and the proportion of the variance in interest rate innovations accounted for by P_1 for each country is quite respectable, ranging from 30 percent for France to 77 percent for the United States under flexible rates.

[10]This is confirmed by an examination of the regression equations used to estimate the innovations in interest rates.

Three general conclusions can be drawn from Tables 2 to 5. First, the degree of association among all four types of variables examined rises from the first to the second period. This appears clearly from comparisons of the cumulative proportion of variance explained by successive principal components. It remains true for both the original series and for innovations, with the single exception of money innovations where the CPVEs are basically the same under fixed and flexible exchange rates. Furthermore, factor loadings on P_1 are frequently reasonably high, especially under flexible exchange rates, indicating that a substantial portion of changes in countries' macroeconomic performance can be accounted for by a common factor. This is particularly true of changes in real output under flexible exchange rates. The strength of the connection in changes in real economic activity, especially in the second period, constitutes our second general conclusion and lends some support to the notion of a world business cycle.

Third, some evidence of regional factors can be garnered from the tables. In particular, a North America versus "Europe" (or "Europe" and Japan) distinction seems relevant for the behavior of changes in interest rates and real output under both fixed and flexible rates. A similar pattern may be sustained, albeit weakly, for money growth under fixed but not under flexible rates. This pattern does not seem to appear in the behavior of inflation rates. Finally, looking at the Federal Republic of Germany's factor loadings on P_1 for the various variables under flexible rates suggests a rising influence of the common factor on that country's economy.

When assessing these findings it is useful to remember that for two reasons principal components will tend to underestimate the common component in the movement of various series. First, as they are based on contemporaneous correlations only, they tend to underestimate the common factor to the extent that it influences national variables with differing lags. Second, to the extent that national variables are subject to measurement error, the latter may lead to the unwarranted identification of a "country" factor and to a decrease in the measured influence of the first principal component. In assessing the findings, it is also useful to remember, again, that they do not allow any inference about causality. Nor do they allow us to attribute a clear cause to the increase in "interdependence" in the second subsample period.

One possibility is that the world economy has been subjected to larger common shocks during the second period, that there has been much more variance to be explained, rather than that "transmission" should have been higher in that period because of a change in the international monetary regime. To get some insight into this issue, the ratios of the standard deviations of innovations in the flexible to the fixed rate period are reported in Table 6. Reading across the lines of the table, it appears that a systematic increase in variance for all countries is present only for interest rate changes. Reading down, it appears that only for the United States (and except for M_1 for the United Kingdom) does the variance of innovations systematically increase in the second in comparison with the first period. The question of why "interdependence" has increased recently thus remains to be explained. Both the change in exchange rate regime and the increased strength of common (e.g., supply) shocks remain candidates.

TABLE 6. RATIOS OF STANDARD DEVIATIONS OF INNOVATIONS
(*Second period/first period*)

	United States	United Kingdom	France	Federal Republic of Germany	Canada	Japan
Consumer price index	1.87	2.74	0.83	0.61	1.29	0.63
Gross national product	1.26	1.32	0.55	0.51	0.71	0.38
M_1	1.50	0.86	0.75	1.23	0.29	1.15
Interest rate	2.25	3.42	2.30	1.98	2.97	...

Two recent studies—one by Genberg, Saidi, and Swoboda (1982), the other by Huber and Saidi (1982)—help shed some light on these issues. The first study analyses in some detail the interdependence between U.S., Canadian, French, and German interest rates (and exchange rates). The data set is different and consists of monthly observations on short-term and long-term end-of-period interest rates. The results, however, are by and large consistent with those presented above. The Genberg, Saidi, and Swoboda paper investigates causality and the dynamics of response by means of causal ordering (Sims) tests and multivariate vector autoregressions (VARs). The results most relevant here are as follows:

(1) U.S. interest rate innovations appear to cause German and, especially, Canadian innovations. U.K. innovations are more exogenous.

(2) The fraction of the variance in foreign interest rate innovations explained by U.S. innovations is significant but not huge.

(3) As in this paper, the variance of innovations (from the VARs) does show an increase for the United States and the United Kingdom from the first to the second subperiod. In contrast to this paper, there is a decrease for Canada and the Federal Republic of Germany.[11]

(4) As indicated by a reduction of the portion of national interest rate variance accounted for by its own innovations, interdependence appears larger in the flexible than in the fixed rate period.

(5) Lags in transmission between countries are small, the largest effect always taking place within two months. Patterns also differ between the two subperiods.

In brief, as far as interest rate changes are concerned, these findings confirm higher interdependence in the flexible than in the fixed rate period. Part of that interdependence does seem to arise from transmission from the United States to other countries, but a substantial (probably more important) part from common response across countries to common underlying disturbances. Finally, that response tends to differ across exchange rate regimes indicating a different role for interest rate changes in the transmission mechanism under fixed and flexible exchange rates.

This last conjecture finds some confirmation in the study by Huber and Saidi (1982). Their results are derived from estimates of vector autoregressions for the United States, Canada, France, and the Federal Republic of Germany. For each country, four variables are typically included at first: money, prices, industrial production, and a short-term interest rate. From our vantage point, the most relevant result of the first part of their analysis is that responses across exchange rate regimes appear fairly stable for the United States, but that the dynamic structure of responses seems to differ across regimes for the remaining three countries. This suggests differences in the transmission mechanism and a

[11]The difference probably arises from differences in the data (smoothed quarterly observations on quarterly long-term rates here and point-in-time monthly observations on short-term rates there) and in estimation procedure.

role for foreign and domestic variables in explaining domestic business cycles. This hypothesis is examined in the next sections of the Huber and Saidi paper, where two "foreign" variables are included in the VAR systems for Canada, France, and the Federal Republic of Germany. The two variables used to capture foreign shocks are deviations from purchasing power parity (the real exchange rate) and movements in the U.S. interest rate. Only a few of the many interesting results obtained by Huber and Saidi can be mentioned here. First, a substantial part of innovations that appeared at first as domestic can, in fact, be attributed to foreign variables. Second, in the authors' own words:[12]

> ... in the flexible rate period unanticipated real exchange rate movements account for a substantial fraction of the variance of domestic variables. The same role is played by innovations in the U.S. T-bill rate in the fixed exchange rate period. The results support the notion that there is a common underlying world business cycle, with an overlying domestic cycle. Differences in exchange rate regimes imply different channels for the effects of the international cycle. More exchange rate flexibility does not imply an insulation of domestic variables from foreign disturbances.

These conclusions are consistent with the evidence presented in this section. It remains for the next two sections to discuss briefly possible reasons for increased interdependence since 1973 and to draw some implications for policy.

II. Why So Much Interdependence Under Flexible Rates?

The preceding section suggests that there has been more interdependence under flexible than under fixed exchange rates. This is perhaps most surprising for the interdependence in real output in view of the main elements of the traditional literature on adjustment under fixed versus flexible rates. This section begins with a brief restatement of the traditional reasons adduced for interdependence under fixed and insulation under flexible exchange rates. It continues with more recent explanations for some degree of transmission under flexible rates. However, as is argued next, neither traditional nor more recent theorizing is entirely adequate to analyze the world business cycles, the existence of which is suggested by the data. The section concludes by sketching briefly the type of a priori reason that might support the world business cycle hypothesis.

[12]Huber and Saidi (1982), Section V.

The integrating characteristics of fixed exchange rates rest in the fact that, if they are strictly fixed and expected to remain so fixed, the world is effectively on a common currency standard. Changes in the currency composition of the public's demand for money are met by adjustments in the currency composition of the supply of "world money" at the going fixed exchange rate. With goods arbitrage and in the absence of changes in barriers to trade, the rate of inflation of prices of traded goods will be uniform across countries; so, eventually, will be the rate of change of prices of nontraded goods in the absence of changes in technology and tastes. Any long-run differences in national inflation rates would thus reflect either measurement error or changes in relative prices due to changes in technology, tastes, or impediments to trade. To the extent that capital markets are integrated and that assets denominated in various currencies are otherwise close substitutes, nominal and real interest rates will tend to be equalized. We are in the realm of interregional economics with all the usual channels of transmission operating. There is some scope for national (state, regional) fiscal policy autonomy but monetary policy must be devoted to the maintenance of fixed exchange rates. Its scope is limited to determining the ratio of domestic to international reserve assets of the central bank within the bounds compatible with maintenance of the parity—that is, within the bounds imposed by the necessity of maintaining credibility of the central bank's commitment to fixed exchange rates.

In such a world, if it is composed of either small or medium-sized countries of roughly equal size, and if international reserves are of the outside variety (gold, SDRs), we should observe close correlation among national price indices and among interest rate movements. For national money stocks the direction and extent of correlation is less clear. It depends on the source of the underlying disturbance and on the time profile of response. Thus, an exogenous increase in the domestic assets of one central bank may result in a negative correlation over some time span, as at first the domestic money supply expands with unchanged money supplies abroad and, then, as the payments adjustment mechanism works itself out, the domestic money supply contracts somewhat while money supplies abroad expand.[13] The pattern of response and correlation would be different if the initial shock had come from

[13]These movements in money supplies may also lead to transitory negative correlations (or lessened positive correlations) in national inflation rates.

a change in the demand for money (general or currency specific) or from a gold discovery. As for output changes, most models predict that a boom at home will spill over into a boom abroad through the trade balance.[14] One may, however, witness different cycles at home and abroad if the cycles are industry specific (or if different industries react with different lags) and if industries are not spread evenly through the fixed exchange rate world. In brief, "target variables" (output, employment, inflation) are closely interdependent and positively correlated; policy instruments are effectively interdependent in the sense that monetary policy loses all but nominal autonomy, but their movements are not necessarily positively correlated across countries.

For large countries and/or reserve issuing countries, monetary policy does have some autonomy. A large country's monetary policy can have a significant effect on the world's money stock and on other macroeconomic variables by dint of its sheer size. A reserve currency issuing country can set the course of world monetary aggregates and of world prices, as its money stock is not constrained by the availability of outside international assets. This is one main juncture at which policy interdependence under fixed exchange rates can lead to policy conflict—i.e., if there is disagreement among the reserve issuing country and others as to the proper stance of macroeconomic (here mainly monetary) policy.

The "real world" differs, of course, from this idealized picture and offers some scope for independent movements in national macroeconomic variables and some autonomy for domestic macroeconomic policy. Exchange rates are not strictly fixed but fluctuate within margins, divergences in national price levels are possible through short-run relative price changes, countries are not all small, substitutability between assets is less than perfect, and some sterilization of reserve flows is possible, especially over the business cycle. The extent of policy autonomy is, however, likely to remain limited to the fairly short run, as long as exchange rates remain basically fixed.[15]

In one sense, the breakdown of the Bretton Woods system was brought about by the policy conflict among the reserve currency issuing country (the United States) and several other countries, as mentioned above. The expectation was that the freeing of ex-

[14]The Mundellian special case of perfect capital mobility and fiscal expansion is a possible exception.

[15]For empirical evidence supporting this statement and a survey of some relevant literature, see Genberg (1977 b).

change rates would lead to greater autonomy in national monetary policy and to less interdependence in both inflation rates and output changes. That floating rates afford more autonomy for monetary policy and more scope for divergence in national price level movements is consistent with common sense, most theoretical models, and facts (no country has experienced an isolated hyperinflation and at the same time kept its exchange rate fixed). That flexible rates should afford more insulation with respect to national output movements is consistent with primitive models of the open economy under floating.

The central feature of these (comparative statics) models that ensure insulation is that net exports are independent, in equilibrium, of the exchange rate. The latter changes until the foreign trade balance is equilibrated (equal to autonomous capital flows). Should domestic expenditure be inadequate to sustain the target of output, domestic monetary and fiscal policies can be adjusted appropriately. Nominal exchange rate changes, however, will affect the terms of trade especially if domestic prices are rigid, and hence real income. Nevertheless output need not be affected unless, as the classic Laursen-Metzler argument puts its, saving depends on the terms of trade.

The Laursen-Metzler article is the first in a long series of theoretical arguments that have questioned the output-insulating properties of flexible rates.[16] It predicts that a boom abroad will create a depression at home; it also emphasizes the possibility for domestic expenditure policy of counteracting such inverse transmission. Another channel for transmission under flexible rates is through the capital account. If the latter is no longer exogenous, neither is the trade account or the net foreign demand for the home economy's output. This channel of transmission is, of course, at the center of the Mundell-Fleming model. Assuming perfect capital mobility (here equalization of nominal interest rates across countries), Mundell shows that a fiscal (investment) boom at home is transmitted abroad, whereas a monetary expansion at home increases income there but reduces it abroad.[17] The reason is that a fiscal expansion that raises the domestic interest rate creates a capital inflow, a depreciation of the foreign cur-

[16]For references, a survey, and some extensions of the standard literature on macroeconomic interdependence under floating rates see the chapter by Michael Mussa in Dornbusch and Frenkel (1979). See also the comment by A. Swoboda.

[17]Mundell's 1964 argument is reproduced in Mundell (1968), chapter 18.

rency, and an increase in net foreign exports which raises output abroad. In contrast, a domestic monetary expansion induces a depreciation of the domestic currency, a capital outflow, and an increase in domestic net exports (and output), the counterpart to which is a fall in foreign exports and output.

One major problem with the Mundell-Fleming model is its static nature, in particular with respect to expectations. Its assumption that exchange rate expectations are static justifies the assumed equality of nominal interest rates across countries but rules out any exchange rate dynamics related to movements in expectations. The asset approach models of the 1970s, notably those proposed by Dornbusch, remedy this deficiency by requiring the equality of the domestic nominal interest rate with the foreign rate *plus* the expected rate of depreciation of the domestic currency. Combined with a model of expectations formation and the assumption that output and/or prices adjust more slowly than exchange rates, such models produce interactions between domestic monetary policy, interest rates, exchange rates, and output and/or prices that appear suggestive of recent experience. In particular, the exchange rate is seen to overshoot, in the short run, its long-run equilibrium value in response to unanticipated monetary disturbances.

Although these models have usually been used to study the effects of domestic disturbances given foreign variables (the small country assumption), their extension to a two-country framework and to the analysis of transmission readily suggests itself. Monetary contraction at home by appreciating the real exchange rate (depreciating the foreign currency in real terms) creates inflation and an expansion of output abroad. This is precisely the example used by Dornbusch (1982) in a recent paper to analyze the so-called dollar problem. Recent monetary tightness in the United States has been cited as a major source of policy conflict between the United States and Europe. High U.S. interest rates have prevented European countries from lowering their interest rates to stimulate output in Europe, as such a lowering of interest rates would result in currency depreciation and inflation. Worse, the tightening of U.S. monetary policy, while it reduces inflation there, increases inflation in Europe without much of an increase in European growth because Europe suffers a terms of trade deterioration that offsets in part the benefits to output from increased competitiveness. Europe is in the awkward position of having to tighten *its* monetary policy to fight the imported inflation (due to U.S. deflation), thus losing the benefits from the added growth.[18]

Traditional and more recent models do play an important role in delineating a number of possible channels of transmission of shocks from country to country and in drawing attention to potential domestic and foreign effects of policy actions. In most cases, however, they predict negative transmission of foreign disturbances, either for output or for price changes. They also point to greater scope for domestic policy to counteract the effects of foreign shocks under flexible rather than under fixed rates.[19] The increased interdependence of both output changes and short-run price changes under floating rates that has been documented above suggests that models endowed with a richer structure and stochastic specification are required to provide an explanation of international and domestic business cycles.[20] Such an explanation is, of course, an exceedingly difficult task; it would, at an empirical level, require the specification and estimation both of the dynamic relationships among macroeconomic variables within and across countries and of the stochastic structure of the shocks to which the international economy is subjected.

Nevertheless, one might suggest that the facts of interdependence under flexible rates support the notion of a world business cycle on which national cycles are superimposed. Transmission is, of course, part of the story but there are several reasons why current models are not entirely adequate to deal with the notion. Among them the assumed structure of output and production figures prominently. The standard models deal with final outputs and with a few homogeneous categories of goods. The aggregation criterion for these composite goods is whether they are exports or imports, traded or nontraded, rather than the structure of their production or the industrial category to which they belong.

The point is that the common element in cyclical behavior across countries may be the result of shocks that affect specific

[18]For the full argument, see Dornbusch (1982), pp. 20–24.

[19]Of course, the autonomy may not have been used and policies may have been so much more similar across countries after 1973 as to produce the greater association in output, inflation, and interest rates. The evidence on money reviewed in Section I, however, does not support this hypothesis.

[20]We may also note in passing that the VAR estimates of Huber and Saidi (1982) do not support the overshooting hypothesis. They find that for France and the Federal Republic of Germany an unexpected increase in domestic money leads to an initial real exchange appreciation of the domestic currency in contradiction to the hypothesis.

stages in the production process and specific industries. Alternatively, these shocks may affect demand across the board but the dynamic response of specific outputs will differ depending on the stage in the production process and across industries. The result of either shock will be the appearance of a common transnational cycle and of national deviations from the common trend, independently of the exchange rate regime. The extent of common cyclical response and of national differences will depend mainly on the distribution of industries across countries; the more even the distribution the greater the coherence with the world cycle—and vice versa. It is still true that the nature of the exchange rate regime is likely to affect the response pattern and that "transmission" will play a role. But, for some purposes, it may be more informative to divide the world into industrial sectors rather than along national borders.

There are a number of obvious examples. The oil price rise is the standard prototype of a shock that has affected most industrial countries simultaneously but differently, depending on the structure of their production. To study the nature of the response requires a model that admits of imported inputs and differing structures of production across countries.[21] Similarly, a number of industrial sectors may be affected in much the same manner, in whichever country they are located. The automobile sector is one example. To the extent that the typical response to changes in aggregate demand is different for automobiles than for other goods, the cycles for countries with a heavy concentration in automobile production will tend to be correlated more closely with each other than with others. Technological change also tends to have industrywide transnational effects rather than country specific effects. In an increasingly integrated industrialized world, common business cycles should arise whether exchange rates are fixed or not.

The increasing degree of economic integration in the last few decades (whether in terms of trade in goods, of trade in assets, or of socioeconomic attitudes and institutions) may account partly for increased interdependence irrespective of the exchange rate regime. In such an integrated world economy, expectations will also tend to show common movements. Industrial gloom (or bullishness) does tend to spread. In addition, common policy re-

[21]For recent analyses and intermediate input shocks (or more generally supply shocks) see Bruno and Sachs (1981) and Jones and Purvis (1982).

sponses to common shocks may reinforce the tendency toward a world business cycle. The policy autonomy afforded by flexible rates in fighting shocks originating abroad is of little avail if the shocks are not transmitted along traditional lines but affect several countries simultaneously and directly.

In brief, the close interdependence in business cycles that was witnessed in the 1970s may well find its origin in a world business cycle in a closely integrated international economy rather than in the transmission of disturbances from one country, or group of countries, to the rest of the world. This is not to deny that traditional channels play a role; but not necessarily a dominant one. World business cycles can occur under both fixed and flexible rates, although the channels of transmission will most likely differ. There is, however, one sense in which the changeover to flexible rates may have altered the dynamics of output changes within and across countries. It has been associated with a basic change in domestic monetary regimes toward fiat money that may have altered the nature and extent of the shocks impinging on the world economy.

III. Some Policy Implications

Strong interdependence and the existence of a world business cycle under floating exchange rates do not imply very novel messages for policy. These findings do, however, provide some background against which to discuss briefly two questions addressed to me by the organizers of this conference: the extent to which a currency union arrangement like the European Monetary System influences the response of countries within the union to external shocks; and the arguments for or against a return to a system of fixed exchange rates between Europe and the United States. These very broad questions cannot be answered satisfactorily here, and the following brief remarks will only touch on them and raise a general question concerning the nature of policy commitments.

As to the first question, the theoretical argument would be superficially that the European Monetary System should help insulate member countries from shocks external to the monetary union, while increasing interdependence and susceptibility to shocks arising within the union. This answer is, of course, predicated on the assumption that flexible rates toward the rest of the world insulate the union as a whole, while fixed rates within the union increase interdependence among the members. The assumption does not receive strong support from the empirical evidence we have reviewed. Of course, it may be that the increased interdependence since 1973 is not due to the adoption of floating rates; interdependence might have been as strong, or even stronger, had fixed exchange rates been maintained. However, for shocks to all industrial countries, such as raw material price increases, there is little that can be achieved by floating against nonmembers.

There is one respect in which a currency union might help reduce the impact of outside shocks. And that is by reducing inside shocks. More specifically, a currency union may reduce uncertainty with respect to the future course of individual members' monetary policy, thus reducing monetary shocks (innovations). The contribution that lowering the monetary shocks occurring inside the union may make to insulate the members stems partly from the role of real exchange rate variations in transmitting shocks under flexible rates (see Section I). With lower unexpected monetary variability there should be less real exchange rate variability. There are two prerequisites for this to occur. First, uncertainty as to individual members' monetary policy should not be replaced by uncertainty as to the union's monetary policy, be it the result of some ill-defined averaging process or that of a deliberate "dollar policy" of the union. The second is that the commitment to fixed rates within the union by individual members be credible.[22] It is left to the reader to decide whether these prerequisites are met in the European Monetary System.

One further aspect of the empirical findings may have a bearing on this issue. The principal component analysis indicated the existence of a regional factor, especially with respect to co-movements in interest rates, on the one hand, and in real output, on the other. The factor suggested that our sample divides into a North American versus European (or rest of the world) group. This might suggest that Europe constitutes an adequate grouping for a currency union. However, note that the grouping holds for the fixed as well as for the flexible rate period and thus does not constitute, prima facie, a case for a currency union for the three European countries.

[22]The credibility issue is discussed briefly below.

Turning to a return to fixity of exchange rates between the United States and Europe, the argument developed in this paper implies that interdependence in real output does not establish a case against such a return. The reason is that output interdependence appears as strong or stronger under flexible as under fixed rates. Moreover, the advent of floating has not diminished the extent to which U.S. variables "cause" European ones (in the VARs mentioned above), even if the channels of transmission are different. And popular views as to recent transmission of U.S. monetary policy indicate that many observers believe U.S. dominance to be even stronger now than it was in the 1960s. The reluctance to return to fixed exchange rates has other grounds.

In the first place, it remains true that price level dependence is much stronger under fixed than under flexible rates and that adoption of the former would enforce much greater convergence of mean inflation rates over the medium term than was true in the 1970s. It is also true that fixed exchange rates would deny countries monetary policy autonomy, however illusory the exercise of that autonomy may be in controlling national business cycles. In the second place, fixed exchange rates are part of a package that governments are loath to discuss let alone agree on, because to work properly, fixed exchange rates require adhesion to a set of rules and agreement on acceptable international reserves and on the process generating their growth. Once these rules are accepted fixed exchange rates force consistency of national monetary policies, at the cost (which may be a benefit) of loss of national monetary autonomy.

The case for not returning to fixed rates between Europe and the United States is, in this perspective, the lack of agreement on such rules. Floating rates have the advantage of letting monetary policy conflicts be resolved by market forces. But inconsistent or unstable policies will also cause an unsatisfactory working of flexible rates—even if that system remains viable during policy conflicts. Hans Genberg and the author have argued elsewhere that floating rates may require as much commitment as fixed rates to work properly.[23] That is, a properly functioning system of flexible rates does not remove the need for rules. The need for policy responses that represent medium- to long-term commitments does not change fundamentally with a change in the exchange rate regime, although the form of the commitment does change. This

[23]Genberg and Swoboda (1982).

conjecture is based on recent work on rules versus discretion and on the inconsistency of optimal plans, notably by Kydland and Prescott (1977) and by Barro (1982). This is not the place to restate the argument. Suffice it to say that the absence of precommitted monetary policies (as would be implied by the pursuit of optimal discretionary policies) might well lead to either increased variability of real exchange rates or suboptimal outcomes from a welfare point of view, or both. Note that precommitted policy does not have to be a set of binding laws but can be the outcome of consistent behavior and the absence of optimal control policies.

The basic issue, in this context, is not so much whether it is preferable to have fixed or floating rates between Europe and the United States. It is, rather, that precommitted and credible policies be adopted under either alternative. Such credibility may be simpler to achieve for nonreserve currency issuing countries under fixed rates. "All" they need to do is to peg and follow essentially gold standard rules. For the reserve issuing country there is no simple precommitted rule that can be readily incorporated into the country's "monetary constitution." To that extent, credible precommitment may be more difficult to achieve for such a country. Be that as it may, the adoption of implicit or explicit rules that are adhered to and are credible can make an important contribution to eliminating unexpected policy shocks as a major source of cyclical fluctuations in world output.

REFERENCES

Barro, Robert J., "High and Volatile Inflation—the Role of Discretionary Monetary Policy," paper written for the Conference on Monetary Policy, Financial Markets, and the Real Economy (International Center for Monetary and Banking Studies, Geneva, June 1982).

Bruno, Michael and Jeffrey Sachs, "Supply versus Demand Approaches to the Problem of Stagflation," in Herberg Giersch, ed., *Macroeconomic Policies for Growth and Stability* (Tübingen, 1981), pp. 15–60.

Dhrymes, Phoebus J., *Econometrics: Statistical Foundations and Applications* (New York, 1970).

Dornbusch, Rudiger, "Equilibrium and Disequilibrium Exchange Rates," paper prepared for the Conference on Monetary Policy, Financial Markets, and the Real Economy (International Center for Monetary and Banking Studies, Geneva, June 1982).

———, and Jacob A. Frenkel, eds., *International Economic Policy: Theory and Evidence* (Baltimore, 1979).

Genberg, Hans (1977a), "The Concept and Measurement of the World Price Level and Rate of Inflation," *Journal of Monetary Economics,* Vol. 3 (April 1977), pp. 231–52.

——— (1977b), "Policy Autonomy of Small Countries" in *Inflation Theory and Anti-Inflation Policy,* Proceedings of a conference held by the International Economic Association at Saltsjöbaden, Sweden, ed. by Erik Lundberg (New York), pp. 183–208.

———, Nasser Saidi, and Alexander K. Swoboda, "American and European Interest Rates and Exchange Rates: U.S. Hegemony or Interdependence?" paper prepared for the Conference on Monetary Policy, Financial Markets, and the Real Economy (International Center for Monetary and Banking Studies, Geneva, June 1982).

Genberg, Hans, and Alexander K. Swoboda, "Fixed Exchange Rates, Flexible Exchange Rates, or the Middle of the Road: A Reexamination of the Arguments in View of Recent Experience," paper presented at the 1982 Wingspread Conference on the Evolving International Financial System.

Huber, Gerard, and Nasser Saidi, "Business Cycles under Alternative Exchange-Rate Regimes: 1960–1981," preliminary draft (Geneva, August 1982).

Jones, Ronald W., and Douglas D. Purvis, "International Differences in Response to Common External Shocks: The Role of Purchasing Power Parity" in Emil Claassen and Pascal Salin, eds., *Recent Issues in the Theory of Flexible Exchange Rates,* Vol. 8 (Amsterdam, 1983).

Kydland, Finn E., and Edward C. Prescott, "Rules Rather than Discretion: The Inconsistency of Optimal Plans," *Journal of Political Economy,* Vol. 85 (June 1977), pp. 473–91.

Mundell, Robert A., *International Economics* (New York, 1968).

Theil, Henri, *Principles of Econometrics* (New York, 1971).

Comments

Jacques R. Artus

One of the interesting arguments advanced by Swoboda is that the interdependence among industrial countries, in part, reflects the integration of their production systems through trade in intermediate products. Another and related argument is that the interdependence among industrial countries, in part, reflects their common dependence on imported fuels and raw materials. When there is a change in the prices of these products, as a result of a supply shock or a change in demand in one of the major industrial countries, this constitutes a real shock rather than a monetary shock. Such a real shock has a similar and simultaneous impact on all industrial countries importing the products affected. Those arguments are not original, but Swoboda is quite right to point out that they have been largely neglected in both traditional and more recent theoretical models.

Swoboda is also quite right to point out that, in an integrated world, it is not only the expectational factors related to economic phenomena that tend to be common but also the political and social factors. He fails, however, to provide us with much explanation or illustration of this important point. I would have liked to see him mention some of the common tendencies that have dominated the evolution of most industrial countries during the 1960s and 1970s. I have in mind the increase in the size of social transfers, the policy of monetary accommodation of wage and price increases, the growth of rigidities in labor markets, and the decrease in the share of income going to capital, mainly in Europe. In my view it is largely because of these common tendencies, and because of the two waves of oil price increases, that industrial countries have all jointly moved into a period of stagflation since 1973. All being in the same situation, it is not surprising either that they have tended to adopt fairly similar policies.

Where I do not follow Swoboda completely is in his argument that there is now a "world business cycle." No doubt activity has tended to go up and down concurrently in the main industrial countries during the 1970s and early 1980s. However, much of this correlation results also from the two waves of oil price increases that followed the Middle East conflict in 1973 and the Iranian revolution in 1979. The increased integration of the production systems of the industrial countries and the common nature of many expectational, political, and social factors are important elements of interdependence, but this does not mean that the amount of interdependence is such as to lead to a world cycle. There, the burden of proof is on Swoboda. In addition, the notion of a cycle implies a certain regularity as to frequency and amplitude, and it is unclear from where this regularity would emanate. As for myself, I would not be surprised if 1983 and 1984 were to be characterized by a marked recovery in the United States and a continuation of stagnation in many other industrial countries, thus bringing about an early death to the notion of a world cycle.

I have even more problems following Swoboda in his empirical work. Both his correlation analysis and his principal-component analysis confirm a well-known fact, namely, that the cross-country correlation of price level, output, and interest rate changes was higher during the 1970s and early 1980s than during the 1960s. What can we conclude from this as to the implications of flexible exchange rates for economic interdependence? We can conclude that the move toward greater exchange rate flexibility did not protect countries from the common real external shocks experienced during the 1970s and early 1980s, or from the common problems inherited from the past. This, however, is not too useful; there have never been any serious beliefs that flexible rates would do this. In particular, as pointed out by Swoboda, it has been recognized for many years that flexible rates would not fully insulate countries from real shocks originating abroad. The meaningful question is whether flexible rates reduce or enhance interdependence, in particular, in the presence of monetary shocks. Swoboda's empirical analysis fails to cast any light on this point.

Swoboda is careful to point out the limits of his empirical analysis. At the same time, he does suggest that there is no evidence that common shocks have been larger during the flexible rate period than during the 1960s, and thus he leaves the reader with the impression that the change in exchange rate regimes is likely to be behind the increase in interdependence. In my view, the argument on the size of common shocks is quite weak. It is based on the observation that the standard deviations of "innovations" in prices and output changes are not larger during the flexible rate period than during the 1960s. But such an observation does not in any way contradict the hypothesis that the shocks are more "common" during the flexible rate period. In addition, because of the way the innovations were obtained,[1] the standard deviations of innovations are more likely to reflect the erratic nature of quarterly series than the size of major shocks. On the whole, it is hard to believe that the simultaneity across countries of the increases in prices, followed by decreases in output, in 1974–75 and 1980–81 was related mainly to the nature of the exchange rate regime rather than to the two waves of oil price increases.

All this is not to say that flexible rates have provided the insulation effects that most economists expected from them, in particular, for external monetary shocks. In fact, as I have argued elsewhere,[2] there are reasons to believe that they did not, and that, in some cases, they even increased the interdependence among countries. To show this convincingly, however, the empirical study would have to separate the effects of exchange rate flexibility from the effects of other factors, including the effects of common real shocks. In particular, the study would have to focus on the problem of exchange rate overshooting, its repercussion on domestic prices, and the tendency for national authorities to adjust their monetary policies to reduce the impact of external monetary shocks on their exchange rates.

Swoboda does refer in his theoretical section to the work of Dornbusch on the overshooting mechanism and on the implications for European countries of the shift to a policy of monetary restraint in the United States. He also refers to the tendency for European countries to fight the imported inflation resulting from the appreciation of the U.S. dollar by tightening their own monetary policies,[3] and explains that this can ultimately lead to a positive transmission of foreign disturbances. But he places little weight on this explanation because he finds no evidence in his empirical analysis of a strong pattern of association among money growth across countries. Here again, part of the problem may be that Swoboda is focusing narrowly on the pattern of association on

[1]The reader will remember that the innovations were obtained by regressing, for each sample period separately, quarterly observations of the variable on a constant, time trend, three seasonal dummies, and four lags of the variable. The residuals were assumed to be the innovations.

[2]See Jacques R. Artus and John H. Young, "Fixed and Flexible Exchange Rates: A Renewal of the Debate," *Staff Papers,* Vol. 26 (December 1979).

[3]It should be observed that during 1979–82 European countries had to fight not only the imported inflation resulting from the appreciation of the U.S. dollar but also, and mainly, the imported inflation resulting from the increase in oil prices in 1979–80 and their own domestically generated inflation.

a quarterly basis, while what is really important is the pattern of association among broad swings in money growth. Chart 1 shows the evolution of the most closely watched monetary aggregates for the United States ($M2$), Japan ($M2+CD$s), and the Federal Republic of Germany (central bank money) from 1976 to 1982, after deflating them by the domestic demand deflators and the levels of potential gross domestic product (GDP) in real terms, and after adjusting them for long-run changes in velocity. It is rather difficult to argue that there has been no pattern of association among these variables over the past seven years.

To conclude, let me look briefly at the European Monetary System (EMS). The theoretical argument is that the System will help to isolate member countries from an external shock, in particular a monetary shock originating in the United States. Swoboda comments briefly that the empirical evidence does not provide strong support for this argument. In a recent paper,[4] I estimated and simulated a small model in order to study the effects of a shift to monetary restraint in the United States on the deutsche mark–dollar exchange rate and the German economy. I concluded that when Germany does not change its interest rates and other EMS countries keep their real exchange rates constant vis-à-vis the deutsche mark, a shift to monetary restraint in the United States of a magnitude similar to the 1979 shift leads to an extremely sharp depreciation of the deutsche mark vis-à-vis the U.S. dollar, a moderate increase in the German domestic deflator, and a moderate increase in the German GDP gap (ratio of actual over potential GDP). If other EMS countries appreciate in line with the U.S. dollar, the increases in the German domestic demand deflator and the GDP gap become much larger, about twice as large as in the previous simulation. There is, therefore, no doubt that, in this case, Germany benefits from constant real exchange rates with other EMS countries.

But the results are quite different when simulation of the model is made under the assumption that Germany chooses to keep its interest rates in line with U.S. interest rates, thus duplicating the U.S. shift to monetary restraint. In this case, if all the other members of the EMS follow suit, then practically all the major

[4]Jacques R. Artus, "Effects of U.S. Monetary Restraint on the DM-$ Exchange Rate and the German Economy," Working Paper No. 926, National Bureau of Economic Research, Inc. (July 1982), scheduled to be published in *Exchange Rate: Theory and Practice,* eds. R. Marston and J. Bilson, (University of Chicago).

CHART 1. ADJUSTED REAL MONEY STOCKS, 1976-82[1]

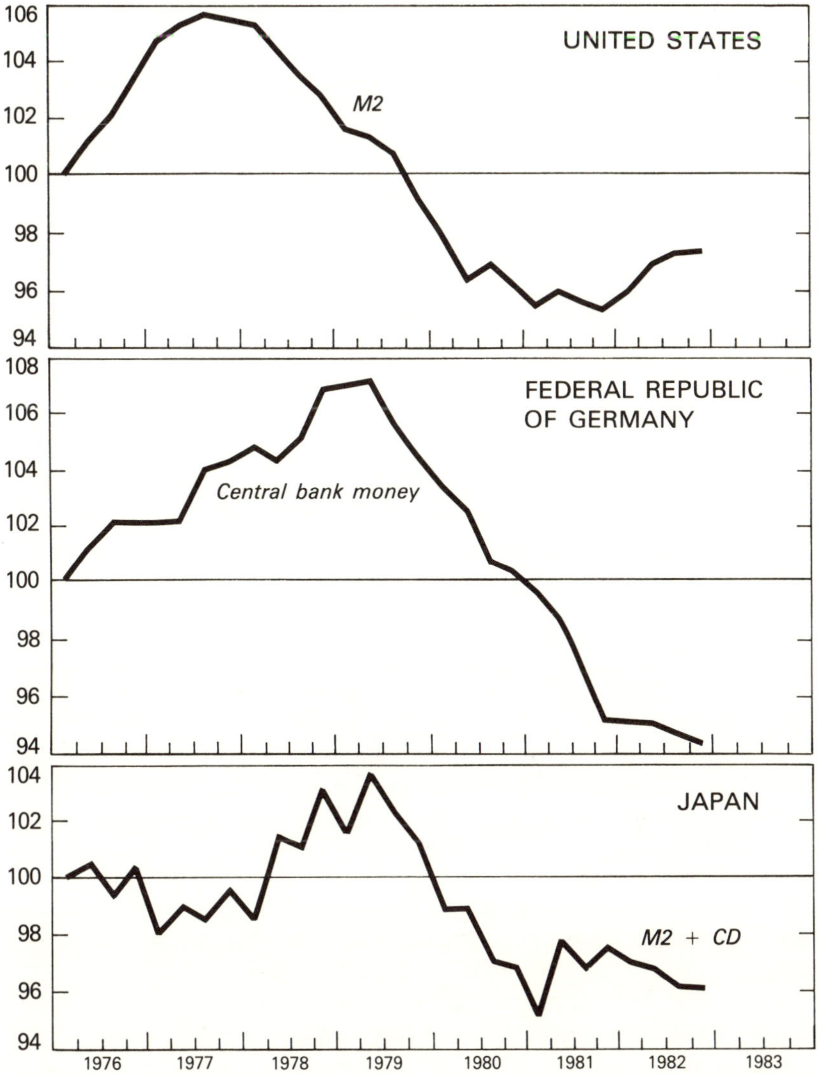

[1]In each country, the nominal stock of money was deflated by the aggregate domestic demand deflator and the level of potential output, then adjusted for the long-run change in velocity. The following annual percentage changes in velocity were used: +¼ percent in the United States, −1½ percent in Japan, and −½ percent in the Federal Republic of Germany. The growth rates of potential output were assumed to be 5 percent from 1976 to 1982 and 4½ percent in 1983 in Japan; 3 percent from 1976 to 1978 and 2¾ percent from 1979 to 1983 in the United States; and about 2½ percent from 1976 to 1980 and 2 percent from 1981 to 1983 in the Federal Republic of Germany.

industrial countries move together toward a policy of monetary restraint and the effects tend to cumulate into a large world recession. To conclude, the EMS helps to isolate activity in member countries when the EMS is floating vis-à-vis the rest of the world. When the EMS implies that most countries adjust their interest rates together, it aggravates the effects of the external shock.

Jacob A. Frenkel

Swoboda's paper on "Exchange Rate Regimes and U.S.-European Policy Interdependence" deals with key issues. It contains useful evidence and stimulating analysis. My remarks are divided into two parts. The first deals with the empirical findings and their interpretation and the second concerns the relevance of the analysis for the choice among alternative exchange rate regimes.

EMPIRICAL FINDINGS AND INTERPRETATION

In comparing the empirical regularities that have characterized the fixed exchange rate period of the 1960s with those of the flexible exchange rate period of the 1970s, Swoboda notes that, generally, the move to the flexible exchange rate regime has been associated with a rise in the mean and in the variance of the rates of inflation while it has been associated with a decline in the mean and in the variance of the rates of growth of real GNP. It is relevant to point out, however, that these changes in the means and the variances have resulted in almost no change in the coefficients of variation of the two series. Therefore, prior to drawing an inference from these findings it would be useful to establish which of the measures of variability are more relevant for such comparisons.

The second set of findings relates to correlation and to the analysis of principal components. Swoboda's computations show that, on the whole, the cross-country correlations among inflation rates, real GNP growth, money growth rates, and interest rate changes have not been altered dramatically by the move to flexible exchange rates. In fact, based on the principal component analysis of these variables, Swoboda concludes that the degree of association among countries has even slightly increased during the flexible exchange rate period. Based on these findings, Swoboda advances the interesting hypothesis that the economic system may be governed by a world business cycle rather than by the traditional mechanism of an international transmission of local business cycles.

Prior to discussing this interpretation of the evidence, it might be useful to ask what are the alternative circumstances that could have caused such patterns of association. In principle, patterns of association that are similar over periods might indicate that, first, the effective exchange rate regime has not changed much over time. That is, the decade of the 1960s was not in practice a completely fixed rate period, while the 1970s was not in practice a completely flexible rate period. Second, these patterns could indicate that, even though the periods were characterized by sharply different exchange rate regimes, the similarities in the associations among countries indicate that the prevailing theory of the transmission mechanism needs revision. Third, it may indicate that the shocks confronting the system during the 1960s were very different from those of the 1970s. Finally, the observed correlations reflect the combination of differences in exchange rate regimes, differences in the nature and origin of the shocks *and* the patterns of government policies that have been adopted in face of the shocks. As the observed data reflect the outcome of the joint influence of the exchange rate regime, the nature of the shocks, and the response of policies, it is evident that one may not ascribe the entire difference between the periods to the differences between the prevailing exchange rate regimes. To avoid any misunderstanding in this respect I would even have suggested modifying the title of the paper from "Exchange Rate Regimes and U.S.-European Policy Interdependence" to "U.S.-European Policy Interdependence during the 1960s and 1970s."

Swoboda's hypothesis that the co-movements of the various series may represent a world business cycle is interesting. It could be explored further by changing the sample of countries in the analysis. At present the countries under consideration represent mainly oil consuming countries. As all have been confronted by a similar external oil shock, it is conceivable that the positive correlation among them reflects the outcome of a common policy response to a common external shock rather than indicating a pattern which is specific to the prevailing exchange rate regime. It would be useful to extend the sample so as to include an oil producing country. If the extended sample also produces a similar pattern of correlations, then the world business cycle hypothesis would receive further support.

Finally, it is relevant to note that if the observed record reflects the reaction of the various countries in the sample to a common set of shocks, then the received theory of the transmission mechanism may still be perfectly valid for the analysis of the mechanisms by which a specific policy shock is transmitted from one country to the rest of the world.

CHOICE OF EXCHANGE RATE REGIME

One of the interesting findings that are reported by Swoboda concerns the regional pattern of variations of the various variables. He finds that, based on the variations of at least some of the variables, one could classify countries into groups, of which one would consist of the North American countries and the other of the European countries in the sample.

There remains, however, the question what does this country grouping indicate? Does it indicate that the countries within each group are sufficiently similar so as to justify a monetary union (or a variant thereof like the European Monetary System)? Or should they consider joining a customs union? Or should they even consider a political union? Since each one of the various forms of integration depends on different considerations, it might be useful to incorporate into the analysis some of the factors that determine whether a specific union is being called for. For example, it is reasonable to argue that prospective members of a monetary union should possess common tastes concerning the common course of inflation. The desired rate of inflation in turn depends, among other things, on the efficiency of the fiscal system. Similarly, one could predict monetary mergers for countries among which there exists a positive correlation of exogenous disturbances, so that expansionary or contractionary policies are mutually consistent with the needs of all members. These and similar considerations might be usefully added before concluding from the patterns of the country grouping whether the European Monetary System does or does not include the appropriate countries.

One of the criteria employed in Swoboda's analysis of the choice of an exchange rate regime is the degree of policy autonomy that is afforded by alternative regimes. In evaluating this criterion, however, three issues need to be clarified. First, a distinction should be made between the autonomy in the *use* of a policy instrument and the *efficacy* of this instrument in influencing a policy target. For example, in principle, a flexible exchange rate regime affords full autonomy in the use of monetary policy—in the same sense that, in contrast to a fixed exchange rate regime, the monetary authority controls the nominal money stock—but one may envisage a situation whereby the control over the money stock does not provide the authorities with the power to alter the course of real economic activity. How should we evaluate such autonomy? Second, is it possible to ask what is so good about autonomy? It is obvious that one needs a criterion with which to evaluate the cost and benefits of policy autonomy. Here it is important to know whether the policymaker is likely to abuse or properly use the autonomy granted to him and, as is evident, no single general answer can be given to this question. Third, the optimal exchange rate regime depends on the nature and the origin of the shocks that affect the economy. It is clear, therefore, that the question of the optimal degree of autonomy that should be granted in the use of various policy instruments cannot be answered properly without reference to the characteristics of the shocks that affect the economy.

Swoboda concludes his paper with a discussion of the issue of rules versus discretion. He emphasizes, correctly, that the commitment to fixed rates must be credible, and that the adoption of credible rules that are being adhered to can make an important contribution by eliminating policy shocks. Granted all these benefits, the intriguing questions that remain are why do these beneficial rules always get broken? and will the world monetary system eventually turn into a regime with a credible stable rule?

In order to gain perspective, it may be instructive to recall that over a century ago, in his *Principles of Political Economy,* John Stuart Mill regretfully concluded that

> So much barbarism, however, still remains in the transactions of most civilized nations, that almost all independent countries choose to assert their nationality by having, to their own inconvenience and their neighbours', a peculiar currency of their own.

In predicting the future Mill believed that eventually the international monetary system would evolve into a unified currency area, a process that would be brought about by "the progress of political improvement."

Mill's prediction has obviously been refuted. National governments have generally preferred to have their own monetary unit and international monetary rules have generally been broken. The apparent inconsistency between what seems to be in the general interest and what is actually being practiced may be rationalized by recalling that, as a general rule, governments tend to discount the future heavily since their time horizons are relatively short. Consequently, faced with a conflict between internal and external targets, elected officials (who wish to be re-elected) will typically sacrifice external obligations to domestic goals by renouncing previous commitments to the international rules of game. In view of this, it is important to choose an exchange rate regime that is capable of accommodating this general tendency of policymakers. Swoboda's reasoning seems to be consistent with this principle. He thus argues that "Floating rates have the advantage of letting monetary policy conflicts be resolved by market forces," and he goes on emphasizing correctly that "inconsistent or unstable policies will also cause an unsatisfactory working of flexible rates—even if that system remains viable during policy conflicts." I fully agree with this argument as it indicates that in comparing exchange rate regimes, the mere survivability of the system under a specific exchange rate regime need not imply the superiority of this regime. Rather, the comparison should be based on the *cost* of sustaining the system under alternative exchange rate regimes. And here one needs to evaluate the cost of the various crises under an adjustable peg regime with the corresponding costs under a regime of flexible rates.

My final remark concerns discipline. It has been argued that the obligation to peg the rate would alter the conduct of policy by introducing discipline. If true, then this argument suggests a strong case for fixed exchange rates. Experience seems to suggest, however, that national governments are unlikely to adjust the conduct of domestic policies so as to be disciplined by the exchange rate regime. Rather, it is probable that the exchange rate regime is more likely to adjust to whatever discipline national governments choose. It may be noted in passing that this is one of the more potent arguments against the restoration of the gold standard. If governments were willing to follow policies that are consistent with the maintenance of a gold standard, then the gold standard itself would not be necessary; if, however, governments are not willing to follow such policies, then the introduction of the gold standard per se will not restore stability, as before long the standard will have to be abandoned.

Policy Interdependence from a Latin American Perspective

RICARDO H. ARRIAZU*

DURING THE LAST FEW YEARS, most Latin American countries have been confronted with increasingly serious balance of payments and economic difficulties. For 1982, practically every country in the region—whether an oil exporter or not—will show a significant current account deficit, accompanied by higher inflation rates and economic sluggishness that will be reflected in very low growth rates or—frequently—absolute declines in economic activity. As a matter of fact, 1981 and 1982 could be best described as the worst economic years the region has experienced in decades.

Numerous attempts have been made to identify and to explain the causes of such a poor economic performance. These have generally been based on evaluations of individual country cases, and the explanations have centered around the misuse of important domestic economic policy instruments: excessive levels of public expenditures, as have allegedly been seen in oil exporters like Mexico and Venezuela, or "unrealistic" exchange rate policies, as have allegedly been seen in Argentina, Chile, and Uruguay. In a few countries, particularly in Brazil, blame has also been placed on some specific external factor, such as oil price increases, or on the external debt burden.

Confronted with these situations, many Latin American countries have implemented, in the recent past, severe external adjustment policies centered basically around massive exchange rate depreciations; included among the adjusting countries are

*Ricardo H. Arriazu is Economic and Financial Consultant to the Banco Comercial del Norte in Buenos Aires. He was formerly an Advisor to the Presidency of the Central Bank of Argentina and an Alternative Executive Director of the Fund. He has written numerous papers on international finance, capital and financial markets, monetary theory, and the problems of small, semi-open economies.

Ecuador and Paraguay, which depreciated their currencies after years of absolute stability.

It is worth mentioning that the majority of adjusting countries have achieved some degree of improvement in the current account (basically through recession-induced reductions in imports) immediately after the devaluations, but the overall balance of payments has, in most countries, tended to deteriorate shortly after, forcing much larger devaluations than were originally envisaged. The cycle of devaluation, inflation, recession, capital outflows, wage increases, fiscal deficit, and further devaluations is well under way in many of the adjusting countries, and it is very difficult to envisage what the end results of these competitive adjustment policies will be. To a certain extent, "beggar my neighbor" policies seem to be in evidence.

In analyzing these facts, the researcher is immediately struck by the strange "coincidence" that most countries in the region have simultaneously applied apparently "erroneous" economic policies (even though their "errors" originated in diverse economic policies); the possibility that one or more external disturbances have simultaneously affected most of the region appears, in these circumstances, to be an *additional* explanatory variable worth exploring. In fact, some individual countries (i.e., Brazil and Chile) and some international organizations have been claiming that at least part of these difficulties have originated in external factors (world recession, high nominal and real interest rates, low primary product prices), but little systematic work has been done on this subject. In particular, there has been little research on the differential effects of these external economic disturbances on the different sectors of the economy and on how alternative domestic economic policies may strengthen or weaken the internal effects of these external disturbances.

A final answer to these questions would require the complete specification of the type of external economic disturbance to be transmitted and the study of the transmission mechanism of such disturbances, the specification of the economic structures of the countries subject to such disturbances, etc.—tasks that lie completely outside the scope of the present paper. It is possible, however, if one uses some simplifying assumptions, to obtain some general answers to questions about the ways in which economic cycles are transmitted, the differential effects of such disturbances, and the possibilities of successfully applying countercyclical domestic measures.

In particular, it is the purpose of this paper to study the effects of a stereotyped cycle—to be described in the section entitled "The Model"—on a small (price taker), semi-open economy under alternative domestic policy scenarios.

I. Outline of Evaluation

After describing the most recent evolution of international transmission mechanisms for economic disturbances (the understanding of which is crucial to the understanding of how these disturbances affect small countries), the paper defines these disturbances in terms of a stereotyped cycle that is designed to resemble real-world business cycles.

In order to evaluate the global and sectoral effects of such stereotyped cycles on small, semi-open economies, the paper defines a model for such economies that is simple but contains enough elements to allow for such sectoral evaluation. This model includes some typical operational characteristics of Latin American countries, and these are described in detail. In addition, the paper emphasizes the analysis of stocks and flows, concentrating on equilibrium conditions rather than on behavioral assumptions. These behavioral assumptions and equilibrium conditions are implicit in the balance sheets in the Appendix.

In order to isolate effects of external shocks from effects of internal disequilibrium, this paper assumes that the external shocks are transmitted into small economies operating in what could be described as steady states—that is, economies operating in global and sectoral equilibrium and subject to no internal or external shocks. The characteristics of the steady state are clearly described.

Two kinds of effects of the stereotyped cycle upon the domestic economy are evaluated: global macroeconomic effects on variables such as prices, nominal and real interest rates, real exchange rates, output, and employment; and sectoral effects in the rentability and competitiveness of each productive sector, as well as the effects of the cycle upon the public sector budget, the accounts of the central bank, and individuals. The effects of the cycle upon the balance of payments are evaluated separately. This analysis is based upon two different assumptions about the operation of the exchange rate system and allows for varying degrees of the economy's openness to capital movements.

Finally, to improve understanding of some of the distortions and real effects introduced by inflation, the paper also deals briefly with the effects of inflation on nominal and real transfers and with the effects of indexation and distorted cost of living measurements on these transfers.

II. Recent Evolution of International Transmission Mechanisms of Economic Disturbances

Economic interdependence is a very old constraint on economic policy; no country, however large or small, can consider itself economically isolated from the rest of the world. International economic cycles are recurrent phenomena in economic history and have been the subject of intense research by specialists.

Recent developments in the world economy, however, have drastically changed the speed and forms of international transmission of economic disturbances. Among the factors contributing to the transformation are the following:

(i) The fast expansion of world trade during the last 30 years that, in fact, implies the expansion of tradable goods in comparison with nontradable goods, as evidenced by the increasing interdependence in commodities markets.

(ii) The internationalization of capital markets, reflected in the phenomenal growth of Eurocurrency markets and offshore financial centers, which has limited national monetary independence significantly.

(iii) The abandonment of the system of fixed parities and the substitution of a hybrid system that could be best described as a system of floating currency blocs, with major currencies floating against each other and secondary currencies pegging in practice (even when a floating rate has been announced[1]) to their major intervention currency. This system of blocs implies a drastic transformation in the transmission mechanism of cycles, since price fluctuations, in terms of intervention currencies, tend to be wider than before.

(iv) Interest rate flexibility and, in particular, floating interest rates have drastically altered the functioning of international cap-

[1]Many developing countries have systematically announced that their currencies were floating freely in moments of crisis, but have generally returned to pegging to their major intervention currencies after very short intervals.

ital markets. Fluctuations in nominal interest rates not only influence capital flows but also have decisive macroeconomic effects via outstanding debt and reserve positions.

(v) The highly inflationary environment underlying the economic disturbances has significantly altered the operations of most markets, particularly capital markets. Higher inflation is always accompanied by larger fluctuations in relative prices, and, in addition, nominal accounting introduces serious distortions into the operations of most markets; financial flows, or transfers, tend to differ from real economic flows. These points need further clarification, but this task will be undertaken in other sections of this paper.

(vi) Easier facilities to finance fiscal and balance of payments disequilibria tend to be reflected in unprecedented levels of floating rate public external debts, a factor that seriously distorts the functioning of the public sector when it is confronted with external disturbances.

(vii) The growing importance of private sector transactions in international capital markets, which is reflected in much larger private holdings of international liquid assets and private external debt. As a matter of fact, in many countries, total private holdings of foreign exchange greatly surpass total private holdings of domestic financial assets, and aggregate private external debt surpasses the aggregate private sector domestic debt. As will become clear later on, the larger the ratio of private foreign assets and liabilities to domestic currency denominated assets and liabilities the larger will be the influence of external disturbances.

(viii) Inter-area trade growth has partly compensated for some of the previously mentioned factors. However, since most countries in the area have become more integrated into world capital markets, external shocks originating there tend normally to reinforce each other.

III. A Stereotyped Economic Cycle

In the last decade, the international economy has experienced shocks more severe than any seen since the Great Depression of the 1930s. Besides the great shocks resulting from the repeated increases in oil prices, the international economy has suffered a series of additional shocks resulting from uncoordinated domestic policies and competitive adjustment policies that exaggerated the cyclical behavior of the international economy.

The most recent cycle seems to have started toward the end of 1978: downward trends in inflation and interest rates came to an end during late 1977 and early 1978, and the dollar started to depreciate faster in relation to other major currencies at the same time that industrial production continued to expand at relatively high rates. Toward the middle of 1978, after a short period of relative stability, nominal oil prices increased sharply, spurring an acceleration in inflation rates and further devaluation of the dollar; the price of commodities other than oil rose during 1979 at a much faster rate (24 percent) than prices of other goods and services (Table 1). Nominal interest rates also rose following the acceleration in inflation, but not by quite as much, so that real rates became slightly negative.

Starting in the first quarter of 1980, the growth rate of commodity prices slowed down. Prices remained stable during the latter part of the year and began to decline sharply beginning in the first quarter of 1981; other prices continued to increase throughout the period, accelerating at the beginning of the year and decelerating later on. Nominal interest rates remained very high during the period, and real interest rates reached unprecedented levels; furthermore, for commodity exporting countries, "real" interest rates (i.e., nominal rates deflated by commodity prices) reached even higher levels (Table 2).

The preceding analysis suggests a possible definition of a stereotyped economic cycle, which can be divided into stages. This characterization of the cycle may facilitate the evaluation of mechanisms for the international transmission of disturbances. No attempt will be made to explain the underlying causes of such an international cycle.

Starting from a situation of equilibrium, the cycle is characterized by the following stages:

1. *First stage:* International prices start to rise as a result of an autonomous shock. Commodity prices rise much faster than the prices of other goods and services; industrial product prices rise faster than nontradable goods. Nominal interest rates also rise following the increase in inflation; real interest rates become slightly negative when deflated by the overall price level, being highly negative when deflated by commodity prices and positive when deflated by prices of nontradable goods.

2. *Second stage:* International prices rise, on average, at a faster rate than in the first stage; most prices rise at similar rates, which implies that the rate of increase of commodity prices slows

TABLE 1: LATIN AMERICAN EXPORT AND IMPORT PRICES, FIRST QUARTER 1979–FIRST QUARTER 1982

(First quarter 1979 = 100)

		Index of Export Prices					
Year	Quarter	Including oil (1)	Excluding oil (2)	Import Prices (3)	U.S. Consumer Prices (4)	Relative Prices (5)[1]	Real Export Prices (6)[2]
1979	I	100.00	100.00	100.00	100.00	100.00	100.00
	II	109.23	108.25	100.00	103.43	108.25	104.66
	III	125.60	117.75	105.80	106.85	111.29	110.20
	IV	141.50	123.94	107.97	109.97	114.79	112.70
1980	I	158.17	131.39	111.59	114.25	117.74	115.00
	II	165.97	134.24	113.77	118.38	117.99	113.40
	III	168.64	135.29	118.12	120.56	114.54	112.22
	IV	177.10	135.86	115.94	128.75	117.18	109.79
1981	I	171.57	123.27	111.59	127.02	110.47	97.05
	II	165.01	112.37	107.25	129.98	104.77	86.27
	III	160.13	102.54	105.078	134.10	97.59	76.47
	IV	165.85	101.31	110.14	135.16	91.98	74.99
1982	I	165.06	97.00	114.49	135.93	84.72	71.36

Sources: Organization of American States, index of export prices; United Nations, import prices (manufactured commodities exported by industrial countries).

[1]Figures in this column are the quotients of the figure in column (2) of the same row divided by the figure in column (3) of the same row.

[2]Figures in this column are the quotients of the figure in column (2) of the same row divided by the figure in column (4) of the same row.

TABLE 2. NOMINAL AND REAL RATES OF INTEREST, 1978–FIRST QUARTER 1982

(In percent)

Period		Nominal		Interest Rates Deflated by	
Year	Quarter	Interest Rates	Consumer Prices	Consumer prices	Commodity prices
1978		8.7	9.7	−0.9	13.5
1979		11.9	12.8	−0.8	−10.8
1980	I	17.1	16.5	0.5	−7.9
	II	11.2	15.3	−3.6	2.0
	III	12.1	7.8	4.0	8.0
	IV	17.1	11.0	5.5	13.2
1981	I	16.3	11.0	4.8	22.0
	II	17.5	9.7	7.1	22.4
	III	18.0	13.3	4.2	22.7
	IV	14.7	3.0	11.4	13.9
1982	I	14.9	2.5	12.1	16.7

Source: International Monetary Fund, *International Financial Statistics*.

while other price increases accelerate. Nominal interest rates tend to rise further, with real rates becoming neutral; sectoral real rates do not show large dispersion.

3. *Third stage:* Commodity prices tend to decelerate, and even to decline, in nominal terms; other price increases also tend to moderate, with the prices of nontradable goods tending to increase the most. Nominal interest rates remain high, and consequently there are very high real interest rates—a turn of events that has a major impact on producers of commodities.

4. *Fourth stage:* The economy tends to return to equilibrium, in terms of both prices and interest rates. Overall prices, however, remain higher than at the beginning of the cycle, partly as a consequence of nominal wage inflexibility.

Obviously, in the international economy, these cycles will be accompanied by large fluctuations in variables such as output and employment, as well as by other sectoral exchange rate and balance of payments effects. However, as this paper covers only the evaluation of the cycle in small, semi-open economies, the principal external repercussions of the cycles will be derived from the preceding description.

IV. The Model

In order to evaluate the global effects of such stereotyped cycles on small, semi-open economies, it seems better to work with a model of a small economy that is as simple as possible while containing enough elements to allow for the evaluation of differential effects on the economy's various sectors and also for the isolation and evaluation of the effects of nominal interest rate variations on financial flows.

The model used in this paper puts emphasis on the analysis of stocks and flows, concentrating on equilibrium conditions rather than on behavioral assumptions. The model assumes the existence of three productive sectors: (1) a sector that produces an exportable commodity that is also sold, in part, in the domestic market; (2) a sector producing commodities that are import substitutes; and (3) a sector producing nontradable goods and services. Imports tend to be those products whose domestic production is either insufficient to meet demand or is nonexistent.

Prices of exportables and import substitutes are basically determined by external prices and the domestic exchange rate, since most small countries are price takers, while nontradable prices are determined by domestic forces of supply and demand. All products are assumed to be, simultaneously, intermediate goods and final goods. Besides these sectors, it is assumed that the economy possesses a well-developed financial system made up of a central bank and one or more financial institutions operating under a fractional minimum reserve requirement system, offering the usual kinds of deposits, and lending to both the private and public sectors.

Finally, the model assumes that the public sector performs exclusively administrative functions and engages in no productive activity whatsoever; it pays for its expenditures by collecting taxes from the productive sectors or direct from the public. If there is a budget deficit, it is assumed that it is financed by borrowing from the financial system, from the central bank, or direct from the public (by selling government bonds). In economies open to capital flows, external financing of the deficit is also allowed.

In addition, in order to focus the analysis on the problems of interdependence, it is convenient, and perhaps essential, to make some additional simplifying assumptions.

(a) All products are assumed to be consumption goods. The capital stock is assumed to be fixed, with no depreciation or additions through investment. Domestic production must be totally sold, either in the domestic market or foreign markets, during the period of analysis.

(b) Domestic production of exportables and import substitutes is assumed to be fixed, with variations in domestic aggregate demand being absorbed by variations in imports and exports and through the nontradable sector.

(c) Changes in relative prices mainly affect consumption while affecting production only marginally.[2]

(d) Changes in aggregate demand affect output and employment in the nontradable goods sectors.

V. Structural Operational Characteristics of Latin American Countries

In addition to the above-mentioned assumptions, some additional operational characteristics common to many Latin Ameri-

[2]This assumption could be justified by differences between the speeds of adjustment, between consumption and production, to changes in relative prices, which imply that producers anticipate cyclical changes in relative prices while consumers do not.

can countries are included in the model; some of these characteristics may also be shared by countries in other regions. The most relevant of these assumptions are as follows:

(1) There is a general practice of nominal wage indexation, with frequency of adjustment varying from monthly to yearly according to the country's experience with inflation. In general, indexation is based upon ex post compensation for inflation as measured by cost of living indices. Ex post wage indexation implies that real wages will tend to fluctuate throughout the cycle; furthermore, nominal wages tend to be inflexible downward.

(2) Tax systems take only partial account of the distortions introduced by inflation in such a way that taxes, measured in real terms, tend to decrease when inflation increases and tend to increase when inflation decreases.

(3) Public sector expenditures on goods and services tend to be maintained in real terms when inflation rises (independently of nominal budgets) but tend to increase when reductions in inflation rates generate fiscal surpluses. In general, public expenditures tend to follow the rule of using "real" budgeting when prices rise and "nominal" budgeting when prices fall.

(4) Most exportable goods tend to be commodities; frequently, these are wage goods.

(5) International reserves tend, normally, to be included in the central bank's accounts rather than in the fiscal accounts. Interest on such reserves does not accrue to the government, so it is not considered income of the public sector. As a consequence, such flows do not generate compensatory domestic currency flows.

(6) Variations in exchange rates generate important changes in real net wealth and alter the domestic currency values of external assets and liabilities. These changes are not, in general, registered in the nominal public sector accounting, and even though they have important macroeconomic consequences, they are difficult to identify and interpret by examining the official figures.

VI. Interest Rates, Capital Flows, Cost of Living Baskets, and Indexation

In an economy that does not permit capital movements, domestic interest rates are determined exclusively by internal factors; in addition, under such an assumption, neither the public sector nor the private sector holds any external assets or liabilities with the sole exception of international reserves held by the central bank.

The total lack of equilibrating capital movements, however, does not imply that international cycles will not be reflected in domestic interest rates; since these economies are semi-open to the movements of goods, international price fluctuations will tend to be reflected in domestic prices and—through their effects on the domestic supply of, and demand for, credit and money—they will also be reflected in domestic interest rates.

The fact that many Latin American countries that have had long experience with inflation have introduced indexed instruments (basically, indexed bonds, deposits, and loans) implies that the above-mentioned tendency to interest rate approximation has also been substantially reinforced.

There are, however, some limits to this tendency toward covered interest rate equalization through indexation. In the first place, implicit nominal interest rates on indexed financial instruments are determined ex post by the actual behavior of inflation, while nominal interest rates are determined ex ante, taking into account expected inflation rates. In the second place, the selection of baskets for "measurement" of inflation plays an even more important role in interest rate discrepancies, since "international inflation" measured by domestic baskets may differ substantially from that measured by international baskets.

International inflation is transmitted to other countries in the form of price increases in tradable goods prices. Domestically, it is reflected in the prices of nontradable goods through its direct effect on costs, its impact on wages and interest rates, and through substitution in demand. Price indices play very important roles through their effects on wages and financial instruments that are indexed and in the formation of expectations. The measurement of the effects of the international inflation using totally different domestic baskets may, therefore, give results that are totally different for different countries.

With partial opening to capital movements, the effects of international cycles on small, semi-open economies are much stronger than in the previous case, but most of the analysis in the preceding paragraphs remains valid. In these circumstances, interest rate changes abroad will be immediately reflected in domestic interest rates because of arbitrage. At the same time, the problems derived from divergences in cost of living indices tend to be augmented; tendencies toward covered interest rate equalization may be distorted by arbitrage between indexed and floating-interest-rate financial instruments or between commodity stocks and financial instruments that generates much larger capital flows than are normally needed for interest rate arbitrage. The main reason for these distortions is that interest rates are transmitted as rates, while inflation is transmitted as price increases that are transformed into inflation rates according to each country's cost of living basket.

VII. Nominal Interest Rates, Real Interest Rates, and Financial Flows

In a system of flexible interest rates and floating-rate financial instruments, nominal interest rates, like inflation rates, tend to adjust in such a way that real rates fluctuate significantly less than nominal rates. As is well known, nominal interest rates can be seen as having two elements—a real interest rate and an adjustment factor addressed to the maintenance of the real value of principal; this distinction is fundamental in the analysis of the real transfer effects of interest rate payments. However, when analyzing financial flows, nominal interest rates are as important as real interest rates, since, besides the real transfers involved in real rates, nominal interest rates payments involve an externally imposed advance prepayment of real capital—a phenomenon that has far-reaching macroeconomic consequences.

In an economy that is semi-open to capital movements, both the private and public sectors may, at any moment of time, hold important amounts of external assets and liabilities; in the last few years, most of these assets and liabilities have been covered by interest rate adjustment clauses. When international nominal interest rates rise, the advance payment of real capital implicit in nominal interest payments generates, ceteris paribus, a reduction in the aggregate demand of net debtor countries coupled with a deterioration in the current account of the balance of payments (and vice versa for net creditor countries). In substance, what is taking place is an improvement in the real wealth of net debtor countries that is derived from a reduction in consumption and is reflected in a reduction of the real net debt.

Recent developments in the world economy have greatly enhanced the importance of these factors. Enlarged private and public external debts, substantially larger private holdings of international liquid assets, wider fluctuations of nominal and real interest rates, and the practically unanimous use of floating-rate instruments in international capital markets have created a set of circumstances in which financial flows frequently play a much more important role than trade flows in the international transmission of economic disturbances. Interdependence seems to have reached unprecedented levels.

VIII. External Shocks and Domestic Economic Policies

As has already been stated, the main purpose of this paper is to evaluate the economic consequences for the economy of a small country of external disturbances exemplified by the stereotyped cycle described in preceding sections, isolating these external effects from the effects of domestic economic policies.

To achieve this objective, a very simple procedure was used—simulation of an external shock in an economy that could, up to then, be characterized as a "steady-state" economy. Specifically, this steady state can be defined as a situation in which domestic and external forces are in permanent equilibrium—that is to say, an economy characterized by

—absolute price stability

—full employment of all productive resources

—balance of payments equilibrium, in terms of domestic currency

—balanced public sector budget

—zero growth rate

—portfolio equilibrium in both assets and liabilities

—similar rate of return on investment in each productive sector

—in economies open to capital movements, equilibrium requires that net interest payments (or receipts) on external positions be compensated for by internal adjustments of consumption (lower imports and/or larger exports).

The Appendix includes an example of such a steady-state situation for an economy open to capital movements. For economies closed to such movements the situation would be similar, but with no external assets and liabilities (except reserves) and with no interest payments or receipts derived from these instruments. Obviously, the numbers used in the example are totally arbitrary, and the modification of any of them requires substantial modification of others in order to return to a steady-state situation. Although the numbers are arbitrary, they have been chosen in an effort to reproduce the situation of a commodity exporting developing country. However, external debt figures—relative to other figures—are extremely small compared with real-world figures. These relatively low figures were purposely selected to emphasize the extreme importance of external debt levels in the analysis of the repercussions of external shocks upon small economies.

Starting from this equilibrium situation, it is easy to reproduce most of the sequences of events that follow an external shock of the type defined by the stereotyped cycle; the advantage of this procedure is that it allows us to observe, step by step, how external shocks affect the economy's different sectors and how these sectoral effects may introduce secondary shocks that either strengthen or weaken the initial external shock. Throughout the analysis, it will be assumed that there is no countercyclical domestic policy and that the only additional exogenous shocks will be those arising from the structural characteristics described in preceding sections.

The evaluation was carried on under two different exchange rate regimes (fixed rates and freely floating rates) and under varying assumptions about capital movements (from partial opening to total exclusion). Such an evaluation poses a variety of methodological questions, and the description of the cycle's first stage will be much more detailed than the descriptions of the others, since it will attempt to clarify some of these methodological questions.

IX. Analysis of Results Under Fixed Exchange Rates

FIRST STAGE

Macroeconomic effects

Effects on prices and interest rates. In this first stage of the cycle, the world economy is subject to inflation pressures that raise the prices of all products as well as nominal interest rates; increases in commodity prices (exportables in our example) tend to be larger than those of other goods and services. Nominal interest rates also rise, but become negative in real terms for all productive sectors. Prices of exportables and importables—expressed in domestic currency—increase following similar increases in international markets. Nontradable goods are also subject to several shocks: increased cost of inputs, increased interest payment flows (derived from the increase in nominal interest rates), and increased aggregate demands (derived principally from the improvement in the terms of trade, the inflow of foreign capital, and substitutions in demand in response to relative price changes). In addition, wage costs also tend to increase as indexation practices are applied. All the above-mentioned factors bring about an increase in the prices of nontradables.

Increases in the prices of nontradables will be higher, the greater the improvements in the terms of trade, the larger the capital flows, the shorter the period between wage adjustments (following indexation procedures), the smaller the interest payments on the net external debt, and the smaller the accumulation of domestic or external financial assets by residents. Global inflation will be the result, therefore, of the strength of those factors and of the proportion of tradables in total goods and services.

Increases in nominal interest rates are spurred by two factors—increases in international interest rates and increases in domestic inflation rates. The relationship between domestic and international rates depends upon the relative force of these two factors, which, in turn, depends upon the degree of the economy's openness to capital movements (arbitrage efficiency). With less than perfect arbitrage, inflation rate differentials tend to determine interest rate differentials. These inflation differentials are basically the result of the different compositions of cost of living baskets and of divergent behavior of the prices of nontradables.

In the first stage of the cycle, inflation rates in commodity exporting countries tend to be higher than those in the rest of the world, and domestic interest rates tend to be higher in the former than in the latter. Nevertheless, "real" interest rates tend to be lower, on average, in commodity exporting countries than in the rest of the world. Capital tends to flow into the country expanding aggregate demand. The growth in demand will exceed the growth that can be accounted for by the expansionary forces derived from improvement in the terms of trade. The strength of these flows and their impact on inflation, interest rates, and output are naturally dependent on the economy's openness to capital movements.

Deficiencies in the selection of cost of living baskets may introduce some distortions of their own. In defining the basic index for purposes of indexation, countries have several options, the main ones being indices whose weights are based on the composition of production or those based on the composition of consumption. In some countries in the region, the measurement of cost of living indices is based upon a special basket of consumption by a portion of consumers—basically, blue collar workers. Consumption indices tend to be weighted in favor of commodities (particularly in partial samples) in such a way that external fluctuations tend to be amplified in the domestic economy and external distortions in interest rates and wages tend to be amplified as well.

Real exchange rates, output, and employment. It should be clear by now that there are deficiencies in the traditional method of measuring real exchange rates. Real exchange rate indices attempt to measure the evolution of the competitiveness of domestic producers of tradables in relation to producers in other countries. Too many factors are involved in the determination of such competitiveness to permit one to determine it using only simple indices; the only sure way to evaluate it is by looking at the tradable producer's complete balance sheet and by observing the evolution of both costs and prices.

Some form of index may, nevertheless, be useful when one is trying to obtain a first approximation of such competitiveness. The traditional procedure of comparing exchange rate variations plus international inflation with domestic inflation would show, in the case under analysis, a deterioration in the real exchange rate, which is absurd in view of the behavior of the terms of trade and of nontradables prices. This is another instance of distortion introduced by baskets. A more adequate procedure is to compare the evolution of the relative price between tradable and nontradable goods, measured in domestic currency. In the case under review, this procedure will show an improvement in the real exchange rate, since the increase in the price of tradables—especially exportables—greatly surpasses the increase in the price of nontradables.

With regard to output, it is clear that under the assumptions of the model, the increase in aggregate demand should be eliminated through increases in the prices of nontradables, the expansion of imports, the reduction of export volume, and the accumulation of nominal financial assets. Marginal fluctuations in the production of nontradables have been allowed as a mechanism for absorbing these changes in demand.

Once again, it is possible to conclude that the larger the improvement in the terms of trade, the larger the inflows of capital; and the smaller the interest payments on the net external debt, the larger will be the increases in output and employment and the increase in the price of nontradables. All the above-mentioned conclusions can be easily verified by examining the example included in the Appendix. This example can also be used to examine other sectoral effects of the cycle.

Sectoral effects

Public sector budget. Starting with the public sector budget, when the reader observes the figures in the example, he will be struck by the fact that in a situation where real expenditures are not increasing, real wages are declining, and the terms of trade, output, and employment are all improving, the budget turns from global equilibrium into deficit. Only a very detailed evaluation of the situation can help to solve this puzzle. Global inflation normally implies that practically every expenditure and receipt item tends to increase in nominal terms. What would happen to the nominal budget if all prices increased in the same proportion, real expenditures, wages, and taxes remained constant, and real interest rates remained the same as in the steady state? It would show a deficit as a consequence of the prepayment of debt implicit in the nominal interest rate increase (based on the assumptions that the government is a net financial debtor and that interest on reserves is not included in the budget). In addition, it should be noted that some of the results in the example are partly derived from the inclusion in the model of elements that tend to describe special characteristics of Latin American countries, such as the lags in wage indexation and in tax receipts.

In general, it may be asserted that as a consequence of the external shock, the *nominal* fiscal deficit will be larger the shorter the period between wage adjustments, the larger the lags in tax receipts, and the larger the amount of net financial indebtedness. Clearly, conditions may be described under which the budget will move into surplus, but these conditions rarely occur in Latin American economies.

Should this nominal deficit be considered a "real" deficit, in the sense of a net transfer of real resources that the public sector financed by increasing its outstanding "real" debt? The answer to this very important question depends on many factors, the main one being the contribution of net nominal interest payments to this deficit. "Inflation adjustment" of budget figures is helpful in evaluation of these real transfers.

Central bank. It is possible to verify that, as a consequence of the cycle, the central bank has, in this first stage, a surplus in both its domestic currency budget and its foreign currency budget; both surpluses originate in increases in foreign and domestic interest rates. Once again, this surplus corresponds to advance repayments on debt instruments held by the central bank. The surplus of foreign currency exists because the central bank's reserves exceed its external debts.

In addition to this operative surplus, the central bank faces a very important flow demand for base money (derived from the increase in prices) that greatly surpasses (given the assumptions) the potential flow net supply (fiscal deficit *minus* the surplus of the central bank). Under a fixed exchange rate regime, this excess demand will be satisfied through the central bank's acquisition of reserve assets, basically through a trade account surplus in those economies practically closed to capital movements and also through external capital flows or dishoarding of foreign assets in more open economies.

The above-mentioned results are normally valid almost regardless of the assumptions made about assets and liabilities. There is a very important case, however, in which the results of the analysis might be quite different; this occurs when the government confronts a very large external debt (in proportion to gross domestic product (GDP)) and in which the demand for base money is extremely weak (also in proportion to GDP), perhaps as a consequence of hyperinflationary circumstances. The increase in international interest rates tends to generate a fiscal "deficit" (and a corresponding need for foreign assets) greatly exceeding the flow demand for base money; as a consequence, the first stage of the cycle might, in these circumstances, generate a large balance of payments deficit notwithstanding the large improvements in the terms of trade.

Financial institutions. Nominal profits (gross or net) of financial institutions will also tend to improve in the first stage of the cycle, basically as a consequence of the increase in nominal interest rates and the maintenance of nominal spreads that occur at the same time as a decline in real expenditures. At the same time, deposits—particularly time deposits—tend to increase in nominal terms (and perhaps also in real terms) in response to a higher price level, relatively neutral real rates, and capital inflows; this increase in deposits is matched by a corresponding increase in credit.

Obviously, the larger the inflow of capital the smaller should be the discrepancy between domestic and foreign interest rates, and the smaller the spread between rates on loans and rates on deposits. Such shrinkage of spreads reduces the profits from outstanding credits, but this reduction is compensated for by the increased volume of credit generated by the capital inflows. However, the most important explanation of the increase in profits of financial institutions is derived from the relationship between the ratio of sight deposits to minimum reserve requirements, on the one hand, and the nominal rates of interest, on the other. In most countries in the region, financial institutions accept sight deposits and pay no interest to depositors on their outstanding balances. These institutions also maintain idle balances in order to comply with mandatory reserve requirements and receive no compensation whatsoever on such balances. Sight deposits, net of minimum reserve requirements, are lent at normal interest rates. Clearly, the larger the differences are between sight deposits and bank reserves, and the higher nominal interest rates are, the larger the nominal profits of financial institutions will be.

In the example, sight deposits substantially exceed bank reserves, and the surplus of funds enables banks to earn large profits as interest rates rise. In substance, financial institutions retain part of the inflationary tax being paid by the public.

Productive sectors. In the three basic productive sectors, it seems clear that the evolution of nominal gross profits depends upon too many factors to permit one to draw a priori conclusions on the subject; in substance, these profits depend on the evolution of the ratio between the prices of finished products and the prices of inputs, the lags in wage and tax adjustments, the outstanding net indebtedness of these sectors in domestic and external markets, and their respective interest rates.

Leaving aside indebtedness problems, it may be concluded that the main beneficiaries in this first stage of the cycle should be the producers of exportables; the results for producers of import substitutes depend on wage and tax lags. With no lags, this sector would suffer a deterioration in its rate of return; while with long lags, it would certainly lose relative position in comparison with other producers but would, nevertheless, increase its profits at the expense of workers and the public sector. Profits of the nontradable sector will tend to be extremely sensitive to the volume of capital flows. The larger these flows, the larger will be the profits of nontradable producers.

However, if elements derived from net indebtedness of producers are added, the main conclusions drawn in the preceding paragraph may be modified. Nevertheless, in considering inflation-adjusted profits, these conclusions are confirmed, and even reinforced, since real interest rates have been assumed to be negative in this first stage of the cycle. Interest payments, therefore, should generate large financial flow problems but no real flow problems. These real flows tend, in fact, to be negative.

Effects on individuals. Among individuals practically all forms of nominal income will tend to increase during the first stage of the cycle. Nominal disposable incomes (after taxes) of savers and investors should increase substantially, while those of wage earners depend upon the lags between wage and tax adjustments and upon employment growth. The larger the flows of foreign capital, the shorter are the lags in wage adjustments, and the longer the lags in tax adjustments, the greater will be the chances of both workers and investors having larger nominal disposable incomes.

Real disposable incomes, however, tend to increase only for savers and investors, and to decrease for workers. The definition of real income itself poses some difficulties. For savers, for example, the situation is complex, since interest flows, deflated by cost of living indices, tend to show large increases; at the same time, though, the real values of assets tend to deteriorate to such an extent that they may bring about a decrease in real wealth (negative real rates of interest) and an increase in real financial flows (prepayments of debt).

Individual expenditure levels are dependent not only on the above-mentioned factors but also on portfolio changes. In the first stage of the cycle, real rates of return on foreign and domestic assets tend to be negative, which leads to a dishoarding of assets (in real terms) and an increase in outstanding debt (also in real terms); real expenditures should therefore increase. The larger the inflow of capital, the larger should be the expansion of aggregate demand.

Balance of payments

The traditional definitions of the balance of payments and its components pose a series of problems when there is widespread inflation and generalized private holdings of international liquid assets. The main difficulties lie in the distinctions between (1) the current account and the capital account, and (2) the central bank's official balance of payments and the national balance of payments, which, in addition to official reserves, includes variations in the external assets of other residents. Examples of the difficulties are the following: Should interest flows on private holdings of international liquid assets be treated as interest income in the current account or as capital flows? Should the "inflation adjustment" component of nominal interest rates be considered interest payments—and, as such, included in the current account—or as advance repayments of "real" debt? Should changes in the private sector's portfolio—matched by corresponding changes in official portfolios (with opposite signs)—be considered capital outflows from a macroeconomic point of view?

Leaving aside these important questions, it seems clear that the most convenient way to evaluate the overall effects of the first stage of the cycle upon the balance of payments is to examine the behavior of the individual components of the balance of payments.

Exports tend to increase, both in value and in volume, owing to three factors: (1) improvement in the terms of trade; (2) a minimum expansion of output; and (3) substitutions in demand that originated in relative price changes. However, income effects originating in increases in national income tend to have the opposite influence on both exports and imports.

Imports also tend to increase, probably by less than exports in nominal terms but by more than exports in volume; as a matter of fact, if capital inflows are large enough, nominal imports will increase even more than nominal exports, and the trade account could move into deficit, notwithstanding the improvement in the terms of trade.[3]

Obviously, as was seen when the central bank figures were examined, the overall balance of payments normally tends to be in surplus in this first stage of the cycle, since the larger nominal interest payments tend to be more than compensated for by a (probable) trade surplus, capital inflows, and dishoarding. The larger the flow of foreign capital, the larger the balance of payments surplus and the smaller the trade account surplus. Only when there are large external debts and weak demand for base money might the balance of payments move into deficit, in this first stage of the cycle, as a consequence of the external shocks.

SECOND STAGE

As the paper has already gone into detail in its analysis of the first stage's repercussions on a small, semi-open economy, it should now be possible to proceed with the analysis of the other

[3]An even stranger development could take place in beef exporting countries, where the improvement in the terms of trade—if thought to be permanent—might induce a retention cycle that would involve a short-run reduction in the volume of exports.

stages of the stereotyped cycle without delving further into such details.

During the cycle's second stage, domestic prices of exportables and import substitutes should rise pari passu with international prices, and those of nontradables are subject to even more violent shocks than those received during the first stage: practically the same, or larger, input costs; even higher interest payments; and substantially larger adjustments in nominal wages and taxes. All these factors necessitate additional adjustments (and larger ones than were required during the first stage) in prices for the sector as a whole. With full indexation, domestic nontradables prices should tend to rise faster than the corresponding prices in the rest of the world.

Nominal interest rates should also rise in response to higher international interest rates, and higher domestic inflation rates are forced upward by the increases in prices of import substitutes and nontradables, but the rate of increase in exportables prices should be lower than in the first stage; the selection of baskets is, again, crucial, since the larger the distortions in favor of exportables, the larger will be the distortions in global inflation indices during the first and second stages. Normally, global inflation rises during this second stage, contributing to the elevation of domestic nominal interest rates. Interest rate differentials with the rest of the world tend to be reduced; and capital flows, although they remain positive, tend to be smaller than they were during the first stage.

Real exchange rates should tend to show a small deterioration when measured by the ratios of the respective prices of exportables and import substitutes, on the one hand, and the price of nontradables, on the other, but the exchange rate should continue to be much higher than it was in the steady state. Traditional measurements may show either an improvement or a further deterioration, depending upon the distortions introduced by the weighting of exportables.

Output and employment may continue expanding marginally, but this result depends basically upon which has a greater effect—nominal interest payments, on the one hand, or capital inflows and dishoarding, on the other. In economies closed to capital movements, output and employment tend to be reduced during this stage.

Turning to the sectoral effects and starting with the evaluation of the public sector budget, it is clear that the budget should show further nominal deficits. The size of these deficits, however, will be larger or smaller than those seen in the first stage, depending upon the following factors: the relative speed of adjustment of wages and taxes in accordance with indexation systems; the increased cost of real expenditures; and, especially, the amount of net nominal interest payments both domestically and abroad. In the example, the size of the nominal deficit remains relatively stable; but in real life, with larger public (domestic and external) debts, further enlargement of the nominal deficit would be likely.

The central bank, though, tends to show a larger operational surplus and larger receipts in its reserves. At the same time, nominal demand for base money should continue to expand owing to higher inflation rates and slightly less negative real domestic interest rates. Total flow demand for base money, however, depends as much on domestic factors as on foreigners' demands for domestic deposits. If capital flows are smaller than during the first stage, global flow demand for base money may also be smaller. Obviously, the counterpart of such a disequilibrium in the domestic money market is the accumulation of international reserves.

Nominal profits of financial institutions should continue expanding, notwithstanding increased costs in the form of wages and taxes and the maintenance of nominal spreads. Basically, these increased profits come from larger credit operations and, in particular, from the increment in the implicit subsidies on sight deposits, which generally increase as nominal interest rates increase.

Net nominal profits of all productive sectors should decrease in the second stage, responding basically to the increase in nominal interest rates. Wage input and tax adjustments are approximately compensated for by increases in finished product prices, but increased interest rate payments involve an additional transfer to savers and to foreign creditors. Obviously, the larger the net indebtedness of any sector and the larger the increase in the nominal interest rate, the smaller will be nominal profits. As explained before, most of these interest payments should be considered advance payments of real debt and, as such, should not modify real profits; nominal accounting tends, therefore, to introduce strong distortions.

Real wages, with nominal adjustments based on past inflation rates, should, in this second stage, maintain levels similar to those reached at the end of the first stage. Deficiencies in cost of living indices may alter this general statement, since nominal wage adjustments will be larger the larger the weight of exportables in such an index. If nominal wages, dividends, and taxes all tend to increase at approximately the same rate, global real consumption will tend to depend exclusively on nominal interest payments, nominal variations in the value of assets and liabilities, and the magnitude of capital flows. In this second stage, capital flows and dishoarding should be smaller, and interest rate payments greater than during the first stage, with the result that consumption should also decrease. This decrease in consumption, in real terms, is reflected in the balance of payments in the form of a larger trade account surplus. The overall balance of payments result depends more on the magnitude of the government's net indebtedness and on the tendency to hoard than on the evolution of real exchange rates.

THIRD STAGE

This is the stage of the cycle when most of the externally generated problems of commodity exporting countries tend to show up. During the third stage, the rate of increase of commodity prices slows down, and prices may even decline in nominal terms. Prices of other goods and services continue increasing at rates slightly lower than those registered during the second stage. Nominal interest rates also remain very high and even tend to increase, while real interest rates tend to reach unprecedented levels.

Domestic prices of exportables and import substitutes tend to rise as a consequence of developments in international markets, and nontradables prices are subject to two opposite forces—on the one hand, increases in wages, taxes, and the costs of some inputs, and on the other hand, a decrease in the cost of commodity inputs and a decline in aggregate demand.

The implicit deterioration of the terms of trade during the stage may also create uncertainties and generate capital outflows. This is particularly so if, during the first two stages, capital inflows took the form of external indebtedness rather than dishoarding (nobody knows the amount of private international asset holdings, while data on total indebtedness are readily available). In these circumstances, domestic interest rates should rise above international interest rates, and real interest rates should become extremely high. Furthermore, the scarcity of domestic credit caused by capital outflows should certainly be reflected in larger spreads and additional external borrowing—that is, net capital outflows might not be reflected in reductions in external indebtedness but, on the contrary, would be reflected in larger private hoardings and smaller foreign holdings of domestic assets.

Global inflation, as measured by indices, should—ceteris paribus—decelerate during this stage, particularly in those countries with commodity-based indices. In these circumstances, real exchange rates, measured by traditional methods, may show an improvement, while those measurements based on the ratio of prices between tradables and nontradables, or based on direct evaluation of producers' balance sheets, should show marked deterioration. During this third stage, output and employment should decline following the reversal of the terms of trade and the outflow of capital.

Debtors should be most severely affected during this stage, and since the public sector is the principal debtor in the economy, it should not be surprising if during the third stage budget deficits tend to become much larger in nominal terms, forcing increases in public indebtedness. If one examines the public sector accounts, it is possible to see why this is so, since while wages, taxes, and nominal expenditures all tend to rise at approximately the same rate (a phenomenon leading to an increase in the fiscal deficit), interest rate payments tend to rise significantly faster, which adds to the nominal deficit. During this stage, there is a tendency to finance part of this deficit by borrowing abroad.

In the central bank accounts, however, an increase in nominal interest rates implies a larger operative surplus; but, at the same time, the larger financial requirements of the government, coupled with a decrease in the growth rate of the flow demand for base money (basically, as a consequence of capital outflows), should lead to a significant loss of international reserves. These increases in the external indebtedness of the public sector and in the registered external debt of the private sector, in combination with reserves losses and a deterioration of the terms of trade, should normally reinforce speculation against the domestic currency.

The financial sector should, in principle, be the sole domestic sector to benefit during this third stage. Larger spreads and higher nominal interest rates should significantly increase the nominal profits of financial institutions, particularly as a consequence of the implicit subsidy on sight deposits. However, credit risks should also be increasing during this stage, especially those on credits to producers of exportables.

With commodity prices falling and production costs rising, the rate of return on investments in the export sector should decline and even become negative. Nominal financial costs should constitute one of the most important elements in this deterioration of profits. Adjustment of the sector's balance sheets for inflation, made on the basis of general indices, might improve this negative result somewhat, but this adjustment would be erroneous, since real interest rates for the sector should be even higher than nominal rates.

Nominal profits of producers of import substitutes and nontradables should also decline, but by less than those of exportables producers, since the prices of the former goods tend to rise faster than those of the latter. "Inflation adjusted" profits should increase, since for the import substitutes and nontradables sectors real interest rates tend to be lower than nominal interest rates. The reduction in aggregate demand for nontradables plays an important role in the profitability loss on these goods.

Real wages should rise marginally during this stage as a result of adjustments based on past inflation rates and the deceleration of inflation during the current stage. However, the decline in employment in the nontradables sector should compensate for part of this increase in wages. With real profits declining, total wages stable, and capital outflows, total aggregate demand and, in particular, consumption should decline compared with the previous period. The more severe the lack of confidence in the domestic currency, the larger should be the outflow of capital and the larger the reduction in consumption. In fact, if capital outflows are large enough, consumption might be even lower than in the steady state.

The balance of payments must reflect all these contradictory forces. Exports should decline, both in value and in volume, following the decline in world prices and substitutability in demand. The behavior of imports during this period depends crucially upon the behavior of capital outflows: the larger the capital outflow, the smaller should be aggregate demand and, therefore, imports. In the absence of commodity speculation[4] and compensatory expansionary policies by the government, imports should decline, both

[4]In moments of exchange speculation, leads and lags in payment for exports and imports tend to reinforce or modify the normal behavior of these variables. Since this model has assumed total consumption during the period, however, commodity speculation is excluded.

in value and in volume. Finally, with larger interest payments and massive capital outflows, the overall balance of payments should be in deficit—a result that would be consistent with money market equilibrium requirements.

These developments at the third stage seem to be totally coherent with developments in the world economy during 1981 and 1982 and, in particular, with the problems faced by Latin American countries.

FOURTH STAGE

During the fourth, and last, stage of the stereotyped cycle, international prices should tend to remain stable. After their decline during the third stage, commodity prices should either remain stable or rise slightly if the decline during the third stage was too large. Nominal interest rates should fall, while real interest rates should decline significantly while remaining positive, especially for commodity producers.

Domestically, with a smaller dispersion of international prices and with smaller wage adjustments (owing to the decline of commodity prices during the third stage), price behavior should be remarkably stable.

Although domestic interest rates should fall, they will probably remain above international interest rates owing to lack of confidence in the value of the domestic currency and to persistent capital outflows.

Aggregate demand should weaken further during this stage as a consequence of capital outflows, and nontradables prices should be very stable. However, wages might play an important role in the maintenance of disequilibria, since the shorter the lags between wage adjustments and the greater the distortions of cost of living baskets, the greater are the chances that nominal wages will overshoot and, because of the downward inflexibility of nominal wages, the greater the chances of a serious balance of payments disequilibrium and of losses in sectoral competitiveness. In these circumstances, exchange speculation might reach massive proportions, amplifying the decrease in demand and the sacrifices implicit in adjustment policies.

The fiscal deficit should be reduced during this stage, since stable nominal expenditures and reduced interest payments, coupled with increased nominal taxes, should more than compensate for the corresponding wage adjustments.

The central bank should also confront a reduction in its operative surplus and a reduction in the excess flow demand for base money. With smaller (but still positive) capital outflows and a smaller (but also still positive) fiscal deficit, monetary equilibrium should only be consistent with additional reserve losses.

Profits of financial institutions should be considerably reduced during this stage, in response to lower nominal interest rates and higher wages. Spreads, however, should remain larger than normal. The main problem for financial institutions during this stage should be increased losses on account of bad loans that are the result of two consecutive stages of serious deterioration in profits for most sectors, and particularly for commodity producers.

Finally, if capital outflows are positive but smaller than those registered during the previous stage, and interest payments are also positive but smaller, the balance of payments should show a smaller global deficit, including a small surplus in the trade account and a smaller deficit in the current account. Imports should decrease, both in value and in volume.

X. Analysis of Results Under Floating Exchange Rates

Up to now, the analysis of the international transmission mechanism for economic disturbances and of the effects of a stereotyped cycle upon a small, semi-open economy has been carried out under the assumption of a fixed exchange rate system. Would the results be altered significantly if the small country operated as part of a flexible exchange rate system? To answer this question, one need only reproduce the analysis of the preceding subsections, modifying the fixed rate assumption.

A floating exchange rate system is defined here as a system in which the monetary authorities abstain from intervening in exchange markets, letting the rate be determined by market forces. A definition as global as this poses serious difficulties in real life, since in most countries the public sector tends to be by far the largest participant in exchange markets, not as a regulator but as a sectoral operator. With large outstanding external debts and increased nominal interest rates, financial transactions considerably exceed trade transactions in exchange markets. Since the government in most countries in the region is the country's major external debtor, the government is also the largest transactor in the market. Consequently, it affects the exchange market and exchange rates, not as a regulator but as a transactor.

Leaving aside this and other problems that would arise in the operation of floating exchange rate systems in developing countries, in order to be able to answer the question posed in this section's first paragraph, it seems convenient to define a floating exchange rate system more precisely as a system in which the existing nominal stocks of reserves and public external debts remain fixed, with the sole exception of accrued interest on such reserves. No other restriction will be imposed on day-to-day official transactions.

It seems clear that assuming no variation in central bank reserves is equivalent—in this model—to assuming that there is no disequilibrium in the domestic market for base money issued by the central bank—that is, if demand for base money is larger or smaller than its flow supply, the exchange rate will tend to adjust until equilibrium in this market is restored.

Returning to the first stage of the stereotyped cycle, the increase in international inflation and the improvement in the terms of trade that are assumed to be taking place during this stage should simultaneously generate, under a floating exchange rate system, an excess supply of foreign assets and an excess demand for base money. At the same time, exports should increase, as a consequence of the improvement in the terms of trade, and import volume and foreign asset holdings should decrease as a consequence of the excess demand for base money. In these circumstances, there is a clear tendency for the exchange rate to be revalued.

With revaluation, domestic prices and interest rates tend to rise by less than they do in the rest of the world and the flow demand for money tends to fall, which contributes to the restoration of equilibrium. If the improvement in the terms of trade is large enough, the revaluation might force prices of imports and import substitutes to fall in nominal terms and thus turn the incipient fiscal deficit into a surplus. If this occurred, revaluation would continue until the reduction in the nominal demand for base money equaled the reduction in supply derived from the fiscal surplus.

With larger interest payments abroad and larger nominal domestic asset hoardings (generated by international inflation), imports (both volume and value) should decline. Because of the private sector budget constraint, however, if the improvement in the trade account brought about by the improvement in the terms of trade is larger than the increase in global interest payments abroad, a decline in imports would be inconsistent with market equilibrium. There would also be a tendency for the exchange rate to be revalued, reducing exports and expanding imports—a tendency that would be stronger the larger the inflow of capital. But, on the other hand, if there were extremely large external debts and an extremely weak demand for base money—a special case mentioned earlier in this paper—the exchange rate would tend to depreciate rather than appreciate.

The new equilibrium in exchange and money markets should also imply much lower inflation and nominal interest rates and—perhaps—absolute declines in some prices. It should also imply a surplus in the public sector budget and a global balance of payments equilibrium.

It is impossible to determine ex ante the sign and size of the trade and current account balances without specifying the behavior and size of capital flows. With large capital inflows, the current account is necessarily in deficit, while the trade account should show a balance exactly equal to the difference between the inflow of capital and net interest payments abroad. As interest payments on international liquidity holdings may, in practice, be registered in either the capital account or the current account, the abovementioned conclusion may be distorted.

In summary, floating exchange rates tend to insulate the domestic economy more effectively against external shocks, such as inflation and interest rate shocks. However, since variations in output and employment, as well as in sectoral competitiveness, tend to be much larger under floating rates than under fixed rates, real sector cycles tend to be amplified.

If the economy is completely open to capital movements, the situation tends to be even more unstable, since capital inflows (undertaken in anticipation of exchange rate developments) will tend to be reflected in larger fluctuations of exchange rates, prices, and aggregate demand. The analysis of the components of the balance of payments in a previous paragraph of this section clearly shows why floating rates tend to generate larger variations in real variables, the principal reason being that under alternative exchange rate regimes, external shocks may also be absorbed by changes in holdings of assets and liabilities.

The evaluations of the other stage of the cycle would be similar to those made in the preceding subsections that assumed a fixed exchange rate system. Obviously, during the third stage of the cycle, capital would tend to flow outward and the exchange rate to depreciate, stabilizing domestic prices and interest rates but amplifying variations in output in the process.

Stabilizing speculation, if it were successful, might dampen exchange rate fluctuations and, in the process, amplify the fluctuations of nominal variables and diminish those of real variables. Distortions derived from the selection of national baskets for cost of living indices might, however, reduce the chances of success for this kind of speculation.

APPENDIX: EXPLANATORY EXAMPLE

Domestic Sectoral Effects of International Economic Cycles Under Fixed Exchange Rates and Partial Opening to Capital Movements

(In arbitrary units of account)

Sectoral liquid assets and liabilities in the steady state

Consolidated Public Sector

		Central bank	50
		Bonds	20
		Financial debt	80
		Domestic	*30*
		External	*50*
		Net financial wealth	−150

Central Bank

Reserves	100	Monetary base	200
Loans to	100		
Public sector	*50*		
Financial sector	*50*		
		Net financial wealth	0

Financial Institutions

Currency	50	Sight deposits	150
Bonds	10	Time deposits	350
Loans to	510	Central bank	50
Public sector	*30*		
Private sector	*480*		
		Liquid wealth	20

Exportables

Currency	20	Debts in	140
Sight deposits	30	*Domestic currency*	*120*
Time deposits	50	*Foreign currency*	*20*
Foreign assets	10		
		Net financial wealth	−30

Sectoral liquid assets and liabilities in the steady state *(concluded)*

Import Substitutes

Currency	20	Debts in	140
Sight deposits	30	*Domestic currency*	*120*
Time deposits	50	*Foreign currency*	*20*
Foreign assets	10		
		Net financial wealth	−30

Nontradables

Currency	20	Debts in	140
Sight deposits	30	*Domestic currency*	*120*
Time deposits	50	*Foreign currency*	*20*
Foreign assets	10		
		Net financial wealth	−30

Individuals

Currency	90	Debts in	130
Sight deposits	60	*Domestic currency*	*120*
Time deposits	200	*Foreign currency*	*10*
Bonds	10		
Foreign assets	30		
		Net financial wealth	260

Foreigners

External debts	120	Reserves	100
Public	*50*	Private holdings	
Private	*70*	of foreign liquid assets	60
		Net financial wealth	−40

Real and financial flows in the steady state

Assumptions: (i) Absolute price stability
(ii) Domestic and foreign interest rates
Time deposits—2 percent
Bonds —3 percent
Loans —5 percent

Public Sector

Wages	99	Taxes	299.1
Purchases of	195		
Exportables	*15*	Deficit (−) or surplus	0
Import substitutes	*30*		
Nontradables	*100*		
Imports	*50*		
Interest on	5.1		
Bonds	*0.6*		
Domestic financial debt	*1.5*		
Central bank	*0.5*		
External debt	*2.5*		
		△ Central bank	0
		△ Bonds	0
		△ Domestic financial debt	0
		△ External debt	0

Central Bank

Wages	1	Interest on	1.5
Purchases of	0.5	*Public sector*	*0.5*
Nontradables	*0.5*	*Private sector*	*1.0*
		Interest on reserves (no monetary effects)	2.0
△ Public sector	0	Surplus	0
△ Rediscount	0	△ Demand for base money	0
△ Reserves (with monetary effects)	0		

Real and financial flows in the steady state *(concluded)*

Financial Institutions

Wages	7	Interest on	25.8
Purchases of	3	*Bonds*	*0.3*
Import substitutes	*1*	*Loans to public sector*	*1.5*
Nontradables	*2*	*Loans to private sector*	*24.0*
Interest on	8		
Time deposits	*7*		
Rediscount	*1*		
Taxes	2.3		
Net profits	5.5		
(Gross profits)	(7.8)		
Δ Currency	0	Δ Sight deposits	0
Δ Loans	0	Δ Time deposits	0
		Δ Rediscount	0

Exportables

Wages	100	Domestic sales	100
Purchases of	115	Exports	150
Exportables	*10*	Interest on	1.2
Import substitutes	*25*	*Time deposits*	*1.0*
Nontradables	*60*	*Foreign assets*	*0.2*
Imports	*20*		
Interest on	7		
Domestic debt	*6*		
External debt	*1*		
Taxes	8.7		
Net profits	20.5		
(Gross profits)	(29.2)		
Δ Currency	0	Δ Domestic debt	0
Δ Sight deposits	0	Δ External debt	0
Δ Time deposits	0		
Δ Foreign assets	0		

Import Substitutes

Wages	100	Domestic sales	200
Purchases of	70	Exports	0
Exportables	*10*	Interest on	1.2
Import substitutes	*15*	*Time deposits*	*1.0*
Nontradables	*30*	*Foreign assets*	*0.2*
Imports	*15*		
Interest on	7		
Domestic debt	*6*		
External debt	*1*		

Nontradables

Wages	450	Domestic sales	600
Purchases of	120	Exports	0
Exportables	*20*	Interest on	1.2
Import substitutes	*30*	*Time deposits*	*1.0*
Nontradables	*50*	*Foreign assets*	*0.2*
Imports	*20*		
Interest on	7		
Domestic debt	*6*		
External debt	*1*		

Taxes	7.2		
Net profits	17.0		
(Gross profits)	(24.2)		
Δ Currency	0	Δ Domestic debt	0
Δ Sight deposits	0	Δ External debt	0
Δ Time deposits	0		
Δ Foreign assets	0		

Taxes	7.2		
Net profits	17.0		
(Gross profits)	(24.2)		
Δ Currency	0	Δ Domestic debt	0
Δ Sight deposits	0	Δ External debt	0
Δ Time deposits	0		
Δ Foreign assets	0		

Individuals

Taxes	273.7	Wages	757
Interest on	6.5	Dividends	60
Domestic debt	*6.0*	Interest on	4.9
External debt	*0.5*	*Time deposits*	*4.0*
Purchases of	541.7	*Bonds*	*0.3*
Exportables	*45.0*	*Foreign assets*	*0.6*
Import substitutes	*99.0*		
Nontradables	*357.5*		
Imports	*40.2*		
Δ Currency	0	Δ Domestic debt	0
Δ Sight deposits	0	Δ External debt	0
Δ Time deposits	0		
Δ Foreign assets	0		

Balance of Payments[1]

Exports	150	Imports	145.2
Interest on	1.2	Interest on	6.0
Private financial assets	*1.2*	*Public debt*	*2.5*
		Private debt	*3.5*
(Interest on reserves)	(2.0)		

[1]The balance of payments expressed in domestic currency is in equilibrium, while the balance of payments expressed in international currency is in surplus. This discrepancy is caused by the fact that interest on international reserves does not generate any domestic monetary creation. The "national" current account balance is also in equilibrium; but, if normal accounting practices centered around the official balance are used, the "international" current account balance may be either in surplus or in deficit, depending on the treatment of interest earned on reserves and, in particular, on private holdings of international liquid assets.

Real and financial flows during the cycle's first stage

Following the framework of the stereotyped cycle, this paper assumes the following behavior of the principal macroeconomic variables during the first stage of the cycle:

(i) International and domestic prices of exportables increase 10 percent.
(ii) International and domestic prices of imports and import substitutes increase 5 percent
(iii) International interest rates on time deposits and on loans rise to 4 percent and 7 percent, respectively.
(iv) International arbitrage, together with indexation practices and other domestic forces, determines domestic interest rates of 5 percent on deposits, 6 percent on bonds, and 8 percent on other loans.
(v) Domestic wages increase 2 percent, on average for the period, responding to indexation clauses and lags in adjustments.
(vi) Domestic nontradables prices increase 5 percent.
(vii) The public sector finances part of its emerging disequilibrium by borrowing in international capital markets.

Public Sector

Wages	101	Taxes	305.5
Purchases of	205.5		
Exportables	*16.5*	Deficit	8.6
Import substitutes	*31.5*		
Nontradables	*105.0*		
Imports	*52.5*		
Interest on	7.6		
Bonds	*1.2*		
Domestic financial debt	*2.4*		
Central bank debt	*0.5*		
External debt	*3.5*		
		Δ External debt	2.0
		Δ Domestic financial debt	2.0
		Δ Central bank	4.6

Central Bank

Wages	1	Interest on	3.0
Nontradables	0.5	*Public sector*	*0.5*
		Private sector	*2.5*
Δ Public sector	4.6	Surplus	1.5
Δ Reserves	8.9	Δ Demand for base money	12.0
(Δ Interest on reserves)	(2.0)		

Financial Institutions

Wages	7.1	Interest on	41.4
Purchases of	3.1	*Bonds*	*0.6*
Import substitutes	*1.0*	*Loans to public sector*	*2.4*
Nontradables	*2.1*	*Loans to private sector*	*38.4*
Interest on	20.0		
Time deposits	*17.5*		
Central bank	*2.5*		
Taxes	2.3		
Net profits	8.9		
Δ Currency	3.0	Δ Sight deposits	9.0
Δ Bonds	0	Δ Time deposits	24.0
Δ Loans to	30.0	Δ Central bank	0
Public sector	*2.0*	Δ Net financial wealth	0
Private sector	*28.0*		
Dividends	8.9	Net profits	8.9

Exportables

Wages	102.0	Domestic sales	109.0
Purchases of	121.2	Exports	166.0
Exportables	*11.0*	Interest on	2.9
Import substitutes	*26.2*	*Time deposits*	*2.5*
Nontradables	*63.0*	*Foreign assets*	*0.4*
Imports	*21.0*		
Interest on	11.0		
Domestic debt	*9.6*		
External debt	*1.4*		
Taxes	8.7		
Net profits	35.0		
Δ Currency	1.2	Δ Domestic debt	6.0
Δ Sight deposits	1.8	Δ External debt	0
Δ Time deposits	2.8		
Δ Foreign assets	0	Δ Net financial wealth	−0.2
Dividends	35.2	Net profits	35.0
Net financial wealth	−0.2		

Import Substitutes

Wages	102.0	Domestic sales	210.0
Purchases of	74.1	Exports	0
Exportables	*11.0*	Interest on	2.9
Import substitutes	*15.8*	*Time deposits*	*2.5*
Nontradables	*31.5*	*Foreign assets*	*0.4*
Imports	*15.8*		

Nontradables

Wages	468.2	Domestic sales	642.6
Purchases of	129.5	Exports	0
Exportables	*22.4*	Interest on	2.9
Import substitutes	*32.1*	*Time deposits*	*2.5*
Nontradables	*53.6*	*Foreign assets*	*0.4*
Imports	*21.4*		

Real and financial flows during the cycle's first stage *(concluded)*

Import Substitutes *(concluded)*

Interest on	11.0		
Domestic debt	*9.6*		
External debt	*1.4*		
Taxes	7.2		
Net profits	18.6		
Δ Currency	1.2	Δ Domestic debt	7.0
Δ Sight deposits	1.8	Δ External debt	0
Δ Time deposits	2.8		
Δ Foreign assets	−1.0	Δ Net financial wealth	−2.2
Dividends	20.8	Net profits	18.6
Δ Net financial wealth	−2.2		

Nontradables *(concluded)*

Interest on	11.0		
Domestic debt	*9.6*		
External debt	*1.4*		
Taxes	7.8		
Net profits	29.0		
Δ Currency	1.2	Δ Domestic debt	6.0
Δ Sight deposits	1.8	Δ External debt	0
Δ Time deposits	3.2		
Δ Foreign assets	−1.0	Δ Net financial wealth	−0.8
Dividends	29.8	Net profits	29.0
Δ Net financial wealth	−0.8		

Individuals

Taxes	279.5	Wages	781.3
Interest on	10.3	Dividends	94.7
Domestic debt	*9.6*	Interest on	11.8
External debt	*0.7*	*Bonds*	*0.6*
Purchases of	589.5	*Time deposits*	*10.0*
Exportables	*48.1*	*Foreign assets*	*1.2*
Import substitutes	*103.4*	Deficit	−8.5
Nontradables	*386.9*		
Imports	*51.1*		
Δ Currency	5.4	Δ Domestic debt	9.0
Δ Sight deposits	3.6	Δ External debt	0
Δ Time deposits	10.2		
Δ Foreign assets	−2.0	Δ Net financial wealth	8.2

Balance of Payments

Exports	166.0	Imports	162.1
Interest on		Interest on	8.4
foreign assets	2.4	*Public debt*	*3.5*
Sales of foreign assets	4.0	*Private debt*	*4.9*
ΔExternal public debt	2.0		
Foreign capital	5.0	Δ Reserves	
		(in national currency)	8.9
(Interest on reserves)	(2.0)	(Δ Reserves)	(2.0)

Comments

Mohsin S. Khan

This is a most interesting paper containing a number of ideas, some of which will be fairly familiar to international economists, and other ideas that may seem unusual, perhaps even controversial. The paper starts with the observation that a number of Latin American countries have experienced similar economic problems in recent years, even though domestic policies and circumstances were quite different in each of them. The author goes on to argue, although in a somewhat conjectural fashion, that these economic problems must be the result of common external factors. This is probably a correct inference, and one can certainly find empirical support for it.

A number of recent studies, some of which have been done at the Fund, find strong statistical relationships between the main macroeconomic aggregates of developed and developing countries. For example, growth rates in developing countries appear to be linked to growth rates in the industrial world (Goldstein and Khan).[1] Most studies of the inflationary process in developing countries also find a significant role for foreign inflation. Finally, it has been demonstrated that changes in the terms of trade have a strong impact on the current account balances of developing countries (Khan and Knight).[2] One could come up with other examples, but it should suffice to say that on balance there is considerable evidence of linkage or, to use the author's terminology, "interdependence" between developing countries and the rest of the world.

The paper makes a reasonably persuasive case for the proposition that such interdependence in the goods and capital markets has increased in the past few years. Whether one can proceed from this to say that this can be attributed to the adoption of generalized floating is, however, not readily apparent. It could be argued that the progressive and deliberate removal of restrictions

[1]Goldstein, Morris, and Mohsin S. Khan, *Effects of Slowdown in Industrial Countries on Growth in Non-Oil Developing Countries,* IMF Occasional Papers Series, No. 12 (August 1982).

[2]Khan, Mohsin S., and Malcolm D. Knight, "Some Theoretical and Empirical Issues Relating to Economic Stabilization in Developing Countries," *World Development,* Vol. 10 (September 1982), pp. 709–30.

on trade and capital flows made developing countries more susceptible to foreign influences in the 1970s than did generalized floating per se. To make the case that floating resulted in a greater degree of interdependence, one would have to abstract from domestic policy changes and exogenous external shocks, such as the oil price increases, and this is quite difficult to do. Consequently, one has to be cautious in making this causal connection between the floating of exchange rates of the developed countries and increasing integration.

The main purpose of the paper is to analyze the nature and degree of interdependence between a small, semi-open (Latin American) developing economy and the rest of the world under alternative exchange rate regimes. Basically, this is done by tracing out the effects—both at the macroeconomic level and, to a limited extent, the sectoral level—of a particular type of external shock. Most of the analysis is conducted for the fixed exchange rate case, and there is a very cursory treatment of the polar case of freely floating rates. In fact, the latter would hardly seem to be relevant to the case of developing countries, particularly the ones in Latin America. It would have been far more realistic to discuss the fixed exchange rate case with some other type of hybrid regime where the exchange rate moved according to a rule, say to maintain purchasing power parity. Variants of some type of exchange rate rule have certainly been utilized by several countries in the region on occasion. The author is well aware of these schemes and in fact was closely involved with the preannounced exchange rate experiment in Argentina during 1979–81.

The issue of interdependence is examined within the framework of a stylized general equilibrium model that is believed to fit a broad range of Latin American economies. The overall structure is quite standard, although there are some interesting features not typically found in such models. The model itself contains three goods—exportables (which are taken to be primary commodities), importables, and nontradables. Demand for each of these is determined by relative prices and, although this is not explicitly stated, by the stock of real money balances or real wealth. The domestic supply of these goods is fixed. Prices of exportables and importables are given by the foreign price level times the exchange rate; excess demand for importables determines imports; and excess supply of exportables equals exports. Any disequilibrium in the nontradables sector leads to changes in the price of nontradables. So far this is all very straightforward, and the model would be relevant for most countries—developing and developed alike.

The economy being modeled also has a reasonably developed financial system, so that it can be assumed that so-called financial reforms have already occurred. Interest rates are determined by market forces, and the private sector can hold assets at home or abroad. The latter assumption is very crucial, since currency substitution and private capital movements in response to changes in actual and expected relative rates of return play an important role in the workings of the model. The public sector can also borrow domestically, either from the banking system or from the public through the sales of bonds, or contract external debt. While there is nothing surprising here, this assumption of a well-functioning financial system relatively free from distortions does limit the applicability of the model to only a few developing countries. Government controls over interest rates, credit flows, and capital transactions are still the norm in Latin America, so that the model would properly fit only a very small number of economies.

The author then takes this model and superimposes three special characteristics regarded as necessary to fit Latin American economies. First, wages and financial instruments are assumed to be indexed in some form to the rate of inflation. Such indexation is fairly commonplace in Latin America and thus must be taken into account. Incidentally, in describing the indexation issue, the author goes into a very interesting discussion of the choice of basket to be used in constructing price indices to calculate the real rate of interest and in defining cost of living changes for wage earners and the rest of the economy. This discussion brings out quite clearly the distortions that can be created by using incorrect baskets to measure aggregate price indices.

Second, lags in government revenues in response to a rise in prices are assumed to be generally longer than the corresponding lags in expenditures. This, of course, creates a negative fiscal drag. As inflation rises, for whatever reason, governments are assumed to attempt to maintain the real level of expenditures while real tax revenues tend to fall behind. This creates a fiscal deficit without any conscious action being taken by the authorities. The negative fiscal drag effect has been documented for Argentina (Tanzi)[3] and other developing countries (Aghevli and Khan).[4]

[3]Tanzi, Vito, "Inflation, Real Tax Revenue, and the Case for Inflationary Finance: Theory with an Application to Argentina," IMF *Staff Papers,* Vol. 25

Finally, the model assumes that even though there are no restrictions on capital movements interest arbitrage is not perfect. In other words, domestic interest rates (adjusted for exchange rate expectations, risk, transaction costs, etc.) tend to be a good deal higher than foreign interest rates on supposedly comparable instruments. The paper does not state explicitly why interest parity does not emerge, but simply imposes this condition artificially on the model. There have been a number of theoretical arguments advanced explaining this lack of perfect arbitrage, but the issue is far from settled. However, even a very casual look at the experiences of countries such as Argentina, Chile, and Uruguay would make one quite sympathetic to the assumption.

Apart from the macroeconomic relationships underlying the model that have been discussed above, special mention ought to be made of the careful spelling out of the intersectoral relationships. The author goes to considerable length in detailing how the government, the monetary authorities, the financial system, the real sector, and the public all interact. This is by far the most innovative part of the paper, and while the relationship and results can be questioned, there is no doubt that sectoral aspects are important and deserve much more attention than they have hitherto received. The author should be commended for having made a start in this direction.

There are a number of problems, of course, with the type of model that the author has decided to work with, and this comment will focus basically on three main ones. First, it seems that all goods in the model are final goods, and there are no intermediate inputs. This is a very strong assumption to make for a developing country that typically relies on intermediate imports (raw materials, capital equipment, etc.) as inputs in the production process. The absence of intermediate imports tends to weaken the external linkage and, at the same time, has a bearing on the effects of changes in external prices (or in the exchange rate) on domestic output. Devaluation, or a rise in foreign prices, could also be deflationary if the economy was heavily dependent on basic or necessary imports. This possibility is excluded from consideration by the model as it is presently specified.

The second problem relates to the treatment of output. It is never made clear whether output is fixed or not. The paper states

(September 1978), pp. 417–51.

[4]Aghevli, Bijan B., and Mohsin S. Khan, "Government Deficits and the Inflationary Process in Developing Countries," IMF *Staff Papers,* Vol. 25 (September 1978), pp. 383–416.

at one point that relative prices do not affect supply, which could be taken to mean that output is constant. As such, there are no real effects of any type of shock, external or internal, and the discussion in the paper about variations in output and employment owing to such shocks does not appear to be pertinent. Later on in the paper, one finds that while the domestic supply of tradables is fixed, the supply of nontradables seems to vary. Certainly in the example presented in the Appendix, the supply of nontradables is variable. What causes it to change is never made clear. One way of dealing with this issue would be to fix trend, or potential, output but let deviations of actual output from this trend value be determined by relative prices. This would be more realistic, since it would allow output to vary in the short run and, at the same time, would make unnecessary the difficult task of specifying sectoral production functions.

Third, the model is strictly speaking an accounting model and has no explicit functions, parameters, or elasticities to speak of. In a sense, the approach is similar to the antecedents of the monetary approach to the balance of payments. The latter also grew out of a set of accounting relationships and identities, with the basic behavioral relationships specified later. The problem with this type of accounting approach is that the results are conditional on the choice of initial values, and one does not know whether the set of values chosen is realistic or not. In such circumstances, it is always advisable to engage in a sensitivity analysis and vary the initial values to see what differences result. It would be useful to know whether this was done and what emerged.

Taking this model, a particular simulation experiment is conducted. The actual experiment is supposed to reproduce the international picture faced by Latin American countries during 1979–82. The author identifies a stereotyped economic cycle in this period that has four stages. In essence, this cycle involves a rise in international inflation and interest rates and then a subsequent fall. Commodity prices, being flexible spot prices, are more volatile than the prices of other goods and services, so that there are sharp changes in the terms of trade for developing countries. Starting from a steady-state position and assuming a fixed exchange rate, this cycle is imposed on the model and a pseudo-dynamic (since the cycle involves the four distinct stages) path is traced out for the system. Since the model is quite complex, the verbal description of the dynamic process following the external shock is quite difficult to follow. One obvious suggestion would have been to put in some simple charts that displayed the paths followed by the variables in question. This would certainly have led to a better appreciation and understanding of what exactly was going on.

Given the model, the results of the simulation seem to be generally sensible. There are, however, a couple of results that deserve mentioning. First, it is interesting to note that an increase in foreign interest rates results in a fiscal deficit because of the rise in interest payments on external public debt. This point has not been widely recognized by model builders and deserves to be. The counterpart to the interest payments is the increased interest earnings of the central bank on its stock of international reserves. Whether these two should be netted out in some sense, perhaps through a transfer to the public sector from the central bank, is an interesting question. Second, in the example in the Appendix, the price of exportables rises by 10 per cent while the price of importables by only 5 per cent. One would have thought that both should have risen at the same rate, given the structure of the model, so this discrepancy deserves some explanation. Last, on the downside of the cycle, foreign interest rates decline but domestic interest rates remain high. However, capital outflows now occur rather than inflows, so that somehow exchange rate expectations seem to have been brought in. This sudden introduction of exchange rate expectations warrants explanation and elaboration.

At the end of the paper, there is a short and quite cryptic discussion of what would happen if, instead of being fixed, the exchange rate were allowed to float freely. Some of the results naturally change, but although the conclusion that floating insulates nominal variables and not real variables from nominal external shocks is not particularly surprising, it does not follow directly from the model. The author argues that variations in output and employment are larger under floating, but as was said before, if output does not respond to changes in relative prices, how can such a conclusion be drawn?

In conclusion, the paper has much to offer from a theoretical standpoint. At the same time, it contains the insights of someone who has been closely involved in policy formulation for a number of years and has obviously thought carefully about the issues. While one may not agree with all of the conclusions, one has to commend the effort to formalize views and judgments about the functioning of a small, semi-open economy. It is certain that some of these ideas will start to show up in the growing literature on stabilization in developing countries.

Michel Aglietta

Mr. Arriazu presented a very substantial analysis of the repercussions of international economic instability on Latin American countries. He rejected the pertinence of internal causes—inadequate exchange rate policies and excessive government spending—and emphasized the importance of external constraints in his explanation of the economic difficulties facing these countries. The special method he used derives from this hypothesis.

An international cycle, according to Mr. Arriazu, takes place in four phases. These phases can be distinguished from the relative evolution of international raw materials prices vis-à-vis other commodities prices and interest rates. This criterion is justified by the hypothesis according to which fluctuations in materials prices constitute the main effect of external shocks on these economies. The effects of the cyclical shock are meticulously analyzed, and the dynamic sequence undergone by the concerned countries is described.

What renders this analysis complex and makes it difficult to follow is also what makes it greatly interesting. The author does not work solely with a global pattern. He identifies the sectoral distortions caused by the great variability of nominal prices. However, this technical and sophisticated paper does not discuss economic policy matters. The impression given is that all Latin American countries are at the mercy of the external forces that dominate the world economy and have no freedom of choice. Such a conclusion may, unfortunately, be right. However, one cannot help wondering if this conclusion is not a fallacious by-product of the method the author has adopted. Indeed, the relationships described are deliberately presented as mechanical. Whatever they do, neither the private sector nor the state seems to be able to counteract these evolutions. Besides, in a framework that pretends to take economic structures into account in order to stress sectoral repercussions, it is odd that no distinction is drawn among countries on the basis of the variation in the resistance of their economic structures to shocks. Such an omission could lead one to underestimate the wide variation in the repercussions of shocks on different countries on account of differences in their exchange rate regimes. It could also lead one to overlook the peculiarities of the present Latin American situation, which is dominated by debt constraints. These constraints can provoke strong reactions—among lenders as well as borrowers—that alter the cycle itself. At present, we are perhaps in a very important, long-lasting phase of declining growth that has resulted from the large amount of debt that has accumulated and that is not the result of standard cyclical evolution.

Now, I shall deal with each of these two points in more detail.

Exchange rate regimes and sectoral distortions. It is possible to take advantage of cyclical phases by investing in the export sector when relative prices are favorable. The accumulation of capital has—as long as it reinforces export production capacity—an irreversible and favorable effect, which ensures that a country's export sector will have expanded when the cycle ends. To convert transitory gains in the world market into a permanent improvement of the productive system, domestic relative prices should be altered to channel profits to economic agents able to decrease the country's dependence on imports or to increase its exports, at least within the following cycle. The success of such measures depends crucially on the state's domestic pricing policy for agricultural products, its control of public spending, and its choice of exchange rate regime. Increased resilience in the face of international fluctuations can only stem from a high degree of food self-sufficiency and from a diversification of industrial production. The achievement of these two goals would allow a reduction in raw materials costs in the production of exports.

Thus, maintaining an overvalued currency—using a fixed exchange rate policy in order to limit the inflationary repercussions of the rise in world prices—can lead to disaster. If it is coupled with high interest rates that attract short-term capital flows and stifle industrial profits, this exchange rate policy weakens export industries and import substitution industries. The gains from the transitory improvement in the terms of trade—in the first phase described by Mr. Arriazu—are not invested in the sectors that could improve the country's competitiveness. They are instead either absorbed by the financial sector or dissipated in imports of luxuries. Moreover, an overvalued currency forces firms in the international sector to put intolerable pressures on real wages.

To alleviate this pressure, the authorities set very low prices on agricultural and food products—that is, they subsidize them. Thus, agricultural income deteriorates considerably. There is a consequent speeding up of the ongoing disorderly exodus from rural to urban areas. Necessities are subsidized in order to keep their prices low, and the continued existence of a large unemployed urban population is assured by minimal assistance. Thus, public spending is increased to the point where the situation becomes hopeless, and the state has to use the gains received from the terms of trade to finance public spending. Such a policy, which weakens the economy during the favorable phases of the cycle, paves the way for a serious crisis during phases when the terms of trade turn against the country. The balance of payments deficit then adds to the budget deficit. The latter is financed by inflationary money creation. Then an exchange rate crisis becomes inevitable, which, in its turn, provokes a brutal recession—the only means of reducing imports.

If the exchange rate is fairly well managed, the pattern can be substantially altered. If this is so, there cannot be a unique pattern, contrary to Mr. Arriazu's hypothesis. The difficulty of carrying out such a policy is how to bring about a regular and orderly depreciation of the currency and maintain an undervalued currency without fostering destabilizing speculation. This aim can only be achieved if internal policies are deliberately geared to production capacities in the labor-intensive sectors in order to make use of the comparative advantage provided by a cheap labor force. The relative price of agricultural products is the crucial variable. If individual farmers can be assured of a decent income, this will make it possible to maintain a balance between rural and urban populations and to reduce the country's dependence on imported food. The experience of Southeast Asian countries is proof of this. Within this context, a high level of productive investment maintains growth, which, in turn, stimulates productivity improvements. These improvements will prevent inflation—which is fed by permanent currency devaluations—from getting out of hand. Also, cyclical evolution could be much smoother than it is when there is an overvalued currency. The high investment rate will give the economy an increased capacity to adapt.

Problems caused by excessive debt. Most of the Latin American countries have overborrowed, leading to the building up of tensions and the creation of considerable uncertainty. A climate of rivalry is fostered between debtors and creditors as soon as default threatens. The appearance on the economic scene of the insolvency problem fosters instability in the behavior of private agents and forces governments to take action. The usual hypothesis of a predictable set of cyclical linkages with given behavior and economic policies becomes highly questionable. Overvaluation of currencies for too long can only worsen the problem by releasing destabilizing speculative forces. It then becomes necessary to look directly at the interaction between the financial fragility of countries and the behavior of foreign lenders. The international financial market can no longer be regarded as a reserve of capital communicating with the borrowing countries by means of variations in the interest rate. On the contrary, overborrowing can lead to dramatic changes in creditors' expectations that can foster instability in the market.

A rupture occurs in the asset and liability structure when no interest rate whatsoever can clear the credit market. This can happen when default becomes likely and leads the two sides of the market to adopt conflicting strategies. First and foremost, debtors are anxious to renew debts or, in other words, to finance assets that do not yield the cash flow that was expected from them when they were bought. Debtors are also compelled to enhance their liabilities in order to pay off increased financial costs.

Creditors do not know whether the money they are lending will be invested productively or dissipated in private or public consumption. This uncertainty alters the nature of the interaction between debtor and creditor. An anonymous market can no longer determine appropriate lending rates. Creditors become obsessed with the quality of their loans, which can lead them to excessively restrict credit. Moreover, the accumulated debt is a factor of uncertain weight that is influenced by the probability of default, which is linked to the amount of future debt. But current creditors ignore what the future debt—which depends on the borrower's strategy—will be.

The more new lenders the borrower is able to attract, the more freedom this strategy permits. Thus, current creditors, who have neither control over nor knowledge of their borrowers' future debts, become very cautious. They require risk premiums and shorten the maturities of their loans. This shortening of maturities increases the debt service burden, which, in turn, causes a deterioration of the current account and a stifling of growth.

When the debtor-creditor antagonism reaches fever pitch, the choice of an exchange rate regime has become secondary. The appropriate method of dealing with the situation is to appoint a mediator. There are two reasons why this would be helpful. First, a mediator would be able to guarantee borrowers a debt rescheduling compatible with their export capacities. Second, a mediator would be able to reassure lenders by putting limits on future loans and by controlling the uses made of these loans by borrowers.

Stopping runaway borrowing without provoking a collapse of debtor countries is a delicate exercise in international monetary cooperation. However, it is the only means of alleviating the negative repercussions of cyclical fluctuations.

Panel Discussion on Southern Cone

Jacob A. Frenkel

This discussion will concentrate on two major issues. The first concerns the optimal design of economic liberalization programs. The key question to be addressed is the proper sequencing of liberalization measures. Specifically, the order of economic liberalization of international transactions in goods and financial markets will be discussed. The second major issue concerns the optimal design of stabilization programs. The key question to be addressed is the choice between gradualistic or drastic applications of stabilization measures. The discussion will close with a few notes on the pegging of a currency to a basket of foreign exchange.

Since this discussant does not claim to possess either specific knowledge of or familiarity with the details of the various economic experiences of the Southern Cone countries, it is relevant to note that the main arguments presented do not apply only to this group of countries. In fact, the arguments are not based on any specific experience of any specific country but rather stem from general basic economic principles. As such, the key issues should also be applicable to other experiences of economic liberalization and stabilization programs.

SEQUENCING OF ECONOMIC LIBERALIZATION

The question of the optimal *process* of economic liberalization involves one of the most difficult aspects of the theory of economic policy, namely, the *transition* toward equilibrium. The prescription of economic theory is very clear when applied to "first-best" situations. Economic theory, however, is much more reserved when it comes to evaluation and comparison of distorted situations. The evaluation of alternative strategies for economic liberalization involves making comparisons among various distorted situations that characterize alternative paths an economy may adopt in its approach to undistorted, first-best equilibrium.

Consequently, views about the "proper" sequencing of liberalization measures should be put forward with great care and modesty; economic theory does not provide an unambiguous answer to that important question. With these reservations in mind, this discussion will state what is likely to be the proper order of economic liberalization.

Consider an economy that suffers from numerous distortions in goods and capital markets and suppose that in the past many barriers to international trade in goods and capital were imposed. Suppose that the government wishes to remove the distortions and to liberalize trade in goods and capital. Under these circumstances, the general rule is that the first step in the liberalization process should be removal of domestic distortions in goods and capital markets and attainment of fiscal order, so as to reduce the heavy reliance on inflationary finance. The second step should be the liberalization of the economy's links with the rest of the world. The external liberalization should also proceed in two phases. The first phase should reduce distortions to the free flow of goods by liberalizing the balance of trade. The capital account of the balance of payments should be opened up and liberalized only in the final phase. In what follows, some arguments are offered in support of the proposed order of liberalization of the trade and the capital accounts of the balance of payments.[1]

The key distinction between the effects of opening up the trade account and those of opening up the capital account of the balance of payments stems from the fundamental difference between goods and asset markets. As is known, the speed of adjustment in asset markets is much faster than in goods markets. Asset markets are more sensitive to expectations concerning the distant future, and new information that alters expectations is reflected in asset prices much faster than in the prices of goods and services. This intrinsic difference in the basic characteristics of goods and assets has several implications. First, since the economy under consideration has been distorted for a significant period, nobody (in-

[1]This order of economic liberalization is advocated in Ronald I. McKinnon, "The Order of Economic Liberalization: Lessons from Chile and Argentina," in *Economic Policy in a World of Change*, ed. by Karl Brunner and Allan H. Meltzer, Carnegie-Rochester Conference Series on Public Policy, Vol. 17 (Amsterdam, 1982), pp. 159–86. The subsequent arguments are adapted from Jacob A. Frenkel, "The Order of Economic Liberalization: Lessons from Chile and Argentina: A Comment," pp. 199–201 in the same book.

cluding economists) can be certain about the precise paths that its various sectors will follow after liberalization. Under such uncertain circumstances, prudence is called for. A program of liberalization that opens up the trade account first has the virtue of providing policymakers with an opportunity to examine the market's reaction and to correct any errors found. A program that opens up the capital account first is not likely to provide such an opportunity, since once the capital account is opened up, the initial reaction is likely to take place very quickly and the resulting capital flows are likely to be huge. Thus, although it is eventually desirable to have an open capital account, prudence calls for a gradual transition to openness so as to facilitate the required change in institutions and the economic structure. An analogy can be made between an economy recovering from a long history of distortions and an individual recovering from a heart condition and a by-pass operation. While the latter's complete recovery may well be anticipated, nobody would recommend that he start his rehabilitation program by running a marathon race.

The implications of the different speeds of adjustment of the trade and capital accounts can be illustrated picturesquely by a carriage pulled by two horses. Suppose that one of the horses is a fast runner while the other is a slow runner. As is obvious, if the two horses were to run at different speeds, the carriage would turn over. To avoid a disaster, the speeds of the two horses must be equalized. This can be achieved by speeding up the slow horse or by slowing down the fast one. It stands to reason that the former solution is not sustainable while the latter can be achieved with little effort. Analogously, the overall balance of payments constraint requires that the trade and the capital accounts be brought into line with each other, and thus, even though the two accounts tend to respond at different speeds, the overall constraint implies that the two speeds of adjustment must be harmonized. It seems that such consistency could be achieved with less effort by slowing down capital flows than it could by speeding up trade flows.

Second, it is easier (and less costly to society) to reverse wrong portfolio decisions than to reverse wrong real investment decisions. This potential difference in social costs also supports the thesis that the proposed sequence of liberalization measures is the correct one. Once the authorities remove distortions in the commodity markets and open up the trade account, real investment in the economy will take place in a less distorted environment—and thus will be more consistent with long-run patterns of real investment. Portfolio investments will continue to be based on a distorted capital market as long as the capital account is not opened up. Once the capital account is liberalized, some portfolio decisions will have to be reversed, but such a reversal is not likely to be very costly. On the other hand, if the capital account is opened up first, portfolio decisions are likely to reflect more accurately the undistorted long-run conditions but real investment decisions will still reflect a distorted environment as long as the trade account is not opened up. Owing to the distortions, the social costs of investments are likely to exceed the private costs. Such real investment decisions will have to be reversed once the trade account is liberalized. Therefore, the trade account should be liberalized before the capital account. In this context, it should be noted that distortions in the flow of goods affect both the trade account *and* the capital account and, by the same token, distortions in the flow of capital also affect both accounts. However, it is likely that the *relative* effects of each distortion on the two accounts differ; distortions in the flow of goods are likely to have a stronger effect on the trade account than on the capital account, while distortions in the flow of capital are likely to have a stronger effect on the capital account than on the trade account. This difference in the *relative* sensitivities of the two balance of payments accounts to the two distortions underlies the recommended order of liberalization.

Third, the cost of a distortion depends on the distortion itself and on the volume of transactions that take place in the presence of the distortion. Thus, when the trade account is opened up first, the cost of the remaining distortion (i.e., the closed capital account) is proportional to the volume of trade, which, owing to the slow adjustment of the market for goods, is likely to be relatively small. One the other hand, when the capital account is opened up first, the cost of the remaining distortion (i.e., the closed trade account) is proportional to the volume of capital flows, which, owing to the high speed of adjustment in asset markets, is likely to be very large. Thus, a comparison of the costs of distortions also supports the proposition that the trade account should be opened up first.

The various arguments that were outlined above rationalized the different treatment of the trade and capital accounts by reference to the different speeds of adjustment in goods and asset markets. In view of the different speeds of adjustment, the synchronization of the two balance of payments accounts was brought about by staggering the liberalization measures. An alternative strategy for coping with the different characteristics of the two balance of payments accounts could be adoption of a dual exchange rate regime. Such an exchange rate system allows for one exchange rate for commercial transactions in goods and services and another (typically a floating) exchange rate for capital account transactions. With this system, the different speeds of adjustment in goods and asset markets are reconciled through an adjustment of the relation between the two exchange rates. It is relevant to note, however, that while a dual exchange rate system may solve the synchronization problem, it starts the economy moving along the potentially dangerous path to multiple exchange rate regimes. The danger of such multiple exchange rate regimes is that they typically involve a complex set of distortions a complicated bureaucratic system, an elaborate structure of rent-seeking activities, and a costly allocation of rents. And, as is typically the case, it is much easier to create distortions than to remove them. Furthermore, experience suggests that a dual exchange rate regime cannot be sustained if the difference between the exchange rates for commercial transactions and for capital transactions becomes too large. In other words, it seems that the dual exchange rate system may be an additional viable effective instrument as long as reliance on that instrument is not too heavy. Since, however, the synchronization problem might be severe during a liberalization program, it is likely that the sustainability, and therefore the usefulness, of a dual exchange rate system might be limited. Under these circumstances, the proposed sequencing of liberalization measures might be more viable.

The removal of various distortions in the market for goods—including various taxes, subsidies, and tariffs—will yield a new equilibrium price level, a new nominal exchange rate, and a new real exchange rate. It is pertinent to note that prior to setting out on such a path, the initial conditions have to be set correctly, so as to reflect the new equilibrium exchange rate and the prices that will prevail following the removal of the distortions. In this context, it is useful to recall that several attempted liberalizations have resulted in uncontrolled inflation. These outcomes can be explained, in part, by the nature of indexation clauses. In order to avoid such failures, it is critical that the initial (once-and-for-all) changes in prices that result from the removal of subsidies and other distortions be excluded from the indices that are used for wage indexation.

As was emphasized earlier, it is essential that the liberalization program be *preceded* by restoration of a fiscal order that reduces the government's dependence on inflationary finance. This restoration is an especially important prerequisite to opening up the capital account. The liberalization of the capital account is likely to encourage the process of "currency substitution." This phenomenon results in an effective reduction of the "tax base" for inflationary finance. Unless the need for inflationary finance is reduced, the opening up of the capital account and the resultant shrinkage of the inflationary tax base may result in an accelerated rate of inflation as the government attempts to collect the needed revenue from a smaller tax base.

It should be recognized that during a liberalization program, some sectors in the economy are harmed more than others. These differential effects are likely to create strong pressures for accommodative monetary and exchange rate policies. It is important, therefore, to emphasize that monetary and exchange rate policies should not be designed to deal with such sectoral difficulties. Monetary and exchange rate policies are aggregate policies that should not be guided by intersectoral considerations. These intersectoral considerations are extremely important, however, and some of them should be dealt with. The proper policy instruments for dealing with intersectoral considerations are *fiscal* policies rather than monetary or exchange rate policies.

Finally, since the success of the liberalization program depends crucially on expectations concerning the feasibility and credibility of the program, it is important that the various measures that are undertaken hang together in a consistent way. Trust and confidence that has been built up with great difficulty can be destroyed very easily. Therefore, it is important not to start the program until all loose ends are tied up. The economic system, through the mechanism of memory that builds itself into expectations, shows little tolerance of errors. Therefore, while a slight delay in the introduction of a program will not be fatal, the premature introduction of an inconsistent plan might be.

GRADUALISM VERSUS DRASTIC MEASURES DURING STABILIZATION PROGRAMS

In many cases, the decision to embark upon a liberalization program coincides with the decision to embark upon a stabilization program. The reason for this coincidence is easy to imagine. Both liberalization and stabilization programs are associated with short-run costs, and both require political courage as well as broad political support. The circumstances likely to generate these requisites are typically serious deep economic difficulties, widespread distortions, and galloping inflation. While liberalization and stabilization programs have tended to be introduced together, it is pertinent to note that the two programs are distinct and need not accompany each other.

One of the central questions concerning the initiation of a stabilization program involves the choice between gradual or drastic applications of the stabilization measures. The case for gradualism is well known; it rests on prudence, and on the fine tuning and mid-course corrections that it makes possible. In what follows, some arguments in favor of drastic treatment are outlined. It should be emphasized, however, that as is the case with liberalization, economic theory does not provide unambiguous guidance to those who must choose between gradualism and drastic treatments. Therefore, it is especially inappropriate to approach this issue dogmatically.[2]

The first argument for drastic treatment is that since there are numerous problems of unsynchronized changes of money and wages in the economy, a major policy shock will minimize the total output costs of seriously reducing the inflation rate. A sharp reversal of policy is likely to ensure that many preexisting contracts will be reopened and that economic agents will adapt their behavior to the likely course of policy; if the policy is well planned, the initial conditions it will produce should be close to the new steady-state equilibrium for the economy.

The second argument for drastic treatment is that gradualism may not, in practice, reduce the inflation rate. Underlying gradualism is the fear that attempts at restrictive policy will produce unemployment. It is precisely these fears that make it likely that any future inflationary shock will not be resisted, but rather accommodated. Under such circumstances, gradualism may well end up gradually increasing the inflation rate rather than reducing it, since inflationary shocks are accommodated and deflationary shocks are allowed to feed into output at the same inflation rate.

The third argument for drastic treatment rests on the recognition that reducing the budget deficit is a vital part of any pro-

[2]Some of the subsequent arguments in this section draw on Stanley Fischer and Jacob A. Frenkel, "Stabilization Policy in Israel" (unpublished, Bank of Israel, July 1981).

gram to reduce inflation. There is little doubt that the single most important factor in reducing a galloping rate of inflation is a significant cut in the budget deficit. Such cuts are, by their nature, very difficult to implement. They are likely to be even more difficult to implement gradually. The short-run pressures are usually to expand the budget deficit for one worthy cause or another. Unless the problem is faced up to directly and as a whole, the budget deficit is not likely to be cut. But once the problem is faced up to, the opportunity is at hand for making a concentrated attack on the inflation rate.

One of the major arguments against drastic measures is that there are uncertainties about the effects of the anti-inflationary package that is put in place. But the basic fact is that any policies that are followed in an economy in a need for a stabilization program have a highly uncertain outcome. It should not be thought that the consequences of pursuing a gradualist policy are certain either. In fact, it is, as argued above, quite possible that gradualism will increase the inflation rate and, consequently, merely postpone the application of drastic treatment.

The central factor determining the success of the stabilization program is its impact on the public's expectations. It is crucial that the introduction of a new policy should be consistent, credible, and broadly based. The main components of any stabilization plans are the fiscal and monetary policy measures that are adopted. It is essential that these measures be viewed as viable, consistent, and sustainable.

One of the difficulties in implementing a drastic remedy is that the existing economic system has grown up over many years and has become deeply embedded. Consequently, any drastic change is necessarily disruptive because it renders many existing investment projects uneconomical. It seems, therefore, that the desirable solution to the problem of the choice between gradualism and drastic measures should be a plan that incorporates the best elements of each option. An example of such a solution could be a *preannouncement* of a *feasible* path for the policy instruments. Thus, if stabilization involves a cut in government spending, a reduction in the rate of monetary growth, and the like, gradual reduction coupled with preannouncement of the entire path will avoid the undesirable consequences of immediate drastic cuts, while the feasibility and the consistency of the plan will indicate the government's long-term commitment, will enhance the plan's credibility, and promote stabilizing expectations.

Finally, any stabilization program must have two chief aims and areas of operation. First, the program must adopt policy measures that rapidly reduce the high rate of inflation. Second, the program must begin the process of institutional reform to reduce the economy's susceptibility to future inflationary shocks and to make it possible to keep future inflation under better control. A key factor in keeping future inflation under better control is the presence of a *nominal anchor* guiding the course of monetary policy. Such an anchor could be the money supply, the nominal exchange rate, or another nominal quantity.

BASKET PEGGING

The large variability of bilateral nominal and real exchange rates resulted in proposals that some of the Southern Cone countries peg their currencies to a basket of foreign currencies rather than to a specific leading currency like the U.S. dollar. These proposals have many positive features, but they also raise some important practical and conceptual issues that have not been fully addressed. In what follows, some of these issues are raised.

First, as should be obvious, all weighted averages (with positive weights that sum to unity) vary to a lesser degree than some of their individual components. Therefore, it is clear that pegging the currency to a basket of foreign currencies will yield a smaller variance of the exchange rate expressed in terms of the basket. But, as is also clear, averages tend to mask great diversity, and the relevant question is whether introducing stability into the weighted average should indeed be the objective regardless of the degree of instability in the components of the average. Specifically, shifting from a bilateral pegging to a basket pegging will stabilize the value of the currency in terms of the basket but will destabilize its value in terms of the individual currency to which it was previously pegged. Is it obvious that the stability of a weighted exchange rate is to be preferred to the stability of a bilateral exchange rate vis-à-vis a major currency? In analyzing this question, it is worth remembering that discussions of the welfare cost of inflation deal with related matters. In those discussions, the distinction is drawn between the cost associated with the variability of the price *level* and the cost associated with the variability of *relative* prices. Drawing on this analogy, one wonders whether those who emphasize the need for stability of the weighted exchange rate instead of the stability of bilateral rates would also place less emphasis on the cost of fluctuations of individual relative prices than on the cost of fluctuations of the aggregate price level. Prior to adoption of a new pegging strategy, the costs and benefits of the relevant alternatives should be specified.

Second, pegging to a basket per se will not eliminate many of the difficulties with, and objections to, flexible exchange rates unless there is an *actual* asset that represents the basket and unless that asset can be traded freely in futures markets.

Third, there is the practical question of choosing weights for the currency basket. The typical procedure has been the adoption of a trade-weighted basket. The choice of the proper weights, however, is not just a technical question, since it begs the conceptual problem of the role of the capital account. Specifically, since a large fraction of international transactions involve international capital markets, what role should these transactions play in determining the proper weights of the currencies that comprise the basket?

The success of a new exchange rate regime, like the success of liberalization and stabilization programs, depends on the adoption of a consistent set of policy tools and on a reasonable understanding of the implications of each course of action. It would be irresponsible to experiment with new systems just to learn how they work out. As is true of liberalization and stabilization programs, the cost of delaying the adoption of a new pegging arrangements until their full implications are understood is likely to be small relative to the cost of a premature adoption.

Rudiger Dornbusch

There are really three ways of stabilizing an economy. One is with financial orthodoxy, another with interventionism, and a third way is that adopted by Latin America, a consequence of which has been that in the last year economic performance in the region has been the worst since the 1930s. Whatever went wrong must have gone wrong in the large countries—Argentina, Brazil, Chile, and Venzuela. What went wrong was that the mix of stabilization and liberalization policies that these countries followed had nothing in common with either the interventionist methods that have often gone wrong or the financially orthodox methods that have often worked. The latter were fashionable in the interwar period, in the 1950s, and even in the 1960s but fell into disrepute when everybody started criticizing the Fund. In fact, the

Fund's financially orthodox stabilization programs have been right in terms of comparative statics, though often not in terms of dynamics.

Looking at the experiences of Argentina, Brazil, and Chile, one observes two problems—a high real interest rate and an overvalued currency. In Argentina and Chile, these problems have been partially solved; in Brazil, similar developments may be expected within the next six months. Each country failed to recognize that an effective stabilization program must (1) correct the fiscal problem, and (2) simultaneously achieve a real depreciation of the currency. In Chile, the fiscal reform was very successful, but policymakers allowed the currency to become more and more overvalued each year, until they were forced to raise the real interest rate extremely high just to finance the current account imbalance. Such a situation was not sustainable, of course, and investors began speculating about how long it would last. While the real interest rate remained high, people praised the new liberalization program, which entailed an across-the-board import tariff of only 10 percent. All things considered, the real exchange rate today (some would even say the exchange rate that prevailed late in 1981) is the lowest for decades. Consequently, now is a good time to acquire importables before the real exchange rate returns to its former level. Not surprisingly, there has been considerable borrowing to finance the acquisition of consumer durables or equipment. The likely near-term consequences are an exchange crisis, a real depreciation of the currency, and a return to the economic conditions of 1975. In the Chilean case, there is little doubt that confusion of stabilization and liberalization, and failure to recognize that fiscal reform must be accompanied by a real depreciation of the currency, have led to the current exchange rate crisis.

In Argentina, commercial liberalization was less extensive, fiscal reform never took place, and an increasing real wage was financed by external borrowing. Of course, the situation was untenable and, in fact, was more severe than in Chile because the real appreciation of the currency had gone much further and the political conditions made it much more difficult to lower real wages enough to offset not only the initial real appreciation but also the debt accumulated during the war in 1982 and the deterioration in external competitiveness brought about the efforts of other developing countries to achieve real depreciation. Looking at Argentina today, one can say that although real wages may have fallen 20 percent, the fiscal deficit has not stabilized and there will certainly have to be another real depreciation to strengthen the current account sufficiently to generate confidence that the economy can be effectively stabilized. Whatever else a country does, an economy cannot be stabilized unless the current account position convinces people that the exchange rate is realistic. Financing, regardless of the amount obtained, is just a gimmick; in the end, the current account will have to service the debt, and the exchange rate will stabilize only when the current account deficit is reduced to manageable proportions.

The preceding remarks provide background for a discussion of Brazil, which really is now in a situation analogous to those in Mexico, Chile, or Argentina before their recent crisis occurred. The Brazilian Government has allowed the real exchange rate to appreciate over the last four years. There has been no real depreciation to make up for the oil shock, the debt accumulation, the higher real interest rates, Southeast Asia's gain in competitiveness, or reduced economic growth rates in the Organization for Economic Cooperation and Development (OECD) countries. The real exchange rate is clearly overvalued, if one allows for the current cyclical situation, though it should be kept in mind that the balance of payments situation is manageable only because the country is experiencing its first recession in forty years. Attainment of a sustainable real exchange rate that was consistent will full employment would probably require a substantial real depreciation.

What happens in these circumstances? It is generally recognized that, with central bank reserves at their current low levels, the real exchange rate will have to fall eventually. The only question is whether the currency can be devalued fast enough in real terms to discourage people from getting into dollars by taking advantage of leads and lags or other means. Again, the problems are caused by failure to achieve fiscal stabilization and a futile attempt to maintain the real wage by exchange manipulation, which leads over time to an incredible overvaluation—incredible because everybody knows that although the deficit can be financed for one year, it certainly cannot be financed for another year.

Central banks have in some way become complacent about such excessive financing and have consequently been able to delay real exchange rate adjustment. Eventually, however, this has led to exchange crises, as have occurred in Mexico, Chile, Argentina, and—most recently—Brazil.

Returning to the question of liberalization and stabilization, it is fair to say there has been insufficient financial orthodoxy in the countries that have been discussed. The traditional approach to stabilization is to correct the budget, to bring about a big real depreciation of the currency, and to establish a controlled capital account program. Of these three goals, Latin American countries have had the most success with fiscal stabilization. Since cutting government subsidies and lowering the real wage are extremely difficult politically, these countries have always tended to avoid lowering the real exchange rate sufficiently, partly because immediate reductions in inflation can be achieved if depreciation is not too fast. This behavior leads first to overvaluation, then to higher real interest rates, and finally—when even these can no longer maintain the exchange rate—to an exchange crisis. The pattern has become very predictable, highlighting the fact that any successful stabilization program must start by *undervaluing* the currency. When the currency is undervalued, there is credibility in employment; once the latter has been established, the country can afford fiscal cuts. Countries can maintain an overvalued currency only by financing the resulting deficit and by forcing up real interest rates; however, in the end, they cannot avoid an exchange crisis.

Not much has been said about liberalization. In all these countries, the problem is one of stabilizing the budget and living with the current account. The worst thing to do is to liberalize the capital account to allow the public to get into dollars before the necessary real depreciation has been achieved. And it is certainly a grave error to try to promote exports and to destroy import-competing industries in world recession. Liberalization attempts have been counterproductive in Chile and would be so in Brazil. They have fostered expectations that real exchange rates were too high and, therefore, have promoted financial instability.

William H. Branson

This discussion will focus on a diagram called Arriazu's box, which looks like an Edgeworth box. It has four sides, along which one measures the degrees of openness in trade and the capital account. One corner of the box represents a completely closed economy, and at the opposite corner a completely open economy. One could even imagine something like a contract curve through the box that would give the optimum degree of openness or the optimum degree of change in openness if he wanted to talk about liberalization in terms of changes in states.

There seems to be a problem in the ordering of liberalization. One can imagine, for instance, a scenerio beginning with liberalization of the capital account, which would generate increased confidence in the country doing so. This, in turn, would generate capital inflows and a real currency appreciation and would be bad for trade, especially in manufactures. On the other hand, if current account were liberalized first, one could imagine a situation where imports would surge. (It takes time to develop export markets.) That would lead to a current account deficit, reserve losses, depreciation, inflation, and the creation of a vicious circle that would destroy the whole experiment. It seems here is a problem that needs to be worked on, and that could be thought about in terms of Arriazu's box.

A funny analytical problem appears when one thinks about the stability of a system that has adopted an accelerating peg. Essentially, when one adopts an accelerating or decelerating peg, he states a schedule of depreciation according to which the rate of depreciation itself is gradually reduced, on the presumption that a stable situation lies at the end of the road. So, basically, one is stating a schedule of the rate of change of the rate of change of the exchange rate. This involves a dynamic analysis that will inherently be very difficult. In technical terms, one will solve second-order differential equations. Making exchange rate stability under such a regime consistent with a financial market equilibrium as the economy is being opened would seem to be an awfully complicated problem.

Ricardo H. Arriazu

I will concentrate my comments on just a few of the questions most frequently raised in relation to these liberalization problems. I will, obviously, base my comments on my knowledge of Argentina.

Basically there are four questions that I would like to deal with. One is this question of what should be open first, the trade or the capital account? Second is the question of preannounced exchange rates. Third is the question of the relationship between fiscal deficits and exchange rates. The fourth is related to the definition of the current account, to which Dornbusch assigns so much emphasis.

Starting with trade or capital liberalization, conventional wisdom says that the trade account should be opened first and only then the capital account, if we want to avoid problems. I share that wisdom, but I would like to emphasize that first we should define clearly what we mean by trade account liberalization. We have at least two possibilities or definitions of trade liberalization: one definition relates to making the economy more open to trade, in the sense of increasing the proportion of goods subject to international competition (proportion of tradables in the economy), and the other relates to liberalization directed at improving the allocation of resources by reducing the effective protection of some sectors while increasing that of others.

The first of these definitions has little to do with the level of effective protection in a country and is much more related to the level of redundant protection ("water") in the tariff structure. As a matter of fact, it is possible to have a product with an effective protection of 500 percent, fully used, which is tradable in the sense of being subject to international competition, while other products with a nominal effective protection of 20 percent behave as nontradable as this protection is not fully used, at least in the short run.

Therefore, when we talk about the dangers of opening the capital account first, rather than the trade account, what we are talking is about the danger of opening the capital account when still a lot of products can be considered as nontradables as a consequence of widespread redundant protection. In these circumstances, if you allow me to use the same box that Branson has just described, we run the risk of moving into the upper left corner, which extreme case defines economies totally closed to the movements of goods and totally open to movements of capital. In this extreme case, the price level may become totally undetermined. Why? Because, under its assumptions, the price level is exclusively determined by the forces of domestic demand and supply, while the money supply is endogenous to the system, which implies that under certain conditions, capital flows may finance any level of domestic prices, even if domestic credit is rigidly controlled. In this sense, it is totally correct to say that to avoid this possibility it is better to open first the trade account (elimination of "water" in the tariffs), then the capital account. It is important to emphasize that this reform has nothing to do with a reform to improve the allocation of resources and which may, or may not, increase the proportion of tradables in the economy. The liberalization process in Argentina, for example, went much further in eliminating redundant protection than in reducing dispersion or effective protection. As a matter of fact, dispersion was one of the main problems of the tariff structure, which provided an average effective protection of 39 percent for the industrial sector, but with wide variations between products from minus 40 percent to plus 400 percent; in addition, a large proportion of the industrial sector confronted negative effective protection; it just happened that the extreme cases of negative and positive protection occurred in the same productive sector. As a matter of fact, existing effective protection structures are the result of accumulated political decisions over time rather than rational decisions on optimal—or preferable—industrial and production structures. The recent tariff reform in Argentina was basically directed in the initial stage to reducing the dispersion of protection between sectors and the level of redundant protection, and only marginally to reducing average protection. One problem in attempting a reform as described is the fact that the authorities normally do not know which sectors have "water" in their tariffs so that efficient reforms take time. The conventional wisdom of opening first the trade account is therefore not easy to implement.

We come now to the second point. Should we control capital movements? And if the answer is affirmative can we really control capital movements? Dornbusch says yes to both questions but do the authorities control capital movements or does the public? My own experience in Argentina makes me very doubtful on the possibilities of controlling capital flows. In 1975, for example, Argentina introduced one of the more severe and extensive sets of capital controls in force in the international economy; during that year the current account registered a deficit exceeding $1 billion, at the same time that Argentines accumulated foreign assets abroad also exceeding $1 billion. How could this accumulation take place with so many controls? Basically, through overinvoicing and underinvoicing.

The experience of 1978 also tends to confirm this fact. At the beginning of 1978, the authorities decided to tighten domestic credit as part of their anti-inflationary program. As reserves had been increasing and covered domestic interest rates had been higher than abroad, the public started to bring capital from abroad at unprecedented rates, in this way avoiding the restrictions on credit. In order to stop these flows, the government decided to introduce an interest equalization tax in the form of a deposit equivalent to 20 percent of the flows—with no remuneration whatsoever; in a situation of 6 percent monthly inflation, this deposit implies a substantial tax. Of course, with this measure, capital flows disappeared as such, but capital continued flowing in, now in the form of exports prepayments. As a deposit was also required for these flows, capital then began to flow in the form of export prefinancing, and when these flows were also restricted, the movements took the form of overinvoicing and underinvoicing. Exchange sales by tourists also increased during the period, even though these "tourists" were obviously Argentines.

After these examples the question remains: can we really control capital movements? It is possible that for some countries the answer would be positive, but in my opinion not for Argentina. This leads us to a final point on this subject. When a country like Argentina has repeatedly introduced strong economic shocks, causing many of its people either to completely lose their incomes and their wealth in very short periods of time, or to accumulate extraordinary profits as a consequence of these shocks, then the association of what is moral and what is legal tends to disappear. The people themselves start to decide what is moral and legal and on many occasions their definition does not coincide with what the government considers to be moral and legal. In these circumstances, it is not rare for the public to challenge what the government decides as illegal if they consider that the decision is not moral, and therefore they do what they consider more convenient. For example, at this moment Argentina has re-established controls on capital outflows, including a dual exchange market, and the country is experiencing very large capital outflows. Unfortunately, persistent economic shocks and frequent income transfers also tend to encourage economic anarchy, which is something very dangerous for the whole social structure of a country. The question is then, if you have capital flows and you are not able to control them, what do you do? Perhaps if you are in the United States or in other countries less used to frequent upheavals, controls could be improved, but if capital flows take place and you cannot stop them, what is the optimal strategy? I think this is a very important problem to discuss, and economists generally tend to forget this structural constraint.

The second subject I want to deal with is related to the meaning of preannounced exchange rates. I have read recently many papers on the subject and most tend to argue that the basic objective of the system is to change expectations in such a way as to help reduce inflation. Since I have been an advisor on this policy in Argentina, let me say that I feel that this aspect of the policy has been overemphasized. Actually, the basic idea was much simpler and comes from the theory of fixed exchange rates. If a country wants to have a fixed rate system and it confronts a large fiscal deficit, it is clear that the end result would be reserve losses and periodic balance of payments crises—with devaluations. In these circumstances, if you cannot have a fixed rate but you want the advantages of a fixed rate system, in the sense of having more transparent markets, less uncertainty, and items like that, then one possibility is to proceed as follows: start by estimating how large the fiscal deficit is going to be and how much monetary base will be created as a consequence of this and other factors. This allows an estimate of how large a flow demand for monetary base is required to be able to maintain balance of payments equilibrium, given the fiscal deficit. Once this disequilibrium is estimated, the reasoning continues as follows: when a country devalues, the prices of tradables also increase as a result of cost increases, indexation practices, and other adjustment forces. This increase in prices will normally be accompanied by an increase in the nominal demand for money, which, in turn, determines an increase in the flow demand for base money. The problem is, therefore, how to estimate the size of a devaluation needed to generate the required flow demand for base money to compensate for the effects of the fiscal deficit. To this estimate, governments always add a security margin just in case the calculations prove wrong.

Once the required devaluation is estimated, the question is whether to keep it secret in order to guide the exchange rate policy without restricting the freedom of the authorities, or to preannounce a schedule of periodic devaluations—making the periods between adjustments as short as possible to reduce speculation—in order to give more certainties to the market. In this sense, preannouncement of exchange rates is equivalent to preannouncement of monetary targets, in countries with floating exchange rates.

Now if it happens that the resulting schedule of adjustments is a declining one, because the calculations show that in monetary terms the country does not need devaluations as large as the ones being implemented, then the declining schedule might contribute to dampen inflationary expectations. However, to try introducing a declining schedule of devaluations, with the express objective of influencing expectations totally inconsistent with the adjustment needs brought about by the fiscal deficit, would have disastrous economic consequences and would be equivalent to maintaining a fixed exchange rate in similar circumstances.

In assessing individual countries' experiences, therefore, the question to answer is whether the authorities were right in their assessment of how much inflationary tax was needed, given the fiscal deficit and the public's hoarding desires, to equilibrate the balance of payments. In the case of Argentina, if you take Harberger's assessment, which coincides with that of the majority of Argentine economists, the answer appears to be that it was wrong, as the fiscal deficit required much larger devaluations than those implemented; the deterioration of the current account and a declining exchange rate are shown as proofs of these points. However, these points are not enough proof to conclude that *nominal* exchange rate adjustments are insufficient, since other problems of economic policies can generate similar results. Here I would like to make use of some of the points raised in my theoretical paper.

Current account deficits are the counterpart of excesses of expenditures in relation to national income. Dividing total domestic expenditures into public and private expenditures, and adding and subtracting the level of taxes, we can divide the relationship between the current account, expenditures, and national income into two parts: a public sector budget (public expenditures minus taxes) and a private sector budget (private expenditures plus taxes minus national income). Since these are real budgets in the sense of measuring real flows, it is clear that the concept of taxes includes both nominal and inflationary taxes; inflationary taxes—as stated in my paper—produce the same macroeconomic effects as normal taxes.

The only way of verifying whether the current account deficit originates in undervaluations of the *nominal* exchange rate, or originates in other factors is to see whether the deficit originates in the public or the private sector budget and, in order to incorporate the effects of the inflationary tax, we have to go below the line and look at assets and liabilities—duly adjusted for inflation—and observe their evolution through time. Disequilibrium must be reflected in variations in each sector's net financial wealth. A deterioration in the net financial wealth—adjusted for inflation—of the public sector is evidence that taxes—including the inflationary tax—were not sufficient, and as such is a priori evidence that nominal exchange rate movements are insufficient to collect the required amount of inflationary tax.

One important question is how to treat the accounts of the Central Bank. If the Central Bank holds reserves and, as a consequence, most of the devaluation taxes accrue to the Central Bank, how are these profits treated? From the accounting system developed in the paper, it follows that the central bank figures should be consolidated with those of the public sector, especially if subsidies are hidden in the central bank accounts. Surprisingly, when these calculations are performed for Argentina, for the period under discussion, the figures show an improvement in the net financial wealth of the consolidated public sector, which implies that, adjusted for inflation, the Government was in surplus. Obviously, there was a nominal deficit, but the amount of inflationary taxes collected was larger than was required to compensate for the deficit. How then did the current account turn into deficit and the real exchange rate appreciate so sharply?

Let me try to give you a possible explanation of what happened in Argentina and what, in my opinion, went wrong. During the last decade, public sector expenditures increased drastically (more than 10 percent of GDP if subsidies hidden in the Central Bank are included), at the same time that taxes—including inflationary taxes—increased even more. This increase in taxes generated the surplus mentioned a moment ago, but increased the tax burden of the private sector, at the same time that—from 1979 on—the Government was pushing real wages upward. This policy coincided with a sharp decline in the terms of trade and an unprecedented high international real rate of interest. This was typical of the Government wanting more guns and more butter, just at a moment when the international crisis required a reduction in expenditures.

The result for the productive sectors caught in the middle was disastrous, as their profits turned to losses, forcing them to borrow to survive. Real interest rates shot up, both as a result of the international environment and as a result of this borrowing, and capital flowed in, financing the emerging disequilibrium. As a consequence, a current account deficit emerged and, since expenditures exceeded income, real exchange rates tended to fall. The system proved inconsistent.

In a situation like this, characterized at the same time by frequent wage adjustments based on past inflation, faster movement of the nominal exchange rate would only have provided the Government with more inflationary taxes, leaving the real exchange rate exactly as before. Obviously, abandoning wage indexation would have allowed the real exchange rate to recuperate, at the expense of real wages. Here, Dornbusch is right in the sense that, if the Government is going to increase public expenditures, real wages have to decline in order to allow the real exchange rate to remain constant.

The final question is related to the definition of the current account. Very briefly, if we are talking about real flows and not nominal flows, we should also talk of the current account in real terms. The balance of payments, as all nominal accounting, is subject to distortions introduced by inflation. Nominal interest payments are composed of two elements: a maintenance-of-value element and a real-interest-rate payment. In measuring real flows, only the latter should be included in the definition of the current account, treating the rest as advance payment of real capital.

Overview

JOHN F. O. BILSON and A. W. HOOKE

MUCH of the literature on exchange rate theory concentrates on the extreme cases of fixed or flexible exchange rates. When a government fixes the price of its currency to the currency of another country, it does so by offering to purchase or sell its own currency for the other currency at the established parity value. It has long been known that, under these conditions, the financial fluctuations in the two countries will be linked and so, as a consequence, will many other macroeconomic variables. Flexible exchange rates were once thought of as a mechanism for limiting this interdependence. If the central bank was not obliged to purchase or sell foreign currency on demand, then it would be able to independently set its own monetary and financial policies. The conclusion, then, is that macroeconomic interdependence would be reduced in a flexible exchange rate regime.

To a certain extent, the lessons from the theoretical analysis have been supported by the experience of the last decade of flexible exchange rates. It has, for example, been possible for interest rates on debt denominated in the major reserve currencies to diverge by over 10 percent and differences in national inflation rates have been far greater than they were under the Bretton Woods system. On the other hand, much of the evidence from the floating rate period conflicts with the predictions of simple exchange rate theories: exchange rates have not simply adjusted to offset inflation rate differentials; interest rate differentials have not reflected exchange rate expectations; and, most importantly, the countries participating in the flexible exchange rate system have experienced strong common movements in their economic performance. After a decade of working within the new international monetary system, most governments retain a flexible exchange rate because they have to rather than because they want to.

The purpose of the conference on exchange rate regimes and

policy interdependence was to explore the channels by which economic disturbances in one country are transmitted to other countries in the post-Bretton Woods system. In the first paper, Mr. Dornbusch synthesized the theoretical contributions that had been made to our understanding of the mechanisms by which international financial markets were brought into equilibrium. He then discussed the channels through which disturbances were transmitted and reviewed the policies that might be adopted to counteract the less desirable features of the transmission process. In the second paper, Mr. Branson considered the structure of the labor, commodity, and financial markets of the industrial world, and he described how changes in the structure of these markets influenced the degree of interdependence when the exchange rate was flexible. In the third paper, Mr. Swoboda examined the evidence on interdependence between the United States and the member countries of the European Monetary System and he discussed the extent to which the formation of a currency union reduced the exposure of individual countries to externally generated disturbances. In the final paper, Mr. Arriazu discussed issues of interdependence from a Latin American perspective. He placed particular emphasis on the sectoral impact on Latin American countries of developments in international financial markets. The conference concluded with a round-table discussion relating to issues of trade liberalization in Latin America.

The purpose of this overview chapter is to provide a convenient summary of the papers presented at the conference and to impart some of the flavor of the discussions that followed the presentations. In undertaking this task, no attempt was made to critically evaluate either the papers or the discussion.

Flexible Exchange Rates and Interdependence, by Rudiger Dornbusch

During the 1960s, flexible exchange rates had been viewed as a way of combining independence of demand management policies with a liberal trade and payments system. However, experience since the breakdown of the Bretton Woods system had undermined confidence in this view: policies aimed at achieving domestic stability had produced large movements in exchange rates when practiced by small or open economies and had interfered with stability abroad when exercised by large economies. In his paper, Mr. Dornbusch reviewed the channels along which the effects of policies in one country affected economic behavior in other countries, and considered ways in which it might be possible to combine domestic policy independence with an open world economy.

Mr. Dornbusch first constructed a macroeconomic model in which assets were perfect substitutes for each other once anticipated exchange rate changes had been taken into account and in which expectations were rational. He then considered how key variables in the model might react to two separate disturbances—a rise in the foreign rate of interest and a reduction in the demand for exports. In the typical case, both caused the currency to depreciate in real terms and unemployment to rise. They also caused, as long as money wages increased, the exchange rate to overshoot its new equilibrium level. The overshooting was greater the stickier were real wages, the lower was the elasticity of foreign trade with respect to the exchange rate, and—for the first disturbance—the greater was the responsiveness of aggregate demand to a rise in the rate of interest.

Mr. Dornbusch then relaxed the assumption of perfect substitutability among assets, thereby introducing a risk premium into the model. The risk premium established a link between the distribution of world wealth, on one hand, and the interest rate and/or the exchange rate, on the other. It thus provided a channel through which the current account could affect the exchange rate. For example, a current account surplus increased home wealth, leading to a rise in the interest rate, an appreciation of the currency, or both. Mr. Dornbusch noted, however, that the current account was likely to be a relatively minor source of changes in wealth. He also pointed out that the risk premium had implications for intervention policy. By giving importance to the composition of domestic assets, it caused open market operations to affect the exchange rate through their impact on the level of debt, independently of their effect on the supply of money.

Mr. Dornbusch discussed three main ways in which expectations might cause the exchange rate to move away from its equilibrium level; he referred to these as "bubbles," "pesos," and "runs." Bubbles occurred when holders of a currency realized that it was overvalued but expected the currency to appreciate further before its price fell. Speculation kept the bubble growing until new information caused it to collapse. The peso problem arose when investors doubted that an announced policy, such as a stabilization program, would be adhered to. By acting on these doubts the speculators might cause their prophecies to be fulfilled. Finally, exchange rates were determined, in part, by irrelevant information, which might give rise to runs on particular currencies as investors shifted their attention from one factor to another.

Turning to prescription, Mr. Dornbusch argued that the exchange rate regime should foster reasonably stable rates in the short run, as well as an equilibrium value of the currency and independence of domestic from foreign inflation in the long run. He then considered three alternatives to the present system: a return to fixed rates, more active intervention, and measures to reduce short-term capital movements.

The restoration of a fixed rate system would be rendered difficult, Mr. Dornbusch claimed, by the large differences in inflation rates among the key industrial countries, the apparent lack of willingness of the major industrial countries to abide by rules, and the absence of stable macroeconomic policies in the United States and the United Kingdom. Intervention aimed at maintaining the exchange rate within a band would encourage speculation; that directed toward dampening fluctuations relative to some notion of the equilibrium rate could cope with disturbances that were clearly financial but would run into difficulties when the disturbances were partly real or when their nature was uncertain. Also, intervention could not be used to deal with cyclical changes in exchange rates due to divergent national policies.

There were three main objections to the use of taxes to discourage international capital flows: that even if they could be made effective they (1) would still allow the transmission of effects through the current account and (2) would introduce distortions into the capital markets, and in any case they (3) would induce tax evasion and therefore would not be effective. Mr. Dornbusch argued that the first objection was the most serious as it implied that the advantages of interest equalization taxes were limited to avoiding the effects of exchange rate changes on real wages and prices. The second objection assumed that the short-term money market rate was equal to the social productivity of capital and was simply not valid. He agreed that there was some merit in the third objection but argued that tax evasion would not be significant for transitory taxes.

Mr. Dornbusch concluded that policy measures had effects on other economies regardless of the exchange rate regime that had been adopted. Nevertheless, the exchange rate regime was important because it determined the distribution of effects between changes in employment and changes in real exchange rates and inflation. The appropriate course of action, he suggested, might be to review the contribution that incomes policies—monetary rules and transitory wage controls—could make toward eliminating the adverse effects of interdependence. In view of the effect the present low level of activity had had on real wages, and the importance of locking in this effect, it might now be an auspicious time to introduce such policies.

* * * * *

The discussion following Dornbusch's paper touched on many subjects, including the factors responsible for the recent international monetary instability, the path to a more stable performance by the international monetary system, the effects of the tight U.S. monetary policy on other countries, and the appropriate response of European countries to this policy.

While Mr. Dornbusch covered many of the factors influencing the recent behavior of the international monetary system, it was argued that attention should also be paid to the roles played by such factors as multiple interest rates and policy strategies. On the first of these, it was pointed out that just as the same time profile of nominal wages might be associated with different perceptions of real wage movements between buyers and sellers of labor services, so might the same nominal interest rates be associated with different perceptions of real interest rates between lenders and borrowers. In particular, movements in real interest rates might look quite different to lenders than to borrowers in the foreign trade sector. Such differences might have been important in explaining developments in the United Kingdom in the early years of the Thatcher Government. Regarding policy strategies, it was observed that not only macroeconomic variables such as output and prices but also policies of different countries were interdependent. Thus, in addition to Mr. Dornbusch's theory of model interdependence, it was necessary to have a positive theory of strategic interdependence to explain developments in the international economy. A normative theory of strategic interdependence was also needed to permit the design of suitable rules of behavior for countries.

Among the policy issues considered were the distribution of emphasis between improving the exchange rate system and improving national policies, the merits of band proposals to improve the exchange rate system, and the use of incomes policies to improve national policies. With respect to the issue of strengthening the system or the policies, it was claimed that it might be as realistic to assume that national policies were given and direct efforts toward improving the exchange rate system as to assume that the system was given and try to improve the policies. However, it seemed more appropriate to consider a third possibility—whether or not a process of circular causation might exist between improvements in the system and improvements in policies; if so, this might be used to seek cumulative improvements in both. Band proposals received some support as a way of strengthening the exchange rate system. It was argued that opposition to these proposals was based partly on the misconception that they involved rather narrow bands placed around central rates and almost continuous intervention. Supporters preferred to use the concept, "target zones," rather than "bands," in order to suggest that there was both a relatively wide range within which rates might be allowed to move and that the authorities were not always intervening in the market. The target-zones approach involved continuous surveillance and occasional intervention. The latter, in contrast to the frequent practice of "leaning against the wind," did not produce the perverse result of slowing down movements back to equilibrium rates. The wisdom of sustained reliance on incomes policies as a means of combating wage stickiness was also questioned. It was suggested that such policies might produce favorable results in the short run and, as the prevailing short-run problems were so severe, that their use should be given very serious consideration. However, it was also argued that over the longer term they might add to the rigidity of wages, thereby aggravating the problems faced by policymakers.

There was considerable interest in the implications of the tight U.S. monetary policy for the economic performance and policies of other countries. It was noted that, while the adverse effects of the policy on other countries have been well documented, not all the effects were unfavorable. The policy had caused the dollar to appreciate and real commodity prices to fall. The dollar appreciation had strengthened the competitive positions of the United States' trading partners, with favorable results for those with initially weak current accounts, and the commodity price declines had benefited—among others—importers of oil and of U.S. wheat, corn, and soybeans. Also, the whole world gained from the progress made by the United States in reducing inflation. Regarding the appropriate European policy responses, it was argued that, if effective demand depended on the exchange rate, European countries should accept the downward movements of their currencies as a partial offset to the depressing effect of the U.S. policies on world demand. However, if exchange rate changes had no effect on real demand, as appeared to have been suggested by the implied stickiness of real wages in Europe, then the only effect of currency depreciation was to increase inflation. Europe should, therefore, adopt policies that would prevent such a depreciation.

Economic Structure and Policy for External Balance, by William H. Branson

For the first 25 years after World War II, the emphasis in macroeconomic studies was on the use of one-commodity models to analyze the interactions between the real and financial sectors of the economy and to examine the role played by aggregate demand in determining the values of such variables as output and the general price level. The version of these models used in international economics was the monetary model of the balance of payments. However, the disturbances experienced by the industrial countries during the 1970s were mainly in the form of changes in relative prices. This development led to increased attention being paid to the roles of structure and supply and to the use of multicommodity models to facilitate analysis of those roles. In his paper, Mr. Branson discussed some of the more important results of these studies.

Mr. Branson provided a framework and a starting point for his exposition by constructing a simple monetary model in which goods were perfect substitutes, wages and prices were perfectly flexible, and domestic and foreign interest earning assets were perfect substitutes. These assumptions ensured, respectively, that domestic and foreign prices were related by the exchange rate, that output was at full employment level, and that with a fixed exchange rate domestic and foreign interest rates were equal. After illustrating the workings of the model, Mr. Branson considered three policy options that the model implied for a country suffering from internal and external imbalance as a result of a budget deficit. These options were (1) the reversal of the budget deficit until the money supply had returned to its initial equilibrium level; (2) the elimination of the deficit, together with a devaluation of the currency that validated the increase that had already taken place in the money supply; and (3) an initial devaluation, followed by further, diminishing devaluations (a decelerating crawling peg) to accompany gradual elimination of the budget deficit. While the simple monetary model suggested that all three were reasonable solutions to the country's stabilization problem, their feasibility in practice was affected to an important extent by structural factors not incorporated in that model. Mr. Branson then proceeded to modify the model and used the modified versions to examine these structural factors.

To incorporate relative price changes, Mr. Branson relaxed the assumption of a single commodity. He examined the effects of a devaluation on the trade balance of four types of economy: a small economy, in which both export demand and import supply elasticities were infinite; a semismall economy, that had some market power on the export side so that the elasticity of demand for its exports was less than infinite; a rigid economy, in which both export supply and import demand elasticities were zero, such as an economy using intermediate imports to produce a supply-inelastic export; and a pure manufacturing economy, which imported intermediate goods and exported manufactures and where the elasticity of demand for imports might be close to zero. Mr. Branson noted that it was only during the last decade that much attention had been paid to intermediate imports, which were important in the rigid and pure manufacturing economies.

In the small economy case, the devaluation had no effect on relative prices but did improve the trade balance. It worsened the terms of trade in the semismall economy case, and might improve or worsen the trade balance depending on the values of the demand elasticities; if the latter were low, the devaluation could produce J-curve effects and exchange rate instability. For the rigid economy, the devaluation had no effect on the terms of trade or on trade volumes; however, it did increase the absolute value of the trade balance in proportion to the exchange rate change, and if the initial balance was a deficit, the devaluation accordingly increased that deficit. It could also lead to a rise in unemployment because of the effect that higher prices had on real balances and that the increased trade deficit had on domestic incomes. In the pure manufacturing case, devaluation could worsen both the terms of trade and the balance of trade. The range of these results, and the possibility that devaluation might worsen the trade balance and lead to exchange rate instability, illustrated the need,

Mr. Branson argued, to pay attention to trade structures when evaluating exchange rate policies.

Next, Mr. Branson relaxed the assumption of perfect wage and price flexibility in order to examine the role of the exchange rate and, to a lesser extent, that of aggregate demand when wage rigidities of various kinds were present and markup pricing was practiced. Reverting to the one-commodity model, he assumed that nominal wages were sticky in one country, say, the United States, and real wages were sticky in another area, say, Europe. In this situation, an expansion of demand in Europe, not surprisingly, increased prices in both Europe and the United States and produced a current account deficit in Europe and a current account surplus in the United States. However, because of the different nature of the wage rigidities, the demand expansion increased output only in the United States; in Europe, the only domestic effect was the rise in prices. In view of this, Mr. Branson observed, it was not surprising that when the United States had supported the locomotive approach in 1977, Europe had rejected it.

In the one-commodity model, an exchange rate change also affected output only in the United States. However, this was not the case if Europe and the United States produced different commodities. In this situation, the relevant real wage for European employers was the nominal wage deflated by the prices of domestic goods, while for European workers it was the nominal wage deflated by a weighted index of the prices of imported, as well as domestic, goods. An appreciation of the dollar, which caused the nominal wage in Europe to rise to maintain the real wage that was of interest to European workers, now increased the real wage that was of concern to European employers, who responded to this development by reducing output. Mr. Branson completed this section by demonstrating that, if wages were fully indexed, an exchange rate change would produce a proportionate change in all other prices and thus would affect output only through its impact on real balances.

Turning to the role played by the structure of financial markets, Mr. Branson first converted the monetary model into a model of exchange rate determination and used this model to show how changes in the money supply could be used to bring about the exchange rate adjustments needed to stabilize domestic prices when the foreign price level was fluctuating. He then relaxed the assumption that domestic and foreign assets were perfect substitutes and showed that price stabilization policy must now pay attention not only to the change in the money supply but also to the manner in which the change was brought about—whether it was through open market operations or intervention. If it was through intervention, the change in the money supply needed to effect the desired change in the exchange rate was smaller than if open market operations were used.

Finally, Mr. Branson observed, the exchange rate of a floating currency was determined in the short run by conditions in the financial markets. Only if these markets were deep and well-integrated with financial markets abroad could the rate be reasonably stable. This helped explain the division of countries into those that could float successfully—mainly the industrial countries—and those for which pegging was the only feasible option.

* * * * *

The discussion following Mr. Branson's paper also touched on a wide range of subjects. Among those that received the most attention were the importance of trade structure in determining the effects of exchange rate changes, the role of financial structure in influencing the feasibility and desirability of floating, the conditions required for successful pegging, the importance of recent fluctuations in current account balances and exchange rates, and some implications of the poor predictive record of exchange rate models.

The importance of trade structure, and the different elasticities it implied for various categories of exports and imports, in determining the effects of exchange rate changes on the current account balance was generally recognized. One participant illustrated this by describing the contrasting effects on the French economy of devaluation of the franc against the dollar, on the one hand, and against the deutsche mark, on the other. France's trade in dollar-denominated commodities was weighted toward intermediate rather than final products. Devaluation of the franc against the dollar produced inflation, a worsening of the current account balance, and a decline in economic activity in France. That country's trade with the Federal Republic of Germany, however, was mainly in final products and the two countries competed strongly for each other's markets. Devaluation of the franc against the deutsche mark, therefore, had little immediate effect on inflation, improved the current account balance, and gave a boost to economic activity in France.

Issue was taken with the argument that devaluation reduced the balance of trade in a country that exported manufactured goods and imported intermediate goods. Japan and Korea, it was pointed out, had this kind of trade structure, but both countries had used traditional exchange rate changes to correct balance of payments disequilibria—revaluations of the yen had reduced Japan's trade balance and devaluations of the won had increased Korea's trade balance. It was suggested, however, that the cases of Japan and Korea indicated not that the conclusions about trade structures and elasticities were wrong but that other factors might have been operating in those countries that had given rise to the particular results of the exchange rate changes.

It was generally agreed that sophisticated financial markets were a necessary condition for successful floating. It was not, however, a sufficient condition. It was pointed out that, beyond a certain point, increased integration of financial markets would render them more susceptible to monetary shocks from abroad. Also, bandwagon and overshooting effects could occur if thick financial markets were accompanied by thin labor and product markets. Participants emphasized that even though financial and other conditions might make floating a feasible policy option, it still might not be the most desirable kind of exchange rate regime to adopt.

Attention was also paid to the conditions that made pegging successful, and indeed preferable, in a small country that was able to exercise some control over capital movements. First, it was stated, the monetary authorities must be able to intervene in amounts sufficient to prevent excessive fluctuations in exchange rates; to do this, they had to maintain a high average level of international reserves in order to permit the necessary purchases of the domestic currency when the latter was tending to depreciate excessively. Second, the authorities must be able to follow a flexible monetary policy and be willing, when necessary, to introduce and persevere with tight monetary policies to make absorption consistent with available supplies. Third, the government must have a strong incomes policy in order to ensure flexibility of real wages. It was easier to pursue the required intervention, monetary, and incomes policies if the country's currency had not been widely used in international transactions.

Participants also questioned whether fluctuations in current account balances and in nominal and effective exchange rates had been excessive since the advent of floating. With respect to current account balances it was argued that such movements had not been unduly large for the industrial countries as a whole and had been smaller for the larger countries than for the smaller countries that pegged their currencies. It was also noted that fluctuations had not been as large since 1974 as they had been in the 1920s and 1930s. Regarding exchange rates it was suggested that, while fluctuations in nominal rates had been larger than had generally been anticipated before the introduction of floating, movements in real rates had been reasonably moderate. Further, fluctuations in exchange rates were not, per se, undesirable. The purpose of having a flexible rate regime was to allow rates to vary. This permitted, among other things, countries to pursue independent fiscal and monetary policies. The conditions that would produce stable rates under a flexible rate regime, including the willingness of countries to assign to monetary policy the role of protecting the exchange rate, would also render unnecessary that kind of regime—they would permit the adoption of a fixed rate system. In this context it was suggested that the wrong conclusions might have been drawn from the fluctuations that occurred during the Great Depression. Rather than aggravating the decline in economic activity, these fluctuations probably reduced its magnitude by cushioning some of the effects of the disturbances that were occurring at that time. It was clear, nevertheless, that regardless of how one assessed recent fluctuations, movements in exchange rates could be excessive. What was needed was a yardstick that would permit judgments to be made about the appropriateness of swings in rates.

Some doubt was cast on the accuracy and usefulness of the assumptions used in exchange rate models and, thus, also of the conclusions derived from these models. It was argued that, based on their predictive records, most empirical models of exchange rate behavior had been failures—in fact, they had been less successful than the spot rate itself in forecasting the exchange rate. In view of this, care should be exercised in accepting the conclusions drawn from exchange rate models, such as the proposition that increases in the money supply led to depreciation of the domestic currency. It was also argued that one possible implication of the inability of economists and exchange market analysts to predict exchange rate changes, namely, that these changes followed a random walk, should not be used to justify inclusion in exchange rate models of the assumption that nominal interest rates were the same across countries. This assumption was not only demonstrably false; using it diverted attention from the real issue, which was to explain why nominal interest rate differentials had been so large. If this question could be answered, it might be possible to narrow interest rate differentials and, through this, contribute substantially to eliminating exchange rate variability. In defense of existing exchange rate models, it was suggested that the poor predictive performance during the 1970s lay not in the assumptions but in the nature of the shocks to which economies were subjected during the period. It was also argued that the poor forecasting record was not surprising to supporters of the asset markets approach to exchange rate behavior, who inferred from it that the role played by new information dominated that of trend factors in determining exchange rate movements.

Exchange Rate Regimes and U.S.-European Policy Interdependence, by Alexander K. Swoboda

Recent theoretical analysis and empirical evidence had cast doubts on the traditional view that economic interdependence was less under flexible than under fixed exchange rates. Mr. Swoboda discussed the relationship between interdependence and exchange rate regimes, considered the implications of his conclusions for economic policy, and examined both the insulating properties of currency unions such as the European Monetary System and the merits of a return to fixed rates between the United States and Europe.

Mr. Swoboda analyzed the behavior of five major macroeconomic variables (prices, output, interest rates, money supply, and government spending) in six leading industrial countries (Canada, France, the Federal Republic of Germany, Japan, the United Kingdom, and the United States) during both the fixed exchange rate period of the 1960s and early 1970s and the flexible exchange rate period from the mid-1970s. The results showed a marked increase in the average rate of inflation and, in line with traditional thinking on interdependence, a widening of rates of inflation from the fixed to the flexible exchange rate period. The average rate of output growth also fell in the latter period but, in contrast with what traditional theory would have suggested, the decline was fairly generalized. No clear patterns emerged for the other three variables and, Mr. Swoboda suggested, there were no a priori reasons why they should.

These results shed little light on such questions as the existence of short-term or medium-term interdependence, the role of common factors in explaining variations in country series, the influence of innovations, the importance of systematic differences in the degree of association among variables as between the two exchange rate periods, and the existence of regional groupings based on interdependence. Mr. Swoboda used correlations and principal components analyses to help answer such questions. These indicated a rise in the degree of association from the fixed to the flexible exchange rate period, for changes in inflation, output, the money supply, and interest rates. They also suggested the probable existence of both a common factor in explaining fluctuations in output and of a regional grouping of countries into North America and Europe for changes in output, interest rates, and—for the fixed rate period only—the money supply.

(Traditional theory suggested that, under a fixed exchange rate regime, macroeconomic target variables were highly interdependent and autonomy in the formulation of monetary policy was extremely limited. Essentially, all countries were on a common currency standard, and economic relationships between countries were, in many ways, similar to those between regions of the same country. Thus, inflation rates and interest rates tended to equality across countries and changes in economic activity in one country induced corresponding changes in other countries. Some autonomy existed for fiscal policy but, except for the reserve currency issuing countries, monetary policy was severely constrained by the need to protect the exchange rate. Under a flexible rate regime, in contrast, differences in inflation rates could be accommodated by changes in the nominal exchange rate and domestic output could be protected from the effects of fluctuations in growth rates abroad by appropriate changes in the exchange rate and demand. For these reasons, it had been widely believed, in the 1960s and early 1970s, that a move from fixed to flexible exchange rates would reduce economic interdependence and would provide greater freedom for the operation of monetary policy.) contrast

The doubts that experience since the mid-1970s had cast on the insulating properties of a flexible exchange rate regime had encouraged the study of transmission mechanisms under flexible rates. Laursen–Metzler had shown that a boom abroad could lead to a slump at home; Mundell–Fleming had demonstrated that fiscal expansion at home could produce an expansion abroad, while monetary expansion at home could lead to contraction abroad; and Mr. Dornbusch had shown that monetary disturbances could cause the overshooting of exchange rates.

However, Mr. Swoboda argued, there were two main difficulties with these approaches: they indicated mainly negative channels of transmission, and they suggested that scope was greater for offsetting the effects of foreign disturbances under flexible than under fixed rates. They did not, therefore, explain the high degrees of association of short-term inflation rates and of output growth rates under flexible rates. While the latter might be due, in part, to transmission, they might also reflect, Mr. Swoboda suggested, the existence of a world business cycle. Such a cycle could arise because shocks were specific, not to countries but to industries and stages of production across countries. In this context, he argued, it might be more useful to divide the world into industrial sectors than into countries.

In his final section, Mr. Swoboda discussed two specific questions that were addressed to him by the organizers of the seminar: how could arrangements such as the European Monetary System affect interdependence? and whether or not fixed exchange rates should be re-established between North America and Europe? The traditional view that interdependence should be strong among currency union countries but weak between these countries and those outside the union was not supported by recent experience. Mr. Swoboda suggested, however, that the formation of a currency union might, by making the monetary policies of members more predictable, reduce the variability of real exchange rates and, through this, the severity of outside shocks. With respect to the choice between fixed and flexible rates, Mr. Swoboda noted that output interdependence and U.S. dominance had been as great since the adoption of flexible rates as they had been before. Nevertheless, the large industrial countries still preferred flexible rates, mainly because these reduced interdependence of inflation levels and appeared to avoid the need for commitment to rules of monetary behavior. However, Mr. Swoboda argued, the appearance of greater policy independence was illusory. Policy commitments were required for successful working of both types of exchange rate system; it was only the form of the commitment that differed.

* * * * *

The discussion focused on the causes of the relative constancy of correlations among major macroeconomic variables from the 1960s to the 1970s and of the general absence of lagged relationships in these variables in the 1970s, the implications of the empirical findings on regional groupings for the feasibility of monetary unions in Europe and North America, the implications of recent developments in Europe and the United States for the usefulness of existing transmission models, and the importance of policy autonomy and policy discipline for the choice of an exchange rate regime.

Considerable interest was shown in Mr. Swoboda's empirical finding that the correlations among major economic variables across countries were largely unchanged from the 1960s to the 1970s. Four possible explanations were suggested for this result: (1) that the differences between the regimes of the 1960s and the 1970s were not, in fact, very great; (2) that the degree of interdependence was not greatly affected by the type of exchange rate regime in effect; (3) that the shocks to which the world was subjected in the two periods were substantially different; and (4) that the data incorporated not only the effects of the differences in exchange rate regimes and shocks but also those of the policies adopted in response to the shocks. There was support for the view that the move from a fixed to a flexible rate regime probably had not significantly influenced developments; the world recessions of 1974–75 and 1981–82, for example, would have occurred whatever the exchange rate regime. However, it was pointed out, the empirical data presented did not permit this view to be tested as they did not separate the effects of the exchange rate change from those of other factors.

The data presented by Mr. Swoboda showed that movements across countries of such variables as output and prices were not lagged, as would be suggested by business cycle transmission theory, but were contemporaneous during the 1970s. It was agreed that this could have been due to the emergence of a world business cycle. However, it was claimed, there was little positive evidence to support this explanation. In particular, the increased interdependence of interest rates in the 1970s should not be cited, as this development could be attributed to the changeover from a fixed to a flexible exchange rate regime.

The findings of contemporaneous correlations could be explained more convincingly, it was argued, by the occurrence of common shocks and common policy responses to these. It was pointed out that the industrial countries had become increasingly integrated over the last three decades as a result of such factors as increased dependency on foreign trade, especially on imports of fuel and raw materials. The greater integration had fostered not only common expectations but also similar political and social policies, as evidenced by the increased government provision of goods and services and by the high employment policies of the 1960s and early 1970s. It had also fostered common structural developments such as the increase in rigidities in the labor market and the rise in the share of wages in gross national product in 1969–75. In view of these developments, it was not surprising that the large increases in oil prices in 1973–74 and 1979–80 had had a major impact on all the industrial countries and that the latter had adopted similar policies in response to them. It was pointed out, however, that the findings of Mr. Swoboda did not indicate that there had been an increased common policy response to common shocks.

It was recognized that the data presented by Mr. Swoboda had provided a basis for dividing the observed countries into a European group and a North American group. It was noted, however, that these data did not imply that a monetary union was feasible or desirable for either group. Before such assessments could be made it was necessary to consider other factors, including attitudes toward and policies for combating inflation, that determined the extent to which monetary policies within the groups could be harmonized.

While most theoretical models predicted negative transmission of the effects of foreign disturbances, especially for output and prices, such variables had tended to move in the same direction in the industrial countries in recent years. It was argued that this did not imply that the models were wrong. In fact, when policy changes were made endogenous, the models, or at least those using the asset markets approach, fitted the facts rather well. This view was illustrated by developments following the introduction of the tight money policy in the United States in 1979. As theory suggested, this policy had had a negative effect on growth and inflation in the United States and a positive effect on inflation in Europe. Because of the largely offsetting effects of currency depreciation and reduced real money supply associated with unchanged policies in Europe, there was little effect on output in Europe. This was not, however, the end of the story. European policies did not remain unchanged but were also tightened in line with those of the United States. The induced change in European policies contributed to the reduction in growth and inflation in Europe that had unnecessarily raised doubts about the usefulness of transmission models.

One of the reasons for favoring a flexible over a fixed exchange rate regime was that the former permitted autonomy in the exercise of monetary policy. It was argued, however, that this autonomy was largely illusory. Policymakers might have freedom with respect to the use of instruments but the latter might not have the potential to reach the chosen policy targets. Specifically, traditional instruments of monetary policy appeared to be ineffective now in promoting internal balance. In the light of this, one participant observed, it might be useful to assign to monetary policy the task of attaining and maintaining external, rather than internal, balance. On the other hand, it was claimed, the argument that a fixed rate regime imposed a firm discipline on the national authorities and reduced the likelihood of irresponsible policies being adopted might also be exaggerated. Rather than adapting their policies to a given exchange rate regime, governments were likely to adapt the exchange rate regime to whatever discipline they chose to impose on themselves.

Policy Interdependence from a Latin American Perspective, by Ricardo H. Arriazu

Mr. Arriazu began his paper by noting that the last few years had been extremely difficult ones for the economies of the Latin American countries. While domestic conditions and policies had undoubtedly played some role in the economic performance of the countries in the region, the general malaise, observed in conjunction with the adoption of very different macroeconomic strategies, suggested that part of the problem arose from the transmission of externally generated economic disturbances into the region. Mr. Arriazu suggested that developments in the world economy, including the expansion of international trade in both goods and capital, the adoption of flexible exchange rate and interest rate policies in the reserve currency countries, and the inflationary environment of the past decade had all contributed to the sensitivity of Latin American economies to externally generated disturbances.

Mr. Arriazu suggested that, given the variety of disturbances experienced during the past few years, it was difficult to build a complete model that would illustrate the impact of these disturbances on a typical Latin American economy. He proposed, as an alternative, to consider the transmission of a stereotyped cycle from the world economy to a stylized Latin American economy. The cycle consisted of an initial increase, and subsequent decline, in world inflation which would lead to a related cycle in world nominal and real interest rates, and the objective of his analysis was to consider the impact of this change on both the macroeconomic and sectoral performance of a model with three commodity sectors—exports, import substitutes, and nontraded—and a developed banking system. The Latin American flavor of the model arose from its concern with widespread indexation of both prices and interest rates and its detailed specification of the linkages between fiscal and monetary policy and the inflationary consequences of the cycle. Mr. Arriazu's small open economy was characterized by private and public sectors that responded endogenously to developments in the world economy.

Mr. Arriazu's analysis of the world inflationary cycle concentrated on the relationship between the inflation of commodity prices and real and nominal interest rates. While other macroeconomic variables were of obvious importance to the center countries, Mr. Arriazu felt that the main transmission channels to the Latin American economies was through price and interest rate effects. In the early stage of the cycle, higher inflation led to an increase in nominal interest rates and a possible decline in real interest rates. However, when inflation declined, nominal interest rates tended to remain high, leading to high real interest rates. In the final stage of the cycle, real and nominal interest rates were assumed to return to their longer-run, equilibrium levels.

The cycle was transmitted to the stylized economy through price and interest rate developments. Mr. Arriazu argued that the growth of world trade had led to a more rapid transmission of inflation from the center countries to the Latin American economies. His analysis of the interest rate transmission channel recognized the fact that private and public debt raised in world capital markets were tending to pay variable interest rates, so that increases in nominal interest rates were leading to additional interest costs for the countries under consideration. In the model, this factor led to a public sector deficit in the early stages of the cycle, even when indexation was complete. However, Mr. Arriazu argued, the fiscal deficit was not likely to lead to a balance of payments deficit in the early stage of the cycle because of the price-induced increase in the demand for the domestic monetary base and the associated increase in the world demand for exportables. In the second stage of the cycle, the world inflation was transmitted, through demand and indexation effects, to the prices of nontraded goods.

When the world inflation began to decline, Mr. Arriazu suggested, public sector deficits would increase sharply. Interest rates on external borrowings would remain high, and domestic tax sources would not automatically increase to offset the high borrowing costs. Given the decline in world commodity prices, in conjunction with a continued domestic response to the previous inflation, world demand for exportables would decline and local demand for import substitutes would increase. Hence, the expanding public sector deficit would, in this instance, be associated with an overall balance of payments deficit. If the prior stock of external debt was sufficiently large, the combination of a public sector deficit with an overall deficit on the balance of payments might lead to concerns over creditworthiness.

Mr. Arriazu suggested that the scenario described in the stereotype model was broadly consistent with the response of Latin American economies to the developments in the international financial system during the past few years. Despite the great differences in the economic policies followed by Latin American nations, the importance of developments in the rest of the world and the increase in the sensitivity of Latin American countries to external developments had led to a number of common features in their recent economic development.

In the final section, Mr. Arriazu briefly considered the modifications that would be required if his model was restated with a flexible exchange rate regime. Mr. Arriazu defined a flexible exchange rate regime as one in which the monetary base was exogenous, so that the exchange rate adjusted to ensure that the demand for the base was equal to the exogenous supply. While a flexible exchange rate regime exacerbated relative price movements during the cycle, and while it consequently created greater volatility in output and employment, the basic lessons from the earlier analysis continued to hold true under flexible exchange rates. Since Latin American debt remained characterized as being denominated in dollars and paying a flexible interest rate, an interest rate cycle would continue to exert real effects on the economy through variations in interest payments on public sector debt.

* * * * *

The discussion of Mr. Arriazu's paper centered on two issues. The first was the extent to which the 1980–81 experience was a good representative case for illustrating the relationship between the Latin American economies and the rest of the world. The second was the extent to which the model's assumption of fixed exchange rates limited its generality.

As far as the representativeness of the 1980–81 experience was concerned, Mr. Arriazu had suggested that the common experience of the Latin American countries was due to the transmission of world shocks through price and interest rate developments. In the discussion, the point was made that major changes in the world economy had taken place when the economic performance of the Latin American countries was extremely divergent. As an alternative interpretation of recent experience, it was suggested that the correlation in the recent performance of Latin American countries might have been due to their similar domestic policy response to the fall in real interest rates in the middle 1970s. It was apparent that many countries borrowed more than they would have borrowed had they known about the future evolution of real exchange rates and real interest rates. If the 1980–81 experience had simply been the result of expectational errors, it might not be an appropriate case for illustrating future relationships between the Latin American group and the world economy.

In regard to the question of the exchange rate regime, a number of the participants observed that Mr. Arriazu's analysis relied too heavily on the assumption of a fixed exchange rate regime. While the response of the economy to an external shock might be similar, in the long run, for both pure fixed and pure floating rate regimes, most Latin American countries did not have pure systems and the distortions introduced by trade and capital controls, overvaluation or undervaluation of the exchange rate, and inappropriate monetary and fiscal policies might have an important role to play in assessing the impact of an external shock on a Latin American economy.

Panel Discussion on the Southern Cone

Panel Discussion with Jacob A. Frenkel, Rudiger Dornbusch, William H. Branson, and Ricardo H. Arriazu.

Mr. Dale opened the discussion of liberalization in the Southern Cone by noting that three Latin American countries—Argentina, Chile, and Uruguay—had, since the mid 1970s, adopted stabilization programs that had included moves toward more liberal exchange rate and trade policies in conjunction with preannounced exchange rate targets. Mr. Dale also noted that these three countries had also encountered difficulties in recent times, and that the issues surrounding liberalization were of great interest, particularly at the present time.

Mr. Frenkel began the discussion by noting that it was generally better to liberalize commodity flows before capital flows, and that it was important that domestic policies be corrected before any liberalization of the foreign sector was implemented. If liberalization was attempted before budgets were balanced and money growth controlled, then it was unlikely to be anything but a temporary phenomenon. The main reason why the goods markets should be liberalized before the capital markets was that goods markets tended to clear more slowly than capital markets. Hence, an external balance achieved through the trade account would be more gradual, and hence less disruptive, than an external balance achieved through capital account liberalization.

Mr. Frenkel subsequently noted that liberalization was often part of a total stabilization package. As far as the stabilization package was concerned, he argued that a rapidly imposed stabilization package would probably be more effective than a gradually imposed one, because a government needed to have a well-defined and consistent change in policy in order for the stabilization package to be credible. If the government demonstrated its credibility through its monetary and fiscal policies, it would find it easier to negotiate incomes policies and capital controls in order to smooth the private sector adjustment.

While Mr. Frenkel recognized that arguments could be made for income policies and capital controls during a transition period, he recognized that these policies could be counterproductive if the transition period did not end because of the failure of the underlying stabilization policies.

Mr. Dornbusch continued the discussion of stabilization policies by noting that the periods of economic crisis in Argentina, Chile, and Brazil were associated with high real interest rates and overvalued currencies. Mr. Dornbusch argued that the source of the problem was the failure to associate a fiscal reform with a real depreciation of the currency. In many cases, he suggested, central banks had used financing to delay adjustment in real exchange rates and had, consequently, established the conditions for a financial crisis. Mr. Dornbusch suggested a return to the more traditional approach to stabilization; an approach based on correcting budget deficits, a substantial real depreciation, and a controlled capital account program.

In his discussion, Mr. Branson returned to the problem raised by Mr. Frenkel concerning the choice between liberalizing trade in goods before liberalizing trade in capital. He suggested that the elimination of capital controls would generate an increase in confidence that would lead to an inflow of capital into the country. The capital inflow would be associated with an appreciation of the real exchange rate and a decline in national competitiveness. However, liberalizing trade would, he suggested, lead to a surge in imports, a current account deficit, and a depreciation of the currency. There were, he concluded, problems to be faced with either approach to liberalization.

Mr. Arriazu began his discussion of the issue of whether to liberalize commodity flows before trade flows by distinguishing between opening the economy to trade and reducing the level of effective protection. In a situation in which there was "water in the tariff," the commodity was so heavily protected that even a substantial increase in its domestic price would not lead to imports of the commodity. Mr. Arriazu argued that opening the capital account in a situation in which many commodities had been removed from the traded goods sector due to excessive levels of effective protection would lead to instability in the balance of payments.

Mr. Arriazu also questioned Mr. Dornbusch's contention that capital controls were a necessary policy instrument. In Argentina, he suggested, it was extremely difficult to maintain capital controls for any length of time because of the ingenuity with which Argentine citizens created methods for effectively evading the controls. Mr. Arriazu also felt that the role of preannounced exchange rate changes was to establish the credibility of the stabilization policy. In Argentina, he suggested that the size of the government deficit determined the extent of the necessary change in the exchange rate and that the preannouncement of the exchange rate changes provided some of the reduced uncertainty of a fixed rate regime.

Concluding Remarks

J. J. POLAK

I WOULD LIKE to respond to a question posed by the Managing Director in his opening remarks as to why the Fund has found it so difficult to make pronouncements on the exchange rates of major currencies. Some ten years ago the Fund did not hesitate to make such a pronouncement. For example, in August 1971 the staff felt sure enough of its ground to propose a new set of exchange rates. In the event, the rates proposed proved wrong: the changes were too small and did not produce enough adjustment. There was, however, a rather comforting explanation: it was not that the Fund's model was wrong but that the size of the 1971 disequilibrium had been seriously underestimated. In the mid-1970s, the Fund staff started to calculate "underlying balances" for the major countries—i.e., balances that would materialize over the medium term with present exchange rates and at reasonably high levels of activity in all countries. The exercise proved generally right in predicting the fall in the deutsche mark/dollar rate from 1976 to September 1978 and it also correctly suggested that the further sharp fall of the dollar in October 1978 went too far. But the model was never good at predicting what would happen to the yen, and it broke down for the dollar in 1980. Since then, interest rates have been so dominant and so volatile over so long a time, with such wide-ranging effects, and with so much bandwagon riding in both the capital and the foreign exchange markets, that the kind of medium-term analysis in which the Fund had engaged has become largely irrelevant to what happens in exchange markets for the short term and also to what can be made to happen through, for example, intervention or any policy of bands or target zones.

In commenting on the conference, I must confess to having a slight bias in favor of ideas in the areas of policy rather than of analysis. However, I appreciate the middle course that Mr. Branson has steered between very simple and very complicated models. By a modest addition to oversimple models, he has introduced quite realistic aspects of countries' economic structure, such as the commodity content of imports and exports, nominal and real wage rigidity, and the presence or absence of effective financial markets. I would like to emphasize two aspects of the Branson approach. First, what may appear as structural characteristics of an economy to the economic analyst need not necessarily be considered in this way for policy purposes. It was true, for example, that full indexation of money wages and the consequential extreme stickiness of real wages were notable characteristics of the economies of many European countries. If one accepts this structural element as immutable, exchange rate policies—and also many other policies of adjustment—become totally ineffective, and any form of adjustment that presupposes the reduction of real wages is by definition impossible. The task of policy in these circumstances then becomes not one of accommodating exchange rate policy to the structure but one of changing the structure so as to make exchange rate policy effective. This indeed has been the main issue of adjustment in recent years in a number of European countries, such as Belgium, France, Ireland, Italy, and the Netherlands, and the key to successful policies in these countries.

Second, Mr. Branson has introduced financial markets as a structural difference between industrial and developing countries. However, I believe that he assumed too readily that the financial markets in the former countries are thick enough for the monetary authorities to trust private speculation to be stabilizing, and, hence, to permit reliance on floating rates. My own impression is that confidence in stabilizing capital movements has gone out of fashion in the last few years, for a number of good reasons, of which Mr. Dornbusch has briefly mentioned the prevalence of irrelevant information, the possibility of changes in the regime that encouraged speculators to hold out for a break in the system, and "bandwagon effects"—all three of which have devastating consequences for the attainment of equilibrium. Quite apart from the trust that can be put in the resilience of financial markets, there was more to structure on this point than whether countries export manufactures or primary products. There is also the need to separate the industrial countries according to their size. There has been remarkably little reference during the day to the concept of the optimum currency area, even though the comparison of the costs and benefits of floating versus fixed rates has a lot to do with the size and openness of a country. Moreover, as we become increasingly less sanguine about the stabilizing nature of speculation, the balance of benefits versus costs as a function of economic size will inevitably shift further in the direction of fixed against floating rates.

One point that has been stressed throughout the day is that, whatever their exchange rate regime, small industrial countries are inevitably exposed to the main economic events occurring in their larger neighbor countries. Should these countries try to exploit whatever freedom they have to control their own business cycle or their own interest rates by following a separate exchange rate policy? Or should they come to terms with the degree of their economic and financial dependence and opt for a fixed rate against the currency of their largest neighbor? A number of medium-sized countries seem to have come to quite different answers to this question; for example, Canada has opted for a floating rate for its currency vis-à-vis the U.S. dollar, while the Netherlands has chosen a fixed rate on the deutsche mark.

I find an absence of dogmatism in today's presentations on fixed versus floating rates and a wide area of parallelism of findings; this is shown by the extent to which all four authors tended to dissent from Harry Johnson's view that flexible rates are essential to the preservation of national autonomy and "independence consistent with efficient organization and development of the world economy." Specifically, Mr. Arriazu has stressed that variations in output and employment have tended to be much larger under floating than under fixed rates, and Mr. Swoboda has observed that floating has not permitted countries to avoid riding, or rather being ridden by, the world business cycle. However, I think it is important not to forget the lesson from the 1930s, when those countries that lowered their exchange rates (such as Japan, Sweden, and the United Kingdom) did notably better in real terms than some of the other main industrial countries. This may have been because nominal depreciations in the 1930s invariably produced *real* effective depreciations, whereas nowadays they often do not. Or it might be another case of confusion of terminology between the general impact of floating and the specific impact of depreciation.

I hope that economists will have a clear idea of what is involved in making a comparative judgment between fixed and flexible exchange rate systems, at least in particular country situations. I must caution against a lowering of standards in making such judgments. Viability, for instance, is being treated as one criterion.

The par value system is not viable in the face of severe policy conflicts, as the events of 1971 and 1973 proved. In a narrow sense, a floating rate system is viable under any circumstances. But the experience of Mexico in the last few weeks has illustrated how shallow this viability can be. I support Mr. Swoboda's conclusion that any judgment about the merits of floating rates must be based on their success in terms of *other* variables, such as inflation, unemployment, cyclical stability, and adjustment. A certain lowering of standards is also visible in the European Monetary System. What else is the rejoicing about the system's ability to survive successive realignments in disregard of the fact that it is the absence of convergent policies—that is, the failure of the European Monetary System in its basic objective—that made these realignments necessary?

I support Mr. Branson's view that we should not look to "better policies" and "coordination" to solve all problems of international policy. Countries have some national instruments, such as the exchange rate, that give them some freedom from the effects of other countries' policies. However, there are limits to the use of any instrument. Living as we do in a period of severe shocks, world inflation, and distortion in the income distribution, is there any point in looking for an exchange regime that will let us get through this period without very unpleasant consequences? Countries cannot escape the consequences of their own policies through their selection of an exchange rate regime.

SUMMARIES

Flexible Exchange Rates and Interdependence—RUDIGER DORNBUSCH (pages 3–30)

The paper reviews the channels of macroeconomic interdependence under flexible exchange rates. The model emphasizes the linkage of international capital markets, expectations, and nominal and real wage stickiness in affecting the impact of disturbances on employment, prices, and the exchange rate. The standard rational-expectations macroeconomic model is extended to facilitate analysis of the role of risk premiums created by imperfect asset substitutability. Peso problems and bubbles are discussed briefly.

In a discussion of third-country effects, the paper addresses the implications tight money has for developing countries. These countries are affected by adverse effects of increased real interest rates on their debt, by reduced real prices of their commodity exports owing to decreased demand and the real appreciation of the dollar, and by reduced demand for their manufactured exports.

The paper discusses two alternative proposals designed to deal with the exchange rate implications of policy interdependence. One is the McKinnon proposal for world monetarism; the other is the band proposal. Both proposals are rejected because they fail to cope with the problems of the transition to a low, common inflation rate. The paper concludes with the suggestion that improved performance of the world economy cannot come from a better exchange rate system but rather from a more systematic use of incomes policies.

Economic Structure and Policy for External Balance—WILLIAM H. BRANSON (pages 39–66)

The traditional macroeconomics of the period since World War II, as well as the more recent rational expectation and neo-Keynesian approaches, analyze one-commodity economies. The international version of this model, in its simplified extreme, is the monetary model of the balance of payments or, more recently, of the exchange rate. During the 1970s emphasis in research has shifted to the supply side and the role of structure in transmitting economic disturbances and effects of policy.

This paper discusses some of the more significant results on the role of economic structure in determining how disturbances are transmitted. It begins with an exposition of the monetary model of the balance of payments, which assumes virtually no structure. This provides a framework for the following sections, which introduce structural differences into the model, one at a time.

The basic results can be summarized briefly. First, supply rigidities or a high ratio of imported intermediate goods to value added in production can make devaluation counterproductive. This can be particularly important for a developing country considering a stabilization program. Second, the effects of changes in exchange rates may be asymmetric between Europe and the United States. Movements in the exchange rate have their main effect on trade in the United States by changing relative prices. This makes the exchange rate an efficient instrument for external adjustment in the United States. But in Europe, changes in the exchange rate may have their main effect on domestic prices, making the exchange rate a poor instrument for external balance.

Third, demand policy in countries with real wage stickiness moves the price level in those countries but influences output only in countries with nominal wage stickiness. Again, there may be a difference between Europe, with sticky real wages, and the United States, with sticky nominal wages. Finally, only countries with developed and open financial markets can expect a floating exchange rate to be stable. This may be the reason why the industrial countries tend to float, while developing countries tend to peg their exchange rates.

Exchange Rate Regimes and European-U.S. Policy Interdependence—ALEXANDER K. SWOBODA (pages 75–102)

This article documents and contrasts the degree of interdependence of key macroeconomic variables across six major industrial economies (the United States, Canada, Japan, France, the Federal Republic of Germany, and the United Kingdom) over the periods 1960–71 and 1974–82. Principal components analysis is the main statistical tool employed. The findings suggest that, although trend inflation rates have indeed become more independent since the adoption of floating exchange rates, short-run (quarterly) changes in inflation, interest rates, and, especially, changes in real output growth have become significantly more interdependent in the later period. This finding holds not only for the original time series studied but also for innovations (unexpected shocks) in these series. In contrast, no very clear difference in the interdependence of policy instruments across countries appears when the two periods are compared.

The evidence lends some support to the notion of a world business cycle, on which national business cycles are superimposed and which is independent of the exchange rate regime, although the channels of transmission differ depending on the prevailing regime. In addition, a weak regional (European) pattern of interdependence appears in the data.

The paper concludes with a discussion of some implications for the choice of exchange rate regime, regional currency arrangements, and the scope for autonomy of macroeconomic policy under floating. It emphasizes the importance of credibility and precommitment of policies and concludes that flexible exchange rates, to work properly, require a set of rules that, although different from those that would apply under fixed rates, are no less constraining for national macroeconomic policies.

Policy Interdependence from a Latin American Perspective—RICARDO H. ARRIAZU (pages 113–52)

During 1982 most Latin American countries faced severe balance of payments and economic difficulties. The paper explores the possibility of a common exogenous origin in these crises. To evaluate this possibility, at a theoretical level, a "stereotyped" international cycle is defined on the basis of the behavior of relative prices and international interest rates, and its effects on small, semi-open economies are carefully evaluted.

The analysis is concentrated on the evaluation of the sectoral effects on the different stages of the cycle, with special emphasis on the effects upon the accounts of the public sector, the central bank, the financial system, the productive sectors (represented by producers of exportable goods, of import substituting commodities and of goods nontraded internationally), and of individuals. The balance of pyaments is then obtained as a residual of the aggregate changes resulting in the net financial wealth positions of each of these sectors.

In order to undertake these sectoral evaluations in conjunction with the usual analysis of the effects of the cycle upon such macroeconomic variables as output, employment, and prices, a method of analysis, based on the technique of interlocking flows, was developed, with special emphasis upon equilibrium conditions rather than on behavioral assumptions, including, in addition, some special operational characteristics of Latin American countries.

The evaluation was performed under two different assumptions in relation to the exchange rate system in operation, in order to determine whether a small economy is better protected from the disturbances brought about by international economic cycles, by fixed exchange rates, or by floating exchange rates.

The results of the evaluation of the behavior of the main macroeconomic variables and of the main sectoral effects show that recent economic developments in Latin America are strikingly similar to those that could be expected, in accordance with the model, as a consequence of recent economic developments in international markets, and as such it can be asserted that most problems in the region have, at least in part, a common origin. The model also proved to be extremely useful for the analysis of sectoral effects of cycles, and some of the results, surprising as they are, contributed new insights into the understanding of recent economic performances; for example, the surprising emergence of a fiscal deficit—as an integral part of the cycle—in spite of an improvement in the terms of trade and higher levels of economic activity and employment. The model also shows that floating exchange rates tend to reduce fluctuations in nominal variables—such as prices and interest rates—better than fixed exchange rates, but tend also to amplify fluctuations in real variables such as output and employment.

RESUMES

Taux de change flexibles et interdépendance— RUDIGER DORNBUSCH (pages 3–30)

L'étude traite des mécanismes de transmission de l'interdépendance macroéconomique en régime de taux de change flexibles. Le modèle souligne le rôle joué par le lien qui existe entre les marchés de capitaux internationaux, les anticipations et l'inflexibilité à la baisse des salaires nominaux et réels dans la transmission des perturbations économiques sur l'emploi, les prix et le taux de change. Le modèle macroéconomique type fondé sur les anticipations rationnelles est élargi de facon à faciliter l'analyse du rôle des primes de risque créées par la substituabilité imparfaite des avoirs. Les problèmes que posent le peso et les vagues d'extrême spéculation sont examinés brièvement.

Abordant les effets ressentis par les pays tiers, l'auteur de l'étude examine les implications d'une politique monétaire restrictive pour les pays en développement; cette politique exerce sur eux des effets défavorables étant donné qu'elle relève les taux d'intérêt réels de leur dette, qu'elle abaisse les prix réels de leurs exportations de produits primaires du fait de l'affaiblissement de la demande et de l'appréciation réelle du dollar, et qu'elle réduit la demande portant sur leurs exportations de produits manufacturés.

L'étude examine deux propositions visant à remédier aux incidences de l'interdépendance des politiques économiques sur le système des changes. La première est celle de McKinnon, qui préconise un monétarisme mondial, et la seconde appuie l'établissement de marges de fluctuation. L'auteur rejette ces deux propositions car elles ne permettent pas, à son avis, de résoudre les problèmes que pose le passage à un taux d'inflation commun modéré. Il conclut qu'une amélioration de la performance de l'économie mondiale ne résulterait sans doute pas de l'adoption d'un meilleur système de change mais plutôt d'un recours plus systématique aux politiques de revenus.

Structure économique et politique d'équilibre extérieur—WILLIAM H. BRANSON (pages 39–66)

La théorie macroéconomique traditionnelle de la période qui s'est écoulée depuis la deuxième guerre mondiale, ainsi que celle des anticipations rationnelles et l'approche néo-keynésienne, toutes deux d'origine plus récente, analysent les économies fondées sur un seul produit. La version internationale de ce modèle, sous sa forme la plus simple, est le modèle monétaire de la balance des paiements ou, plus récemment, celui du taux de change. Pendant les années 70, les recherches ont été davantage axées sur l'offre et le rôle de la structure de l'économie dans la transmission des perturbations économiques et des effets de la politique économique.

La présente étude analyse certains des principaux résultats concernant le rôle de la structure économique sur la façon dont les perturbations sont transmises.

Elle commence par une description du modèle monétaire de la balance des paiements, qui ne pose par hypothèse pratiquement aucune structure. Cette présentation sert de cadre aux sections suivantes qui introduisent, une par une, des différences structurelles dans le modèle.

On peut résumer brièvement les principaux résultats. Premièrement, en présence de rigidités au niveau de l'offre ou d'un ratio élevé entre les biens intermédiaires importés et la valeur ajoutée à la production, la dévaluation peut aller à l'encontre des buts recherchés. Cette constatation peut être particulièrement importante pour un pays en développement qui envisage un programme de stabilisation. Deuxièmement, les effets de variations des taux de change peuvent être asymétriques en Europe et aux Etats-Unis. Aux Etats-Unis, les variations du taux de change agissent essentiellement sur le commerce en modifiant les prix relatifs. Ainsi le taux de change est un instrument efficace pour l'ajustement extérieur aux Etats-Unis mais, en Europe, les variations du taux de change pourront se faire sentir principalement sur les prix intérieurs, faisant du taux de change un piètre instrument d'équilibre extérieur.

Troisièmement, la politique de la demande dans les pays où les salaires réels sont inflexibles à la baisse fait varier le niveau des prix dans ces pays; elle n'influe sur la production que dans les pays où ce sont les salaires nominaux qui sont inflexibles à la baisse. Là encore, il y a peut-être une différence entre l'Europe, où les salaires réels sont inflexibles, et les Etats-Unis où ce sont les salaires nominaux qui sont inflexibles. Enfin, seuls les pays dotés de marchés financiers développés et ouverts peuvent s'attendre à ce qu'un taux de change flottant soit stable. C'est peut-être la raison pour laquelle les pays industrialisés tendent à pratiquer le flottement, tandis que les pays en développement ont tendance à déterminer leur taux de change par référence à d'autres monnaies.

Régimes de taux de change et interdépendance des politiques économiques en Europe et aux Etats-Unis—ALEXANDER K. SWOBODA (pages 75–102)

A partir de données statistiques, le présent article compare le degré d'interdépendance des principales variables macroéconomiques entre six grands pays industrialisés (Etats-Unis, Canada, Japon, France, République fédérale d'Allemagne et Royaume-Uni) pendant deux périodes : 1960–71 et 1974–82. L'analyse en composantes principales est le principal outil statistique utilisé. Les résultats indiquent que si les taux tendanciels d'inflation sont effectivement devenus plus indépendants depuis l'adoption des taux de change flottants, les variations à court terme (trimestrielles) de l'inflation et des taux d'intérêt et surtout, les variations de croissance de la production réelle sont devenues nettement plus interdépendantes pendant la deuxième période. Cette constatation vaut non seulement pour les séries chronologiques initiales étudiées, mais aussi pour les éléments nouveaux (chocs imprévus) dans ces séries. En revanche, une comparaison entre les deux périodes ne fait apparaître aucune différence très nette quant à l'interdépendance des instruments de politique économique entre ces pays.

Les résultats appuient l'idée qu'il existe un cycle économique mondial auquel se superposent les cycles nationaux, et qui est indépendant du régime de change, encore que les voies de transmission de ses effets diffèrent selon le régime en vigueur. En outre, les données mettent en évidence un schéma régional (européen) d'interdépendance assez peu prononcé.

Dans la dernière section de l'article, l'auteur examine certaines implications de ses conclusions pour le choix d'un régime de change, les accords monétaires régionaux et l'autonomie des politiques macroéconomiques en régime de taux de change flottants. Il souligne l'importance de la crédibilité et de l'engagement préalable en politique économique et conclut que les taux de change flexibles exigent, pour fonctionner convenablement, un ensemble de règles qui, si elles diffèrent de celles applicables en régime de taux de change fixes, n'en sont pas moins contraignantes pour les politiques macroéconomiques nationales.

Interdépendance de la politique économique dans une perspective latino-américaine— RICARDO H. ARRIAZU (pages 113–52)

En 1982, la plupart des pays d'Amérique latine se sont heurtés à de grave difficultés économiques et de balance des paiements. L'article examine l'hypothèse d'une cause exogène commune à ces crises. Pour évaluer cette possibilité, sur un plan théorique, un cycle international "stéréotypé" est défini sur la base du comportement des prix et des taux d'intérêt internationaux relatifs et les effets de ce comportement sur les petites économies semi-ouvertes est soigneusement étudié.

L'analyse est centrée sur l'évaluation des effets sectoriels sur les différents stades du cycle et met plus particulièrement l'accent sur les effets au niveau des comptes du secteur public, de la banque centrale, du système financier, des secteurs productifs (représentés par les producteurs de biens exportables, de produits de remplacement des importations et de biens ne faisant pas l'objet d'échanges internationaux), ainsi que des particuliers. Les données de balance des paiements sont alors obtenues en tant que résidu des variations globales qui définissent la position patrimoniale financière nette de chacun de ces secteurs.

Afin d'effectuer ces évaluations sectorielles parallèlement à l'analyse habituelle des effets cycliques sur les variables macroéconomiques telles que la production, l'emploi et les prix, une méthode d'analyse, fondée sur la technique des flux entrecroisés, a été mise au point et met tout particulièrement l'accent sur des situations d'équilibre plutôt que sur des hypothèses de comportement, et inclut, en outre, certaines caractéristiques opérationnelles particulières aux pays d'Amérique latine.

L'évaluation a été effectuée sur la base de deux hypothèses différentes en ce qui concerne le système de taux de change en vigueur, afin de déterminer si une petite économie est mieux protégée des perturbations provoquées par les cycles économiques internationaux, selon qu'il s'agit d'un système de taux de change fixes ou d'un système de taux flottants.

Les résultats de l'évaluation du comportement des principales variables macroéconomiques et des principaux effets sectoriels montrent que les événements économiques récents survenus en Amérique latine présentent une similarité surprenante avec ceux auxquels on pouvait s'attendre, d'après le modèle, à la suite de l'évolution économique récente sur les marchés internationaux; on peut dès alors affirmer que la plupart des problèmes de la région ont, au moins en partie, une origine commune. Le modèle s'est également avéré extrêmement utile pour analyser les effets sectoriels des cycles et certains résultats, pour surprenants qu'ils soient, ont apporté des éléments nouveaux contribuant à la compréhension des performances économiques récentes; par exemple, l'apparition inattendue d'un déficit budgétaire—en tant que partie intégrante du cycle—en dépit de l'amélioration des termes de l'échange et des niveaux plus élevés d'activité économique et d'emploi. Le modèle montre également que les taux de change flottants ont tendance à réduire davantage les fluctuations des variables nominales—telles que les prix et les taux d'intérêt—que les taux de change fixes, mais ont également tendance à amplifier les fluctuations des variables réelles telles que la production et l'emploi.

RESUMENES

Tipos de cambio flexibles e interdependencia—RUDIGER DORNBUSCH (páginas. 3–30)

En este artículo se examinan los cauces de interdependencia macroeconómica en un régimen de tipos de cambio flexibles. El modelo destaca la vinculación entre los mercados internacionales de capital, las expectativas y la inflexibilidad de los salarios nominales y reales como factor que afecta al impacto de las perturbaciones en el empleo, los precios y el tipo de cambio. Se amplía el modelo macroeconómico normal de expectativas racionales a fin de facilitar el análisis de la función de las primas de riesgo creadas por la sustituibilidad imperfecta de los activos. Se examinan brevemente los problemas de "pesos" y de "burbujas".

En un análisis de los efectos en terceros países se hace alusión a la importancia que tiene la política de dinero escaso para los países en desarrollo. Estos países resultan afectados por los efectos adversos del alza del tipo de interés real que se les cobra por su deuda, el descenso del precio real de sus exportaciones de productos básicos debido a una menor demanda y a la apreciación real del dólar, y por una menor demanda de sus exportaciones de manufacturas.

Se examinan dos propuestas alternativas para hacer frente a la repercusión de la interdependencia de las medidas de política en el tipo de cambio. Una de ellas es la propuesta de McKinnon de un monetarismo mundial; la otra es la propuesta de bandas de fluctuación. Se rechazan ambas propuestas porque no logran resolver los problemas de la transición a una tasa de inflación baja y general. Finalmente se sugiere que el mejoramiento de la economía mundial no puede basarse en un mejor sistema de tipos de cambio sino en una aplicación más sistemática de políticas de ingresos.

Función de la estructura y política económicas en el equilibrio de los pagos—WILLIAM H. BRANSON (páginas 39–66)

La macroeconomía tradicional posterior a la segunda guerra mundial, así como los enfoques más recientes, el basado en la expectativa racional y el neokeynesiano, analizan las economías monoproductoras. La versión internacional de este modelo, simplificado al máximo, es el modelo monetario de la balanza de pagos o, más recientemente, del tipo de cambio. En la década de 1970 la investigación se orientó hacia la oferta y el papel que desempeña la estructura en la transmisión de las perturbaciones económicas y los efectos de política.

En este estudio se examinan algunos de los resultados más significativos con respecto al papel que desempeña la estructura económica en la determinación de la forma en que se transmiten las perturbaciones. Se expone al principio el modelo monetario de la balanza de pagos, que supone la ausencia prácticamente total de estructura. Esta descripción ofrece un marco de referencia para las secciones siguientes del estudio, en las cuales se incorporan una a una las diferencias estructurales en el modelo.

Los resultados básicos pueden resumirse brevemente. En primer lugar, las rigideces de la oferta o una elevada relación entre los bienes intermedios importados y el valor agregado en la producción pueden hacer que la devaluación resulte contraproducente. Esto puede tener especial importancia en el caso de un país en desarrollo que desee aplicar un programa de estabilización. En segundo lugar, los efectos de las variaciones de los tipos de cambio pueden ser asimétricos entre Europa y Estados Unidos. El efecto principal de las variaciones del tipo de cambio en el comercio exterior de Estados Unidos es la variación de los precios relativos. Esto hace del tipo de cambio un instrumento eficaz para el ajuste de los pagos en Estados Unidos. En cambio, en Europa las variaciones del tipo de cambio pueden tener su efecto principal en los precios internos, con lo cual el tipo de cambio resulta un instrumento deficiente para lograr el equilibrio de los pagos.

En tercer lugar, la política de demanda en los países con salarios reales inflexibles eleva el nivel de precios en dichos países, pero sólo influye en el producto de los países en los cuales haya inflexibilidad de los salarios nominales. También en este caso puede haber una diferencia entre Europa, con salarios reales inflexibles, y Estados Unidos, país con salarios nominales inflexibles. Finalmente, sólo los países con mercado financiero desarrollado y abierto pueden esperar que sea estable un tipo de cambio flotante. Esta podría ser la razón por la cual los países industriales tienden a poner su moneda en flotación, en tanto que los países en desarrollo tienden a vincular el tipo de cambio de sus monedas.

Régimen cambiario e interdependencia europeo-estadounidense en cuanto a sus medidas de política—ALEXANDER K. SWOBODA (páginas 75–102)

En este artículo se documenta y compara el grado de interdependencia de las principales variables macroeconómicas de las seis economías industriales principales (Estados Unidos, Canadá, Japón, Francia, República Federal de Alemania y Reino Unido) en los períodos 1960–71 y 1974–82. El análisis de los componentes principales es el instrumento estadístico primordialmente empleado en este trabajo. Las conclusiones indican que, si bien las tasas de inflación básicas se han hecho más independientes a partir de la adopción de tipos de cambio flotantes, las variaciones a corto plazo (trimestrales) de la inflación, de los tipos de interés y, sobre todo, del crecimiento del producto real, se han hecho mucho más interdependientes en los últimos tiempos. Se llega a esta conclusión no sólo en el caso de las series cronológicas originales estudiadas, sino también en el de innovaciones (choques inesperados) de dichas series. En cambio, cuando se comparan los dos períodos no aparece una diferencia muy clara en la interdependencia de los instrumentos de política en los distintos países.

Los datos corroboran en cierta medida la noción de un ciclo económico mundial al cual se superponen los ciclos económicos nacionales y que es independiente del régimen cambiario, aunque los mecanismos de transmisión difieran de un régimen a otro. Además, aparece en los datos una tenue interdependencia regional (europea).

Concluye el artículo con un examen de algunas de las consecuencias en cuanto a la selección de un régimen cambiario, de regímenes monetarios regionales y el ámbito de autonomía de la política macroeconómica en un régimen de flotación. Se hace hincapié en la importancia de la credibilidad y la determinación previa de las políticas y se llega a la conclusión de que los tipos de cambio flexibles requieren, para funcionar adecuadamente, un conjunto de normas que, si bien han de ser diferentes de las que se aplicarían en un contexto de tipos de cambio fijos, no son por ello menos restrictivas en lo que a las políticas macroeconómicas se refiere.

Interdependencia de las políticas económicas de los países latinoamericanos
—RICARDO H. ARRIAZU (páginas 113–52)

En 1982 la mayoría de los países latinoamericanos tuvieron serias dificultades económicas y de balanza de pagos. En el artículo se estudia la posibilidad de un origen exógeno común de estas crisis. Para evaluar esta posibilidad a un nivel teórico, se define un ciclo internacional "estereotipado" basado en el comportamiento de los precios relativos y los tipos de interés internacionales, midiéndose cuidadosamente sus efectos sobre economías de reducida magnitud y semiabiertas.

Se centra el análisis en la evaluación de los efectos sectoriales que producen las diferentes fases del ciclo, con atención especial a los efectos sobre las cuentas del sector público, el banco central, el sistema financiero, los sectores productivos (representados por los productores de bienes exportables, de productos sustitutivos de las importaciones y de bienes que no son objeto de comercio internacional) y a personas. Se obtiene después la balanza de pagos como valor residual de las variaciones agregadas que dan por resultado las posiciones netas de riqueza financiera de cada uno de estos sectores.

Con el fin de abordar estas evaluaciones sectoriales de forma conjunta con el análisis habitual de los efectos del ciclo en variables macroeconómicas como la producción, el empleo y los precios, se elaboró un método de análisis, basado en la técnica de los flujos intervinculados, prestándose especial atención a las condiciones de equilibrio más bien que a los supuestos de comportamiento, incluidas además algunas características operativas especiales de los países latinoamericanos.

Se efectuó la evaluación bajo dos supuestos diferentes en relación con el sistema cambiario en vigor, a fin de determinar si una economía de magnitud reducida está más protegida contra las perturbaciones causadas por los ciclos económicos internacionales mediante tipos de cambio fijos o tipos de cambio flotantes.

Los resultados de la evaluación del comportamiento de las principales variables macroeconómicas y de los efectos sectoriales principales indican que la evolución económica reciente en la América Latina es sorprendentemente similar a la que cabría esperar, de acuerdo con el modelo, como consecuencia de la evolución reciente de los mercados internacionales y que por lo tanto puede afirmarse que la mayoría de los problemas de la región tienen, al menos en parte, un origen común. El modelo resultó también sumamente útil para analizar los efectos sectoriales de los ciclos y algunos de los resultados, aunque sorprendentes, contribuyeron a comprender mejor el comportamiento económico de estos últimos años; por ejemplo, la aparición inesperada de un déficit fiscal

—como parte integral del ciclo— a pesar de una mejora de la relación de intercambio y de niveles más altos de la actividad económica y de empleo. El modelo muestra también que los tipos de cambio flotantes tienden a reducir las fluctuaciones de las variables nominales —como los precios y los tipos de interés— en mayor medida que los tipos de cambio fijos, si bien es verdad que tienden también a ampliar las fluctuaciones de las variables reales como, por ejemplo, las de producción y empleo.